"Good Evening!"

Other books by Raymond Swing

Forerunners of American Fascism
How War Came
Preview of History
In the Name of Sanity

"Good Evening!"

A Professional Memoir by Raymond Swing

Harcourt, Brace & World, Inc. / New York

to Meisung

Contents

PART TWO

/*Part One*

Chapter 1 / Oberlin Days

What is to follow will be mostly about myself and what happened to me in my profession. I am not setting out to write the history of the remarkable times which as a news-paperman and broadcaster I have been privileged to observe and report. It would be much more to my credit if I were able to write such a book. But to do so would entail research for which I have neither the inclination nor the time. I shall write about my memories and my experiences. I have sometimes speculated about writing a book detailing in full candor what happened to me to make me the person I am, which I believe I know something about. But I have chosen not to do this. My life has been built up, in part, of intimate personal relationships, most of which provided me both the beauty I experienced and the splinters of wisdom I may have acquired. I only own a share in them, and to write about them fully would be exploiting something only partly mine. And I have no intention of compiling my confessions.

As a child I did not realize that I was anything but a unique entity with my own peculiar difficulties, and under constant pressure to live up to the arbitrary standards of others, my father and mother and Oberlin itself, the Ohio college com-munity where we lived. The pressure was not often violent or unkind, but it was unrelenting, and I recall my childhood as having been severe. To be sure it was filled with rewards, such as hearing my mother play Beethoven sonatas after I

3

had gone to bed and listening to the great Second Church choir which later I was to join—not to mention the affection, comradeship, and fun that all children have and so easily forget. What I did not realize was that I was the carrier of genes from before my time which were molding my personality. Now I am able to identify the traits of my heritage. They are an admixture of New England Puritanism and the like Puritanism of the Alsatian Huguenots, both mobilized by the fervor that brought my forefathers on the two sides of the family to this country. These genes were not making me a duplicate of these predecessors. Like all else, Puritanism had to change, and I was to emerge as a modified type, in some respects almost an antithesis of my forebears.

Oberlin itself was founded by New England Puritans in a wooded and uninhabited plain thirty-three miles beyond Cleveland, and it was a remarkable combination of austerity and liberalism. Even in my student days, boy and girl students were not allowed to dance together, card-playing was prohibited, and smoking was sternly forbidden. Yet Oberlin had the distinction, unmatched by any college in this country, of having been the first to have given degrees to women on the same terms with men, and to Negroes on the same terms with whites.

Long before Oberlin was founded, my mother's ancestors had been active Puritans in New England. The family names are among those known in their time: Billings, Storrs, Edwards, Mead, Mather, Wells. Among my ancestors was Richard Mather, brother of Cotton, also the grandfather of Jonathan Edwards. It is a family legend that every generation in this New England and post-New England procession produced at least one clergyman. My own did not.

My grandfather Hiram Mead was a Congregational pastor in South Hadley, Massachusetts, the town where Mary Lyons conducted her Female Academy to pioneer in women's education. He then went to Oberlin Theological Seminary as professor of Homiletics. He died before my mother married, and his widow, Elizabeth Storrs Mead, was to be the first president of Mt. Holyoke College, to which the Female Seminary was changed. After her retirement, she came to live in our Oberlin home with her spinster twin sister, Harriet Billings, who had spent her life as a congenial teacher in New

England private schools. My father rebuilt the second floor of our home on South Professor Street so as to provide a two-room suite for them, which greatly impressed me because it had a private bathroom, and Oberlin at that time did not have many suites with private baths.

As for my father, Albert Temple Swing, his ancestry went back to Samuel Swing, who had emigrated from Strasbourg in the early 1700's. The Strasbourg Swings (then called Schwing; and to this day, as I was to learn later, there are scores upon scores of Schwings in the Strasbourg telephone directory) were Huguenots. Samuel was followed to this country by other Huguenot Swings seeking religious liberty as well as a better living in a new country. My father's father moved to Ohio, near Cincinnati, where he farmed and preached. And this combination of farming and preaching helped make my father the man he became, a powerful six-footer who rowed in the Yale crew as a divinity student. He earned his tuition at Oberlin by teaching in country schools. He was ten years my mother's senior and at Oberlin was five years ahead of her scholastically. I do not know anything about their courtship, an ignorance that must have been due to their own reticence, for I was an inquisitive child and surely asked about it. My mother, Alice Mead Swing, had been a brilliant student. She could read the New Testament in Greek at twelve and learned later to read it in Hebrew.

I have always believed the marriage between my father and mother was built on more than the formal devotion of upright Christians in the bonds of matrimony. My father had humor, though I would not call him an affable man in those years. He was too sternly conscientious, and he was a strict disciplinarian of his children. My mother was gifted and charming. I happen to know that my grandmother, imparting to my mother the facts of life as a young woman, told her that the physical intimacy of marriage was solely for the enjoyment of the husband. But I believe this was not true of my father and mother, a conclusion based on conclusive and not intentionally indiscreet evidence supplied by my sister, Betsy. Belief that this was so helped reconcile me to the stern seriousness of my father. I now believe he was more preoccupied than stern. But it was something of an experience to pass one's father in the street, as I often did, without his saying a word, only silently nodding, and striding on without a smile or a halt. In his later years my father completely mellowed and became a political and theological liberal of great effectiveness. In those years we became close friends. But in my childhood he believed in hard work and self-discipline, and insisted on them from me as well as himself. There was no pleasure-seeking he would not forbid if it meant that schoolwork would not be done or done as well as was possible.

When I was a junior in high school, our class voted to stage a play for public performance to raise money for a graduation present for the senior class. I was chosen to produce the play, which was to be "Mrs. Wiggs of the Cabbage Patch," which I dramatized and then saw through its rehearsals. I kept all this a secret from my parents, for I was sure my father would forbid something which was so sure to take time from my studies. I had to invent pretexts to explain the absences from home at rehearsal times. The nearest my participation came to discovery was on the night before the first performance when a problem arose over obtaining chairs for the auditorium in the Town Hall, where the performance was taking place. Jimmy Brand, son of the pastor of the First Congregational Church, who lived across the street, came to see me for a whispered consultation. (He became justice of the Oregon Supreme Court and one of the Nürnberg trial judges.) My father was suspicious. High-school mates did not pay visits to our home after supper. But I concocted a reason having to do with my Latin assignment, and, like so many of my falsehoods, it passed muster. "Mrs. Wiggs" was duly performed to a full house and even had to be repeated. How it came about that none of my father's acquaintances attended the play and mentioned my part in it to him I cannot say, but it was my good fortune that they did not do so.

Before coming to Oberlin as a professor, my father had had to go through three years of preparatory study in church history, the subject he was to teach, and somehow saved enough money from a pastor's salary to take his family—then consisting of a wife and three children—to Halle, Germany, where he attended the university for the entire three years. I was three years old when we went, and by six I could speak only German. After we were established in Oberlin, my mother tried to maintain German as the home language so that it would not be lost. Obviously I had only a child's limited vocabulary, a limitation that I did not appreciate. For when I went to spend a winter in Munich, shortly before becoming Berlin correspondent of the Chicago *Daily News*, I learned to my dismay that while I could understand about seventy per cent of what was being said in conversation, most of the meaning was concentrated in the thirty per cent I did not understand. My mother, however, mastered the language and taught it in the Academy. She also translated a theological work by Albrecht Rietchl, a liberal teacher who had greatly influenced my father.

As I now look back on it, a great part of my life at Oberlin was devoted to a conflict within myself between good and bad. I wanted to be good, but it was too much for me. Right down to my freshman year in college, when I was on probation for almost the entire year, I oscillated between mischief and prayer. By no means all the mischief was of a sort to be extenuated. My chief shortcoming was dishonesty, with myself and others. But I should say that a fair share of the misdemeanors of those years was attributable to my age, and no influence of my father, home, or community could have kept them in check.

Naturally, my brother Harold and sister, Betsy, and I were not allowed to play cards. But I earned a little money doing work and running errands for neighbors, and I invested some of it in cards. We usually played with these upstairs in the barn, until we were caught at it. Then the cards would be confiscated, and we would be punished. This happened time after time. One day I remarked to Harold that Father, being innately frugal, would destroy nothing of value and must have hidden the confiscated cards. If we were smart enough, I was sure we should be able to find them and not have to buy any more. The opportunity to test this theory came one day when my father went to Cleveland to attend a meeting of the Congregational clergy. This meant that he would be absent the entire day, so we waited for my mother to be out of the house and set out on our search. We first explored the mysteries in the closet in my father's study. Here we found his rifle, which we handled with some awe—it was one with which we knew he had once shot a deer. But there were no cards. We went through the drawers in my father's desk with no success.

But in the chiffonier in his bedroom, in the bottom drawer, covered with layers of his underwear, we came upon the treasure we sought—eight decks of cards. After that we bought no more cards. When we felt it was safe to play, one of us crept into my father's bedroom, removed a deck from the cache, and when the game was over carefully put it back.

I might add that I have been a devoted card-player all my life. Whether my avidity sprang from the forbiddance imposed by my father, I cannot say. Oberlin being what it was, I think I understood even then that my father could not sanction the breaking of a college rule in his own home, for after all he was a pillar of the Oberlin edifice of virtue. As children we did not limit ourselves to simple card games, for I bought a Hoyle's Games, and we learned all the principal varieties. Poker later was to become my favorite, but only if played seriously. To this day I am annoyed if there is too much conversation not having to do with the play itself except during shuffling and dealing. That is, I even play cards like a Puritan, earnestly and dogmatically. I never played for high stakes, which I can also attribute to my genes. Later on I liked to play regularly with the same group, and some of my closest friendships were cemented around the poker table in London and later in Washington.

The struggle between good and bad which so beset me at Oberlin, I now realize with some astonishment, was devoid of any consecration to Eros. At Oberlin in my last two years, affairs were certainly outranked by pranks. I ascribe this in part to my immaturity and ignorance, and also to the fact that all the girls I knew well at the time were rigidly respectable. There were good companions among them, and I may have hankered after one or two of them. But I would not have dared disclose it. Not that all girls in Oberlin were rigidly respectable. The distinction could be made between the town and the college, and certainly some of the town girls were less fastidious than those in the college. For some time I made a point of chumming with town boys as well as with my special friends among the faculty families. I liked the vulgarity of the town boys and what I took to be their greater sophistication. I was fully accepted by them, but their acceptance did not extend to the point of winning me intimacy with the town girls. And the few times I did try to get close to one of them,

I think I was considered a little ridiculous. I did not know how to conduct myself.

While I definitely was a "bad" boy, I was not wild. My Uncle Edwards, as I called Dr. William Edwards Park, who retired from a New York State Congregational pastorate and spent the year at Oberlin when I was a freshman, was astounded and perplexed when I went into debt that year, saying he did not know how a boy could spend so much money except on wine and women. Dr. Park, I should add, was a warmhearted patron to me during my childhood. His two children were much older than I and were headed for lives of distinction, his son, Dr. Edwards A. Park, becoming chief of the Department of Pediatrics at Johns Hopkins, his daughter, Marion Edwards Park, becoming president of Bryn Mawr College.

I was a great disappointment to him, and if I did not spend my borrowings on wine and women, I was "bad" in other ways. I lied and cheated at home, and I smoked cigarettes by the time I was fourteen, which somehow my parents did not discover because I accompanied the smoking with assiduous brushing of my teeth with minted toothpaste. Among my sins at the time was some shoplifting in the town drugstores, called "snitching" or "swiping" by the town boys, and not considered heinous. But I was not courageous or confident enough to express myself frankly with girls.

I am sure my father believed in children having fun, but I also am sure he believed it belonged at a low level in the range of values. Consequently, summer vacations were not spent at formal or informal camps or in visiting relations. The summer I was sixteen, I was encouraged to take a job on a farm. It was situated about four miles from Oberlin on the interurban electric railway that ran to Cleveland. I was to earn ten dollars a month—in today's money, perhaps thirty or thirty-five dollars. My work lasted from dawn to dusk. I began each day by milking twelve cows, and ended each day milking them again. I still have good strong hands as a result of this exercise. The farm work reached a climax at haying and harvesting time. I learned how to stack wheat and cock hay, also how to load a hay wagon and stow hay in the barn loft.

But my unforgettable memory of the summer was my discovery of the reality of infinity. It was when I was given a hoe and put into a ten-acre cornfield to hoe the entire field. I never had imagined anything so unfathomably vast. My father was sure the farm work would build up my body, and no doubt he was right about it. But the two months left me only recollections of joyless drudgery.

The next summer my father softened, and allowed me to take a job in a soft-drink concession in a public park on the lake front near Lorain. I had a better time of it here. I learned to swim and did some boating and fishing in off hours. And the work in the drink concession was not dull, for there is a degree of low creativeness even in mixing soda syrups and making ice cream, and a pleasant amount of social intercourse in serving customers.

The summer before entering college, I invested in a bicycle and undertook to solicit subscriptions to a home encyclopedia in a country territory in western Ohio. Going from farmhouse to farmhouse, I tried to induce farmers' wives to sign up for the encyclopedia. This turned out to be unremunerative and distasteful, and I came to loathe doing it. For one thing, I was not a good salesman. I knew the life of a farm family from experience and refused to press a prospective customer into buying what I knew he or she could not afford.

Finally I deliberately smashed my bicycle and headed for home. To get there I surreptitiously boarded a boxcar in a freight train and headed for Toledo. In that city, I knew, one of my father's students was pastor of a Congregational church. I counted on his lending me enough money to get to Oberlin by train. A tramp soon joined me in the boxcar, and as night fell it became uncomfortably cold, so that the tramp and I slept in each other's arms to share our bodily warmth. We arrived in Toledo before dawn on a Sunday morning. I had to find a telephone directory to look up the address of the pastor I was seeking. But first I begged an early-morning dairy-cart driver to give me a drink of milk, which he did. I found the address of the pastor, which, on inquiry, I discovered was on the other side of the city. But I set out to walk to it, grimy and unwashed.

I reached the pastor's house well before church-time, and received a puzzled but cordial welcome. I was allowed to take a bath and was fed a good breakfast. The pastor told me that my arrival was opportune, for his church organist was unavoidably absent, and he would be glad to have me play the service for him, which I did. He then paid me a few dollars to take the train to Oberlin, and my commercial vacation came to an end.

I owe Oberlin as a college community two debts, only one of which I realized at the time. That was an appreciation of music. The other was its liberal view of the equality of women and Negroes. As a youngster I did not think Oberlin was liberal at all, and had only contempt for its rigid rules. But my attitude toward the rights of women and persons of other than the white race was shaped at Oberlin without my being aware of it. One of my best friends in my senior Academy year was a talented Negro musician who was to become an outstanding composer. We took long walks and had long talks. Oberlin had been a station in the Underground Railroad before the Civil War and had helped in the escape of slaves. The college was abolitionist to the core. That also means it was passionately intolerant of the South. But that was part of its hatred of slavery, which I recognize as more important than a tolerant understanding of the point of view of Southern whites. Just being a part of Oberlin gave me an innate sense of the political equality of men and women, all men and all women. I was not a little surprised when the appellation *liberal* first came to be applied to me. My father had been a Republican. I started out thinking I was one. After I left home, the Republican party split, and I went with the progressives. But I was no more liberal than slightly left of center in my school days. I debated against trusts on the Academy debating team; this is as far as political radicalism at Oberlin reached at that time.

Oberlin was a great place for music, and I took piano lessons in the Conservatory while still in high school. When I entered the Academy for my senior year, I studied both piano and harmony. My piano teacher was a musicologist of renown, and I learned from him more about music than how to play it. This was well, for I did not have the manual dexterity nor the power of self-application to become a performer. The following year I studied organ with Professor George Whitfeld Andrews, reputed to be the best organist in the country and also the best musician in the Conservatory. He was a well-known composer in his day, and he was conductor of the Musical

Union, the student chorus which concertized twice each year. This professor had played the organ in the church which my family attended throughout my childhood, so that I was familiar with organ classics if not always carried away by them. He was an unusually tall and angular man, cordial, considerate, and extremely pious. He made it a rule to ask every student who studied with him if he had "given his heart to Christ." In due course it was my turn to answer the question, and I felt only embarrassment, for despite the sincere religious observance in our home, I did not understand what it meant to give one's heart to Christ, and I certainly had not made any such formal gift. I did not learn to play the organ well, but it was a privilege to be studying with this great master. I sang in the choir for which he played the organ, being the first boy to pass the entrance examination, as an alto before my voice changed, then later as a bass. I also sang under him in the Musical Union.

My freshman year at Oberlin brought all my troubles to a head. My father took a sabbatical leave for the year with my mother, so that the new experience of college began with the removal of all home restrictions. I had longed to go to an Eastern college, preferably Amherst. An English professor from that college had once visited our home and said he was sure that if I did well at Amherst, I could count on a teaching appointment at the American college in Beirut, Syria, where he had connections. This excited me. I wanted to live and work abroad. But it was much more economical for me to stay at Oberlin. When my freshman year came around, two rooms were fitted out for me and my roommate, who was to be my best friend from the Academy. It was also arranged at the college boardinghouse adjoining our home that I was to wash dishes in exchange for my meals. As I now recall it, this house had twenty-seven boarders, and it took me forty minutes to wash the dishes when no gravy was served and at least an hour when it was.

School had no sooner started than my roommate and I decided to organize a secret society of seven members—partly for social reasons, but partly because fraternities were forbidden at Oberlin. We were to meet regularly in our rooms during the school week and camp out on weekends at a shack in the woods we had found. At the shack we built a bonfire, cooked our supper over the coals, smoked, and slept out under blankets. We usually took Paul Griswold Huston, our freshman English instructor, on these excursions, not as a chaperon, but as a fellow-conspirator. He was a Princeton graduate and did not think well of the rules at Oberlin. He also smoked beside the bonfire and camped out for the night. We loved this teacher. He introduced us, with simplicity and fervor, to English literature and gave us our first appreciation of it. He stimulated me to writing to the point that I often wrote most of the themes for most of the seven in his English class (without his knowing it). Obviously a teacher who would go out in the woods and smoke with freshmen did not "belong" to the Oberlin of that day. Yet he was a born teacher, and for my part I have always felt an enormous gratitude to him. Before the end of the year his behavior was discovered, and he was not re-employed the following year. He went on to a well-known boys' academy, where he spent the rest of his life as the most beloved member of its faculty.

The pranks in which we indulged in my freshman year were markedly juvenile in the way underclassmen's pranks in a college tend to be. The first one was designed to break up the sophomore class Thanksgiving party, which was being held in the chapel of the First Congregational Church. As soon as dusk fell we went into the chapel cellar with plumbing tools and plugged the gas pipes with putty, so that the room could not be illuminated. (This was before electricity had come into use.) We were not successful in breaking up the party, for the sophomores obtained candles and enjoyed themselves all the better. And we were found out—I don't know how. All of us were put on probation forthwith. My own case was considered particularly serious because it was known that I also smoked, and I was ordered to report to the Dean of Men every Monday morning and tell him whether I had smoked during the preceding week. From then on I appeared each Monday at his office in Peters Hall and duly stated that I had smoked. The Dean was a genial man and did not at first read me lectures about my duty to my parents and to the Oberlin tradition. As a small boy I had for years been a member of his wife's Sunday-school class. Probably he knew, as some Oberlin authorities did not know, the difference between evil and wrongdoing.

The next prank was even sillier than the first. There had been some policy disagreement in the sophomore class. We went into the colored quarter of the town where we had espied an old baby carriage on a porch, "borrowed" this, made a mannequin which we arrayed in sophomore class colors and suspended from the baby carriage, and then with considerable risk—my daring roommate had laid a ladder from the roof of the Conservatory of Music to the top of its big chimney—dragged the carriage across and placed it there with a banner proclaiming that " '08 Has Had a Falling Out." It took the authorities nearly a day to remove the baby carriage, so that the "stunt," from our standpoint, was a singular success. But once more we were found out, and this time we were given a tongue-lashing by the Dean because the colored woman who owned the baby carriage was unable to collect washing in it to make her living, and we were required to pay her five dollars' damages.

With all the fun I was having, I did poorly in my studies, excepting English and German. Early in the fall term I simply walked out of freshman math, a required course, because it was totally incomprehensible to me. My grades in high-school algebra and geometry had been good, but calculus and trigonometry were a closed door I was unable to open. Freshman Bible was another required course, and was taught by the Dean of Women, whose father, as it happened, had been a classmate of my father. I may have tried to exploit any favor she may have had for me on that account by cutting her class. But in time she reported me, and my absence from freshman math and my being on probation all added up to shortcomings that could not be overlooked. I was called to the Dean's office and told that my work was not satisfactory; I should have to drop my organ lessons and reduce my studies to three majors—English, German, and French; and in these I had to obtain a grade of 4 (a "B" in present-day colleges) if I were to be allowed to return in the following year. In English I was well toward the top of the class. In German I had little trouble because of my childhood knowledge of the language. French and my French teacher were to be my nemeses. I had done fairly well in the subject, but I did not work hard. Moreover, the professor was disgusted with my behavior during the absence of my parents. He thought I was a bad boy and that Oberlin would be better without me. I am sure of this because of the way he handled my spring-term grades. I had had a bout of flu which kept me out of classes for a week. When I recovered I took an extra two weeks' absence from French. This work had to be made up, and the professor, who knew quite well that I had cut his class for two weeks, told me that if I did perfectly in making up the work for all three weeks, he would grade me only a 3 (comparable to a "C"). I did perfect work, but the 3 for the absent weeks brought my term average down to a 3.9, and that simple decimal point was enough to doom me to suspension from college for a year.

I do not censure the professor. He was right enough about me. I had wasted most of my year, and I had disgraced my parents. Long before I was suspended I grieved, as I so often was to do over myself. I knew I was weak and without self-discipline, and I went to the eminent theologian who lived next door—a great theological liberal whom I had known all my boyhood. I asked him to help me, which he tried to do by going down at once on his knees with me in prayer for divine assistance. I also went to the President of the college, a classmate and close friend of my mother, and the father of one of my best friends. I asked him for help, and he likewise prayed with me. Nowadays I am sure that Oberlin knows of other therapies for mixed-up boys than punishment and prayer. But I cannot criticize the pedagogues of Oberlin for not being ahead of their time. They were not too distant in years from Charles G. Finney, the celebrated evangelist of the mid-nineteenth century, who preached hell-fire for sinners with great eloquence and effect, and who was to become one of Oberlin's early presidents.

It was not until later that I realized how much Oberlin had given me, in music, in the first interest I had in the other arts, in the basic liberalism of racial and sexual equality. My parents' home had been a center of culture where many well-known figures in education were guests at our table, so that I listened to enlightened conversation, with my parents and my grandmother taking a lively part. As for my French professor, it was not until after I had rushed through my newspaper apprenticeship and had become a foreign correspondent of the Chicago *Daily News* in Berlin in 1913, and so had been privileged to cover the first years of World War I, that I knew what a godsend he had been. If I had stayed in college to graduate with my class, I should have missed this career altogether.

Chapter 2 / The First Newspaper Work

I owe my first newspaper job to the interest of a man who was to be a friend—if geographically not a close one—most of my life. He was Grove Patterson, who was editor and editor emeritus of the Toledo *Blade* most of his life and served a term as president of the American Society of Newspaper Editors. We also were to be trustees together of Oberlin College.

He was a senior in college when I was a senior in the Academy, and I came to know him because he was head of the college debating team and took on the task of coaching the Academy team on which I was an alternate. We struck up a friendship, took long walks together, and he was generous enough to discuss at length the affairs of the world. When he graduated he took the post of editor of a small-town daily in Lorain, a steel community on Lake Erie not far from Oberlin.

When calamity befell me at Oberlin, I went to Lorain to look for work. The first two jobs I obtained were as cashier in a barbershop and clerk in a men's clothing store. At the same time, I was employed to play the organ at the Disciple Church. This musical occupation turned out to be more than I had foreseen, for I had to play every night for a six-week campaign of an evangelist named the Reverend Mr. Violet. Night after night I listened to his exhortations to repentance and played the hymns that stressed that theme. And as the

17

weeks progressed, scores went to the altar and accepted baptism by immersion.

I considered myself a Congregationalist by tradition, since the Puritans had been Congregationalists. Moreover, I had joined the Second Congregational Church at Oberlin at the time that my best boyhood friend joined. I did it, I confess, not out of any stronger desire than to do everything together with him. Congregationalists were not baptized on joining the church. Baptism by Congregationalists is performed in infancy by sprinkling, as it was in my case by my father, and was considered to be an act of the parents consecrating the child to God. But baptism in the Disciple Church was a formidable operation. It was performed in a tank specially introduced for that purpose, filled waist-high with water in which the pastor and the converts stood in special robes and in which, to the accompaniment of suitable holy words, each convert was completely immersed by the pastor for a brief moment. By this act the convert became a member of the Disciple Church.

As the six weeks of the Rev. Mr. Violet's crusade drew to a close, I found myself more and more challenged by the evangelist's exhortation to repentance. I had listened closely to his sermons, which had deepened my conviction that I was a sinful person. But they somehow failed to convince me that my redemption would be any more assured as a Disciple than as a Congregationalist. The Rev. Mr. Violet, however, had a telling issue in baptism. He argued that immersion clinched salvation, and anyone not having been immersed had foregone the certainty of that blessed state. I was not sure that I was at all eligible to salvation, but I was subjected to two pressures, the nightly plea of the evangelist and my own uncertainty as to whether there could be any truth in the dogma that baptism by immersion was a factor in salvation. In the end I succumbed, first to the Rev. Mr. Violet's nightly exhortations and then to the doubt in my own mind about the sufficiency of baptism by sprinkling. If there was any question about it, I told myself, it was easy to be safe and be immersed. So on the final night of the crusade, I rose, came to the altar as a supplicant, and was immersed. I recognize that spiritually the action had virtually no significance. It did not result from my having become a better person, though it may have registered a desire to be better.

My most interesting memory of Lorain is not of my immersion by the Rev. Mr. Violet, but of the steel mill where I obtained employment as clerk of the blacksmith shop. This shop was a huge iron-roofed shed containing two steam forges where the repairs on machinery requiring forging were done. My work as clerk was to trace and register every repair made, which gave me the run of the mill and an easygoing relationship with foremen and men. The mill was staffed chiefly by Hungarian immigrants, whom I liked and who soon showed friendliness to me, inviting me to their homes when they celebrated national festivities.

I saw Grove Patterson from time to time and told him my ambition to be a newspaperman. His Lorain paper had a reporter, but was not prosperous enough to afford a second one, even at a beginner's salary. However, the editor of the Cleveland *Press* was a friend of his, and he promised that the next time he went to Cleveland, he would be glad to see him and recommend me. Before the summer ended, he did this, and I was summoned to Cleveland for an interview.

The job offered me was the most modest one existent on a newspaper—to be night man on an afternoon paper. It paid ten dollars a week, which was enough in those days to rent a room, provide modest meals, pay for laundry, and supply me a little pocket money. Cleveland was the home town of John D. Rockefeller, already an elderly man. I had a good many services to perform as night man on the *Press*. I had to "make the rounds"—that is, telephone all the police and fire stations in the city to find out if anything had happened, and if anything sounded important enough I was to wake up the city editor. I "made the rounds" every four hours through the twelve-hour night. I had to go to the post office at midnight and bring back the mail and sort it, and had to read and clip the state newspapers for items which were published as "State Briefs." But above all I had to call up the editor in chief, the managing editor, and the city editor, no matter what the hour, if John D. Rockefeller died. They then would set the wheels turning to get out an extra edition. During my stay, and for years to follow, John D. Rockefeller did not die. But no one in the United States could have been more alerted at that time to the possibility of such an event than I.

The contrast between the life of a professor's son at Oberlin and a fledgling newspaper employee in Cleveland at night was incalculable. The Cleveland *Press* set up no rules to be observed. It maintained no standards of behavior. It imposed no discipline. There were no teachers, no student body, no classrooms; there was no social life. On the contrary, I did my work in a vast plant at night which, excepting for janitors, I had to myself. The work was elementary; I really was only a kind of super office boy. My only editorial function was to write the State Briefs and cut up the morning papers and sort out the clippings, city news for the city editor, telegraph news for the telegraph editor, and so on. The rest of the routine was even more elementary. However, I felt fortunate to be doing it, and I organized my work so as to be finished, all told, in about five hours carefully interspersed in the twelve.

I was not to be lonesome for long. "Making the rounds," as I recall, required about a hundred telephone calls, to all the city's police precincts and fire stations. As the call was answered, I would say: "This is the *Press*. Is there anything doing?" It took, all told, a few seconds. I made these calls always in the same order, and having a good memory in those days, I knew the numbers by heart and did not have to read them off. What pleased me was that the same telephone operator took the call and that she also memorized them, so that when I was finished with one number, she was ready with the next. Ultimately, when it came to making the rounds, I simply called to this operator, and she called my numbers.

This, it is easy to understand, was the start of a fellowship. When I was finished with the rounds, I chatted with the operator. That led to my chatting with several—in fact, all that were on the night board at the telephone company, including the long-distance operators. I even had some acquaintances on long-distance boards outside Cleveland, in Columbus, Cincinnati, and Toledo, being introduced by one operator to another. To begin with, this conversation was idle, but before long I did most of my talking with a few operators with whom I conversed quite seriously for hours at a stretch. This was real communication. I shall not say it was erudite, but it was thoughtful and became quite intimate. It was as good talk as I would have had as an underclassman at Oberlin. After I developed these marathon conversations, I made accommodations for them and held them lying in comfort on the top of two flat desks softened by newspapers. I wore earphones with attached mouthpiece and could talk for hours without fatigue.

Finally my interest centered on two young women: one, the night chief operator on the long-distance board; the other, the operator who "made the rounds" for me. We became exceptionally well acquainted, as one can do in the security of distance, even better, perhaps, than in the actual presence of the other person. Mary, the long-distance operator, and Rose, her friend, were devoted to each other. Mary came from the better family, in fact her home was on Euclid Avenue, and she was working nights at the telephone company so as to be able to help discreetly put her brother through college. Rose was a village girl who had come to Cleveland to find work.

It was not long before I began suggesting that we meet on one of our days off. Both Mary and Rose resisted this idea, putting up meaningless objections, but putting them up. One reason, they said, was that they were too shy. How would we recognize each other, and how could we arrange our meeting? I asked the theater editor one morning if he could get me three free tickets to the local vaudeville house for a Saturday afternoon. He said he thought he could if I gave him advance notice. This solved the problem. Mary and Rose were to have their tickets, I was to come in after the house was darkened, and in that way we could have our first glimpse of each other after the theater lights went on.

Even so, the girls held out for some time, it seemed to me unreasonably, but I pleaded endlessly, and they finally assented. The tickets were obtained and distributed, I entered a few minutes late, found the seats in the dark, and was aware of two young women adjoining me whom I could not clearly see. We exchanged whispered greetings in the dark. It was exciting and unusual to be meeting in person for the first time two girls whom I knew so well. It was as if spirits were materializing.

When the lights went up I ventured to look at them. Rose was sitting next to me, and Mary in the seat beyond. I had no sooner seen them both than I understood why it had taken so long to induce them to meet me. Rose was unusually tall and angular and extremely plain. Mary was blooming with attractiveness. And Mary, who was attached to Rose, knew that what was to happen would happen: I would thereafter concentrate my attention on her.

I did talk to Rose at nights after that, but not for hours. There no longer was any mystery about her. I talked more with Mary alone, and arranged finally to spend an evening at her home, Rose not included. It was a happy and intimate evening. I liked Mary, but she was several years my senior and presented me with what I considered to be a serious ethical problem. I knew I would not want to marry her. She was affectionate toward me, and I did kiss her that night. But because she was a nice girl, I knew I had no right to kiss her unless I expected to marry her. So I thought I must never do it again. Thereafter, the long night conversations with both Rose and Mary shortened and finally ended. Oberlin may have dismissed me, but I had not yet dismissed Oberlin.

No one could have been more impatient to be promoted to the day side at the *Press* than I. I talked about this incessantly when the day staff came on before I went to my lodgings for my sleep. I was told there was only one chance: some night, something would happen, like a murder, on which I would do all the reportorial labors, get the photographs and all the facts, and have these on the city editor's desk when he came to work. I waited for that murder with impatience. But Cleveland was going through a law-abiding spell, and my nights were without opportunities to develop my journalistic ability. The only unusual event in my life was obtaining a job as luncheon waiter at the exclusive Cleveland Club, for which I was rewarded by being allowed to eat any meal on the menu. This cut down my expenses and also proved to be interesting work, for I repeatedly had the experience of serving members who had been guests at my Oberlin home. I recognized them easily enough and wondered if any of them would recognize me. I had to wear the club uniform at mealtimes, and thought it would be embarrassing both for the member and for me if this recognition were to take place. I realized it might give me a higher status with the headwaiter, but still would be an awkward occurrence. However, it never happened.

Instead, something happened that put an end to my services

at the club. Word about my work at the club reached the editor of the *Press,* and he left a message that I was to call on him as soon as he came to work. What he had to say was to commend me for working at the club and to tell me that I should keep my ears open while serving club members and pick up and report any news that I overheard. He said it was a great opportunity. Evidently he thought he had a confidential agent disguised as waiter in the city's most exclusive social club, which was a unique journalistic advantage. But that is not how the situation appeared to me. I did not tell the editor so. I tried to show interest in his suggestion, but I was shocked by it, and I resigned my job at the club that noon. In the years to come I was frequently to defend the freedom of the press. But this is surely the only time I defended the freedom of club waiters from unethical exploitation by the press. Whether the editor learned that I had quit, I do not know. The subject was never referred to again.

In due time a murder was committed which was to give me a chance to exercise my faculties as a reporter. It was not a particularly exciting murder. A worker shot his middle-aged mistress, in her very shabby bedroom. I visited the room soon after the crime. The woman's baby was still lying asleep on a pillow in the corner, and that was the only feature of the story. I had hours to work on it, to get pictures of both principals and to write an account of the facts. I had all on the city editor's desk before his arrival, and had reported the murder itself to him as soon as I learned about it from the precinct where it had taken place. I did not tell the city editor I was covering the murder for him. That was to be my surprise.

As I now remember the episode, I was dismayed by the sordidness of the tragedy, but all the same I was elated. For this was my chance. Everyone had told me that someday there would be a night murder and I would have all the facts on the desk by the time the city editor arrived and would be promoted to the day side. Now it was to come to pass. And indeed I was promoted, though without a rise in salary.

However, my time with the Cleveland *Press* was not to last long, owing, I must say, to my repeated requests for an increase in salary on being promoted to the day side. I was still a greenhorn, but I was importunate. The city editor did not make much use of me, perhaps believing I was not yet to be trusted to cover an assignment. But the day-side reporters were paid a minimum of twelve dollars, and I kept asking for it. Finally the editor gave me a kindly talking-to and dismissed me. He said I was a bright boy and would make a good news-paperman and was to come back to the *Press* when I had had more experience.

The next years were dedicated to obtaining the experience the editor told me that day I needed. I should add, they also were spent in trying to get an education without going to college. I did not actually peruse textbooks or work over problems. I simply read voraciously. I knew I would never understand freshman math and never tried to again. But I could acquaint myself with the great literature of the world, and this I did. I felt keenly that my suspension at Oberlin not only disgraced me, but might limit my career. So I read avidly. Probably it would have been better for me to study than to read. I might have tried to keep abreast of my class at Oberlin, but I did not. I had no intention of returning to Oberlin or going to any college. The world of literature was there before me, and I gratefully entered it. I took no advice, I simply followed my own interests.

After being dismissed from the *Press* I did not at once find another newspaper job, but worked at one thing or another through the summer. I had one employment for a single week as salesman in a shoe store. In Oberlin one of my money-earning jobs had been to clerk in one of the town's shoe stores. I worked occasional hours during the week, and then all day Saturday. I came to know the stock and how to show it to customers. This experience obtained for me the Cleveland employment. The reason it lasted only a week was that when I knew that the store did not stock what the customers wanted, I told them so. On being fired, I was informed that it was not my function to co-operate with customers in that way, but to make them want what they did not want. This in its way was also educational. It taught me I was not cut out for a commercial career.

But in the autumn my luck broke, and I was hired as reporter by the Cleveland *News*. I was put at once on the court beat, the poorest of the beats, but it took me into courtrooms, where I listened to many trials. Most trials are dull, but a courtroom is a window opened onto reality, and while I did not get much news, I had a view of a world and its petty conflicts I had never seen or imagined at Oberlin. Now and again I also filled in at police headquarters, and here the view of reality was even more sordid. Morgues, prison cells, police courts, and all the other places of contact in the municipal system are in themselves depressing, and newspapermen who are required to frequent them usually become cynical. But unless one has been in attendance at them, one does not know what the city is like. If one knows these places and what they represent, one can at least start one's own social thinking at scratch.

I did not stay a full year at the Cleveland *News*, owing to a want ad, in one of the Cleveland dailies, seeking an editor for a small-town weekly newspaper not far from the Cleveland area. I applied and was accepted. If experience was what I needed, I could not get it more usefully than in producing a small newspaper by myself. I spent a year in Orrville, Ohio, editing the Orrville *Courier*. The town had about 3,000 inhabitants, and its existence depended on its being a junction and repair point of the Pennsylvania Railroad. The proprietor of the chief hardware store in the town was chairman of the small company that owned the *Courier*, and after visiting him I realized that the job was as different as could be from anything I had learned in Cleveland. What counted in Orrville was not news, but names. My work was to consist of getting as many names into the paper as possible, each identified with some activity, such as a visit from or to some relation or a trip to another locality. Local events had to be reported, always with names, and while I was to be permitted to write a few editorials in which I expressed opinions, this was an indulgence only. The *Courier* had a circulation of 1,300, which it was my duty to increase. There was a rival weekly with about the same circulation published by a tired old man.

At the end of the year the owner of the hardware store told me flatly he did not think I was working hard enough and I had better find myself a new job. He would allow me time to relocate myself. The editor of the *Press* had discharged me, and now I was to be dismissed in Orrville. I believe I was working hard enough to keep my Orrville job. I certainly concentrated on getting names into the paper. During my year the *Courier* changed from a weekly to a biweekly, grew a little in circulation, and made a little more money than before. Soon after I left, it was bought out by the rival newspaper, and the tired old man took charge of the merged papers. My dismissal may have been one of the terms of the deal, though this only occurred to me later on.

My experience with small-town life was highly satisfactory. I was engaged for five dollars a week to conduct the choir of the First Presbyterian Church, which I enjoyed enormously. (The pastor had been a student of my father.) The organist was the most attractive young woman in town, and I fell heir to her as a "steady" because her previous "steady" had gone off to college. As winter came, I was nominated to be the local official at basketball games. And as spring came I found myself manager of the baseball team, which was better than a sand-lot team because we had a small income from gate receipts and could pay the best players from surrounding localities.

Two Orrville friends stand out in my memory. One was the German-born head of the printing shop. He undertook to teach me how to hand set type and correct it in the galleys. He also appointed himself my intellectual mentor, and I shall never forget holding forth to him enthusiastically on the flight of the Wright brothers, about which there had been newspaper reports, but which finally was confirmed in detail in one of the national magazines. I was greatly excited by this. If man could learn to fly, I knew the very nature of social life would be changed. But my printer squelched me completely. I must grow up, he said, and learn not to believe everything I read in the national magazines. Man had never flown in all his past, and he was not learning to now. I cannot say how long it took me to unlearn what the printer tried to teach me about the impossibility of flying. But I am still grateful to him for teaching me to read type in galleys.

The other friend, Heber Blankenhorn, was the son of the town's leading physician, whose acquaintance I did not make until he returned from college for the summer vacation, when we became close pals. He was a little older than I and knew the world correspondingly better, and I looked up to him. I recall one of our undertakings, which was to walk all night from Orrville to Oberlin. The distance was at least thirty-three

miles, and it took us eleven hours. My new friend was to go
into newspaper work after leaving college. Many years later
he was city editor of the New York *Herald,* in the time of
Frank Munsey's ownership. When I wanted to return to Europe after the end of World War I, he interceded with Munsey
for me and obtained my appointment as Berlin correspondent.
Ultimately he was to be on the staff of the National War Labor
Board, and became one of the best-informed men on the activities of labor unions in the country.

I found my next newspaper job also through a want ad. A
city editor was sought for a small daily newspaper in Indiana.
I applied and was accepted. The appellation "city editor" was
on the grandiose side. The entire news staff consisted of three
persons, the second one being a reporter who knew the community, the third, a student correspondent in a college situated in that city. In addition there was an editor, a fiery little
nervous redhead who had ability well beyond the requirements of his post. The newspaper was the *Evening Item,* and
the town was Richmond, the seat of Earlham College, founded
as a Friends' school, staffed by teachers of ability. This gave
Richmond an intellectual level above the run of Indiana
towns. J. Bennett Gordon, the editor, would today be called
an outstanding liberal, a term not then in vogue. I learned a
great deal from him about politics as well as newspaper work.
He studied public issues, something I had still to learn, and
I became a disciple as well as an employee. The *Item* stirred
up community opinion. Contrary to expectations, Mr. Gordon backed the "wets" in a local-option election on the ground
that it was better to have law-enforced drinking than boot-
legging. However, the "drys" won. It was the first election I
saw close at hand, and while I was a bit startled to have the
Item supporting the "liquor interests," I was greatly excited
by the campaign.

The *Evening Item* received the state wire of one of the national news services, so in contrast with the Orrville *Courier,*
news counted more than names. As general editorial fac-
totum, I edited this telegraphic news as well as the local and
college items produced by the two reporters. So I obtained experience and actually produced a small daily newspaper,
with the exception of the editorial page.

In my off-duty hours I again earned a little extra money

conducting a choir, this time in an Episcopal church. This assured me some social life. By now Oberlin and the disgrace of dismissal were three years behind me. I still had not rid myself of all my Oberlin conventionality. I still was mixed up about what was good and what was bad, and considered myself bad while wanting to be good. But I had been rehabilitated as a member of my family, and my parents thought I was proving to be a credit to them. They were now reconciled to the certainty that I never would have a college education.

Chapter 3 / The Meads—and Then Europe

The most influential man in my life at that time and, I think, in all my life, was my mother's brother, Professor George Herbert Mead, of the University of Chicago.

He was married to a Castle, daughter of the business agent of the missionary pioneers in the Hawaiian Islands who had built up for himself a family fortune in sugar. My Aunt Helen was a spirited woman of wide cultural interests, and possessed a lively and persistent conversational talent. Through my childhood the Meads came regularly to Oberlin, particularly while my grandmother was alive. The visits were always stimulating. An undercurrent of religious differences was noticeable in some of the talk between my father and George Mead, who had ceased to be a Christian. But this was kept within bounds. George Mead was becoming a notable personage in the academic world. He was an intimate friend and associate of John Dewey, and is now recognized and studied by scholars as the pioneer of all social psychologists. But he was more than an original thinker; he and his wife were persons of uncommon generosity and selflessness who influenced hordes of young people. I have spoken of the sugar fortune in the family. It enabled the Meads to travel, back and forth to the Hawaiian Islands and to Europe, but that was their only self-indulgence. To the end of their days they never owned an automobile. They spent their money doing things for others, chiefly young persons needing an education. They maintained two large apartments in Chicago which became boarding-houses for students they were putting through the university. Professor Mead presided over the common table at mealtimes, leading the conversation into all the opening fields of human knowledge. He was a man of great humor and geniality, so that these sessions were spiced with laughter as well as wisdom. He himself kept abreast of world thinking and world affairs, and was capable of expounding both with simplicity. He was tall and handsome and wore a short chestnut-hued beard that curled up at the tip. He had bulk, and kept his weight down by running in shorts around the Midway before breakfast, which to me seemed to prove an enormous amount of character and determination.

When I was thirteen, the Meads took me back to Chicago for a winter. They recognized my musical interest and saw to it that I had my first piano lessons. They also entered me for a term in the experimental school John Dewey had established at the University of Chicago. I did learn to play one or two presentable piano works by the time I came home, to the delight and satisfaction of my parents. What I derived from the Dewey School during my brief stay would be impossible to estimate. Certainly it gave me prestige in Oberlin, for the name of Dewey already was becoming one to conjure with. But all I can recall of the time spent in the school was my becoming enamored of Professor Dewey's daughter Evelyn, whom I determined someday to marry, an idea which, at the time, she approved. The aspiration, however, came to nothing. I only saw Evelyn Dewey once or twice on subsequent visits to Chicago, and the romance quickly withered.

The scholarship of my father was traditional, though for an Oberlin professor he was out in front. But the modernity of the Dewey thinkers was beyond his favor in those years. Professor Mead was aware of the blossoming of science, was erudite enough to understand it and to expound what was going on in the experimental laboratories. My Aunt Helen was just as comprehensive in her knowledge of the arts, old and new. So it always was a stirring time when the Meads came to Oberlin, and after I left the college it was just as stimulating to me to visit the Meads in Chicago, which I was to do regularly. It was many years later before I came to appreciate fully the content and flavor of my uncle's mind. But even then

I derived from him faith in the benefit of social action in dealing with the great problems of ignorance and poverty. He was a friend of Jane Addams at Hull House and a member of her governing board. He and Aunt Helen were also greatly interested in my sister, Betsy, and her capacities as a designer and artist. And it was at their prompting, I am sure, that she became a resident and teacher at Hull House, where she was to make many friends. Unfortunately, she also was to succumb to a combination of ailments. This was after I had gone to work in Europe. After her death a drinking fountain in her memory was installed at the Hull House entrance.

I captured from Uncle George some of the light of promise which shone in his thinking. The world of Oberlin, liberal though it had been, at that time was being left behind by inquiries of the sciences and psychology. And while I now realize that even George Mead was committed at that time to a doctrine of progress that the speed of change in the present-day world has twisted out of shape, I could not have become a conscious member of my generation without his influence.

I moved from Richmond to Indianapolis within a year, having been offered a reporting job on the *Star* at much better pay, and within a few months was covering the statehouse for that newspaper. I certainly was getting experience! At that time Thomas R. Marshall was governor. Later he was to become vice-president under Wilson, and authored the universally known aphorism "What this country needs is a good 5-cent cigar!" He deserves to be better known for being a thoughtful and constructive leader and should have renown for having doggedly refused to take over the functions of the President during Mr. Wilson's long illness, which was a demonstration of self-control and modesty. I became well acquainted with him at the governor's office, and always found him communicative and stimulating.

Another Indiana figure prominent in national life was Senator Albert J. Beveridge, who had a reputation as an orator and a progressive, and later was to do his best work as a biographer of Justice John Marshall. I did not get to know that played an important role in my life. By then I had been him until he was running for re-election, a campaign promoted to be night city editor of the *Star*. A young and wealthy tin-mine owner, Rudolph Leeds, who had lived in

Richmond and was a friend of Bennett Gordon, the *Evening Item* editor, was a Beveridge enthusiast and decided to buy a newspaper in Indianapolis to help his campaign. He employed Gordon as editor, and Gordon chose me as managing editor.

In that way the Indianapolis *Sun* came into existence. I put together a staff of newsmen, most of them colleagues on the *Star*, and, with what now seems to me hardly any effort at all, we appeared as a full-blown newspaper. I was twenty-three, the youngest man on the staff. One of my first undertakings was to cover a speechmaking tour of Senator Beveridge, for which I was to meet him at the station. I barely made the train on time because of a visit to the men's room. The Senator, who was sententiousness itself, chided me solemnly with the words: "Young man, you must never pee on the eve of battle."

I worked much too hard on the Indianapolis *Sun*—fourteen and fifteen hours a day—and I must say my colleagues worked hard, too. We were, to be sure, interested in the re-election of Senator Beveridge. But we were much more interested in creating a newspaper, and I think we put together a pretty good one. But before a year was out I was on the point of a breakdown, and I was sent away to a summer cottage on the eastern shore of Lake Michigan with my youngest brother—Herbert, later known as Dolf, and eleven years my junior—as companion, with orders to rest for six weeks.

Before taking another newspaper job, I was to have a summer in Chicago, engaged in a research assignment which my uncle arranged. It went under the heading of a vocational-guidance project. I was given a list of school children on the West Side—the poorest district in Chicago—who had quit school at fourteen, and was to go to each home to find out the precise reasons the child had quit school. This brought me into the most squalid homes I had ever seen. I found that virtually all the children had left school because their earnings were needed to help feed and clothe the family. One of my duties was to find out just what the family budget was in each case. The point of the survey was to demonstrate the need of providing vocational training and guidance in the public-school system, to keep children there long enough to develop earning skills. But it taught me a far wider lesson about the poverty and ignorance in Chicago slums, and for me it constituted an increased awareness of the realities of American city life. Fifty years later the nation was to be markedly better off. How much devoted and unselfish interest on the part of civic leaders was needed to help raise the standards of living and education is more than I can say. But the United States did not reach its present standards—such as they are—by abstract economic forces alone. It became better also through the unceasing interest of the Jane Addamses and the George Meads.

Having been a managing editor, night city editor, statehouse reporter, and responsible for a dozen newspaper departments, I had no fear of not finding a good newspaper job after leaving the Indianapolis *Sun.* When the research project in Chicago ended, I became desk man on the Cincinnati *Times Star,* a newspaper owned by the brother of William Howard Taft, who was to become the next President of the United States. I was glad to go to Cincinnati, a region in which my father and his father had lived. Two Swings were on the bench there at the time, and I did not want for friends. But my sojourn in Cincinnati was not to be long. On one of my regular visits to Chicago, I became violently ill while dining with my uncle at the University Club. It was a stomach upset accompanied by severe leg cramps, and I remember walking up and down the private dining room, cursing like a sailor. The Meads had first-class medical advisers, and an examination showed that I had an inflamed appendix. I was instructed to return to Cincinnati, wait until I felt quite well again, as I was assured I would, and then enter the hospital and have the appendix removed. I carried out this program. I appeared on a Sunday morning, with my bag packed, at the hospital, announced that I was there to have an appendectomy the next morning, went cheerfully to bed, and was operated on the following day.

It was at this point that the Meads gave me the greatest boon of my life thus far: they offered me a year abroad—a "year of study," it was called—which was to be combined with my marriage to a young Frenchwoman, Suzanne Morin, who had been a Mead protégée, and whom I had met at their great student boarding establishment. This was in 1912.

My wife and I planned to divide the year into quarters, one each to be spent in Paris, Munich, Berlin, and London. In

Paris the "study" was to be for me the French language, which, I regret, I studied then and since then without mastering. In Munich the focus was to be on music; in Berlin and London it was to be on world affairs.

The months spent in Paris were uneventful beyond the recurrent delight I felt in living in so handsome a city, with its treasures in art and architecture. It was eventful in my getting to know Paul Scott Mowrer, Paris correspondent of the Chicago *Daily News,* who became a dear friend.

Munich, then capital of the kingdom of Bavaria, was also a kind of cultural capital, with a noted opera company, a good orchestra, and fine art galleries. It was a tidy sort of minor metropolis. Living there was for us an admixture of the brows, the high one artistic, the low one spent with the congenial Bavarians in their vast beer gardens. It was in Munich I was shocked to discover that the knowledge of German I had come by as a child was illusory, and I set myself to learn at least to read the newspapers.

Munich meant music first of all for me. We had been provided money enough to go regularly to the opera and attend concerts, and we had introductions to Munich homes where musicians, including music critics, gathered. I had imagined myself to be a musically educated person. It is true I had heard *Tristan and Isolde* only once, when the Metropolitan came to Cincinnati. I had heard *Madame Butterfly* as an Oberlin student, and I had only once heard *The Ring,* while waiting in London for the family to gather there for my wedding. So, my operatic knowledge was next to nothing. I enjoyed music, but I certainly was no judge of it, a fact I was to learn in those evening social gatherings in Munich. For I would attend some operatic performance and then the next night listen to its being discussed by the experts. I had thought the performance wonderful. The experts tore it to pieces. This amazed and troubled me, for, literally, I did not know what the experts were talking about. All I could assume was that they had knowledge about music, its interpretation and proper performance, of which I did not have an inkling. In the years to come, when I grew better acquainted with the masters and their masterpieces and how they should be performed, I was to learn that the musical experts sometimes tore performances to pieces without being as wise as they sounded. But in

Munich I learned something about listening to music. I also plunged headlong into my Wagner period, something every young music-lover at that time had to go through. I listened to Wagner incessantly in Munich, and attended the festival at Bayreuth. I memorized all the leitmotifs of the operas, and pored over their texts, and read biographies of the master. I experienced a mounting enthusiasm for everything Wagner wrote that did not leave me for several years. Later, in Berlin, where as foreign correspondent I was able to obtain free tickets to the Royal Opera, I heard the Wagner operas so often that I finally began to tire of them; and to this day, when I still consider *Die Meistersinger* one of the greatest of all operas, I doubt if I could manage to sit through more than one or two performances of it. Similarly, I might be able to listen to a few sessions of *Tristan* and of *Götterdämmerung*, but not of many others of the works I once so devoutly worshiped and came to hear so often. Before I was to leave Berlin in 1917, I was listening to Strauss and other moderns and finding Wagner, though still indubitably the greatest musical genius of his generation, somewhat tedious.

Chapter 4 / I Become a Berlin Correspondent

The third quarter of the year's holiday brought us to Berlin. We found it as tidy as Munich, but with less character than either Paris or Munich. It boasted to be a city without slums, but this virtue was offset by the tedious similarity of most of its residential streets, and it had but few arresting and historic monuments and edifices. Such as there were, like the Siegesallee, were more spectacular than impressive. But Berlin was a great world capital for other reasons than its past and its architecture. William II was one of the dominant actors on the world stage, and the busy German capital expressed power if it did not possess great beauty. We did not realize in Paris or Munich that the cloud of a world war was already discernible on the horizon. Nor in Berlin did we at first notice it, but we felt an energy and assertiveness that bespoke the Prussian quality of the emperor as well as of the city.

I was to find my professional luck working for me in Berlin. It was not to be unadulterated luck, as things turned out. One of the correspondents I met was the representative of the Chicago *Daily News*, a person of charm and culture, whom I liked immensely. He became ill while I was there. It was reported to be a serious illness, and his friends told me he probably would not be able to work again for months. The idea came to me that I might be engaged as a substitute till he was well again, and I went to Paris to suggest it to Paul Mowrer. He liked the idea, said he would take it up with Edward

Price Bell, the London correspondent and titular head of the foreign service, and I might hear more of it. I did. I was invited to London to meet Mr. Bell, and he appointed me acting Berlin correspondent. What I did not know at the time was that the Chicago *Daily News* had its own reasons for wanting a new Berlin correspondent altogether, and, on finding the incumbent could be replaced with a promising substitute, got rid of him.

When it became known that he had been dismissed, his friends vented their spleen on me. They carried their displeasure to the Society of Foreign Correspondents in Berlin, where they opposed my election as member on the ground that I had conspired to take a colleague's job away from him. Mr. Mowrer came from Paris to set the record straight, testifying that I had never asked for more than a fill-in appointment while the correspondent was ill. But I was blackballed all the same. I was shocked and resentful, for there was no justice in it. But I learned a lesson or two from it. One was that newspapermen can be uncommonly immature in conducting an organization of professional members. Another was that it was a mistake to meddle with another man's job, even with the most innocent of motives. I did not appreciate the value of this second lesson until many years later, when I was about to be appointed chief of the London bureau of the Philadelphia *Public Ledger*. The Berlin experience unexpectedly justified itself on that occasion, as I shall relate in due course.

The foreign service of the Chicago *Daily News* was to win high plaudits in the years to follow, but at that time it was a somewhat naïve creation that could only have come from the Midwestern mind of Victor F. Lawson, the publisher. Mr. Lawson did not care a hoot about foreign news. He was not interested in the state of the world, in the rising perils that darkened the political horizon, or in the prestige that pioneer foreign correspondence might bring to him as a publisher. The reason he had a foreign service was to have Chicago *Daily News* offices in London, Paris, and Berlin where Chicago subscribers could register in the visitors' book and have their names cabled each day for publication in the paper, thus keeping their friends in touch with their travels. This required the maintenance of presentable offices in the heart of the three leading European cities. They had to be offices that impressed the Chicago visitors with the opulence and solicitude of the *Daily News*. And, in theory, a correspondent had to be in charge to greet and advise the visitors. It happened that the three correspondents were experienced newspapermen, but they never cabled anything to the *Daily News*—other than the names of registered visitors. They did write news features, which they sent by mail. Mr. Lawson was a superb business-man. His only journalistic concepts were those he was sure would sell papers, for which I am not inclined to blame him. He once told me that the feature he would rather pub-lish than anything he could think of would be the auto-biography of Mary Pickford, then rising to stardom. Readers of the Chicago *Daily News,* he told me, were more interested in Mary Pickford than any person in the world. Unfortunately he probably was right about it. But Mr. Lawson had no idea that World War I would break out in 1914 and that the United States would be in it by 1917 and that this would surpass the importance to *Daily News* readers even of Mary Pickford. It was due to no foresight of his that by the time the war came the Chicago *Daily News* had the framework of a foreign news service which in due course was to make the newspaper one of the leaders of the American press.

I had a wonderful time in my first year as Berlin cor-respondent of the Chicago *Daily News.* I was not wise as to world affairs and was not expected to demonstrate wisdom. I was to supply a feature service by mail. Nobody told me what to write. Germany was my field, and I could describe anything and interview anybody I chose. The mail service from abroad was used exclusively in the inside pages of the newspaper, though I aspired to write something so important one day that the editor would have to publish it on page one. Among my interviews, I recall, was one with Professor Albert Einstein in which he told me that he had undertaken to write a populariza-tion of the relativity theory, and that after each chapter he called in his sixteen-year-old daughter and read it to her, thinking that if she could understand it the general public also would be able to. She always said she understood. But when the book was finished, the public did not understand it, and, as Professor Einstein told me, he again questioned his daughter, who confessed that she had not understood anything her father read to her, but had been afraid to tell him so.

I also interviewed Arnold Schönberg, then teaching composition in the Berlin Hochschule, and I remember his saying in effect that it was genius, not modernity, that characterized great new work. If the genius wrote great new works in the language of Beethoven, he said, the style of Beethoven would guide the moderns. This sounded plausible at the time, but since no modern has cast his masterpieces in the mold of Beethoven or any other classic, I have come to doubt the statement.

Among the features I wrote about were the talking horses of Elberfeld and Rolf, the talking dog, which filled the German press at the time. I saw the celebrated Arab stallions, but only in a pasture. They no longer performed, but at one time one of them had been able to extract fifth roots on sight, something humans would have great trouble in doing. Their owner was experimenting with another stallion, which I did watch as he identified letters in the alphabet by stomping his feet in a slow kind of telegraphic code.

I did not see Rolf, the talking dog, for he was dead, but I did interview his owners. This remarkable Airedale had worked out a code for the alphabet and spelled out—always phonetically—brief sentences of communication. He did this for only a few weeks, when he succumbed to brain fever. He had apparently obtained his education lying in the home schoolroom where the crippled mother who owned him taught her children. Once when a child was unable to answer some elementary question, the mother exclaimed: "Why, Rolf knows that!" whereupon the dog leaped up and showed so much excitement that his owner asked him if he wanted to learn how to talk. Subsequently, the dog went through the alphabet and chose his own signal for each letter, one or more pats with the left paw, one or more with the right. The climax of the story came when he was watching his mistress make a painting. She finished it, and the dog leaped up to spell out the words: "Picture finished. Picture lovely." Several psychologists tested Rolf and confirmed his abilities, in fact he was pestered with so many that when one came he refused to answer any questions, which led the psychologist to twit him for being stupid. Rolf retorted: "Rolf not stupid. The man

can go to the devil!" (*"Herr soll mir den Bugel steigen!"*)
Enough German scientists had confirmed the feats of Rolf
and the Elberfeld horses to lead me to believe in them, and I
still think Rolf's comment "Picture finished. Picture lovely" is
the most remarkable communication to come from an animal
to a human being, assuming—as I do—that it was made.

One of my memorable visits was to Bayreuth, where I met
Eva Wagner, the daughter of my then musical hero, Richard
Wagner, and granddaughter of Franz Liszt. I had begged for
the interview by letter, and it was to take place in the evening
at Villa Wahnfried, the Wagner residence in whose grounds
the master lies buried. I was enormously impressed simply to
be received by Eva Wagner and to set foot in her father's
mansion. The interview itself was brief and not very produc-
tive. Meeting an American journalist was no event for Fräulein
Wagner, and she went through it with excusable diffidence.
My first questions dealt with the Bayreuth Festival. She answered them politely; I did not have the courage to break
through her cold reserve, and she soon gave me to understand
that I was to leave. After thanking her, I let myself out of the
front door.

It was a dark night, and the entrances of the house and the
grounds were not illuminated. I had started down the path
to the high iron gate when I was terrified by the onslaught of
what seemed a horde of hounds. Probably there were not more
than four, but they were huge and ferocious, and they made
for me. I had known the grounds were guarded by hounds
protecting the grave of Richard Wagner, but it had not occurred to me that they would be free to attack a guest of the
villa. The front door of the villa was closed, so I could not
take refuge there. There was nothing to do but to make a dash
for the gate. To my horror, it was locked, and my only safety
lay in trying to climb over it or at least get out of reach of the
dogs. The gate must have been eight feet or more high, made
of wrought iron ending in pointed spikes. I threw myself upon
it and managed to climb high enough to be safe from
the snarling hounds.

Fortunately for me, the dogs made so much noise that they
were heard in the villa, and someone realized that the young
American visitor must be trying to get away out of the locked
gate. A light went on, the door opened, a manservant called

to the dogs and walked down to the gate. Keeping the dogs at bay, he unlocked the gate and bowed me out.

This was not my only experience with a member of the Wagner family. Siegfried Wagner was at that time a composer of considerable ability if not genius. Had his name been Hauptmann or Schmidt, he probably would have received some praise and encouragement. But as his father's son, he was merely indulged. He did not measure up to his name. An opera by him was being staged at the Staatsoper in Berlin, which he came to conduct. I asked him for an interview. He told me over the telephone that if I called for him at his hotel the following morning, we could take a walk together in the Tiergarten, Berlin's Central Park. As a young correspondent, I was not unaware of the sad lot of a great man's son, but I was delighted to be privileged to meet him.

I duly called the following morning, and we set out for the Tiergarten. Then followed the most extraordinary interview I can remember ever having taken part in. It was not extraordinary for what Siegfried Wagner said, but for what he did not say. I did not press questions on him, for I was shy. But I gave him an opening to converse, as a reporter should. He declined to use it. We walked together but we did not talk together. I tried again to start a conversation. Siegfried Wagner looked away into the distance as though searching for a comment. He did not find it, and we walked on in silence. I tried a third time and was rebuffed once more, whereat I gave up and decided to keep my mouth shut. We walked, all told, half an hour. On returning to the hotel, he shook hands with me, still in silence, bowed, and smiled. Not a word had been spoken by him. Herr Wagner could at least tell himself that he had kept his promise to me: we had walked together in the Tiergarten. He was a vain-looking man, and, as Wagner's son, that would be understandable. I do not know if he thought he was conferring a favor upon me by simply taking me for a walk with him, the son of the great Wagner, in the Tiergarten. If so, I did not feel honored. I thought it was one of the oddest and rudest experiences of my newspaper life, and somehow on a par with the aggression of the hounds at the Villa Wahnfried. I should add that the two events did not affect my appreciation of Richard Wagner, nor of Cosima, and Siegfried's grandfather, Franz Liszt, who to this day remains one of my favorites in the gallery of the great.

Chapter 5 / The Coming of World War I

As the year 1914 progressed, my attention turned more and more to world affairs, and I made one major effort to interest the Chicago *Daily News* in the mounting danger of war. This was when Chancellor von Bethmann-Hollweg, as a counter-move to France's adoption of the three-year military service, introduced a bill increasing the German army by two army corps. I attended the session of the Reichstag when the bill was introduced and listened attentively to the Chancellor's speech. I realized that war might well be an imminent possibility. And while I had to write my report of this event and its possible significance for the *Daily News* to be sent by mail, I was sure that for once I would have a story on page one. I wrote several thousand words; I quoted von Bethmann-Hollweg at length, explained the power struggle that dominated Europe, and frankly foresaw the possibility of war. I waited for the four or five weeks to pass which it would take to deliver my solemn and warning article to Chicago and for it to appear on page one and be delivered to Berlin. Four weeks passed, then five and six, and finally eight. And then I was to discover an article of mine on an inside page, with von Bethmann-Hollweg's speech omitted, along with all reference to the danger of war. It carried a headline about "a picture of the German Reichstag when the government brings in a bill." Subsequently I was told that Charles Dennis, the managing editor, had said he was not going to put up with any nonsense about the danger of war from his "youngsters" in the European bureaus. But August came, and brought the outbreak of war. A few·weeks were to pass before the *Daily News* changed from mail stories to cables, and I was later given a relay man in Holland to whom I sent my telegrams for forwarding to London and reforwarding to Chicago, and also authorized to send messages via wireless to New York.

In the immediate days before the war, I tried to send cables to Chicago, cables about mobilization, about declarations of war, about passports being given departing ambassadors. All of these efforts to report the early days of crisis in August were fruitless. Not a dispatch of mine arrived in Chicago. I paid out countless German marks for sending them. I don't know where they were held up. They simply vanished. It was three or four weeks before a by-line of mine appeared over cable or wireless dispatches from Berlin.

The first two or three weeks of August were not concerned solely with trying to send news to Chicago. I had to devote a great deal of time to helping stranded Chicagoans and other Americans trying to get out of Germany. The *Daily News* office on Unter den Linden was stormed by these frightened people. Fortunately, the home office had supplied me with a bank account that enabled me to advance money to worthy Chicagoans. I became a travel agent, booking space on the crowded steamers bound for New York, and for years to follow I was to receive thanks from individuals I did not recognize, who blessed me for helping them get out of Berlin. Before the war, international travel did not require passports, a condition which one must assume will not return before the final stages of disarmament have been passed. But in the crisis, passports were introduced, and I spent considerable time at the embassy helping to issue them. My relations with the embassy at that time were most friendly, in particular with an attractive young attaché, doing his first tour of Foreign Service duty, named Chris Herter, later to become Congressman, Governor of Massachusetts, and Secretary of State under President Eisenhower. Ambassador James Gerard and his charming wife were always cordial.

The post office was not far from the Kaiser's palace, and in those first August days he was in residence. So the trips to the post office brought me repeatedly into contact with the im-

mense crowds gathered around the palace. They were singing crowds, and over and over they repeated "The Watch on
the Rhine." I found something incongruous in this. The enemy
in those early days was not considered to be France. It was
Russia. But the Germans had no songs against Russia, though
they were deeply alarmed by what was known as the Slavic
peril. The Russians were far more numerous, and they were a
tread or so below the Germans on the ladder of progress. Germans had been indoctrinated in the value of German *Kultur*
and in despising Russian backwardness. They believed that a
Russian victory would ruin their civilization. The word *Kultur*
is not completely translated by its English counterpart—culture. It stood for a civilized status of a law-abiding state, for
widespread education and the beginning of a welfare community. *Kultur* was to become a war slogan used both by and
against the Germans. After the viciousness of German reprisals in Belgium, it became for the Allies a word of scorn.

In those first days of crisis, certain simple facts stood out:
the origin of it had been the assassination of the Austrian Archduke by a Serbian. This had led to overly stern
Austrian demands. The Hapsburg kingdom was not doing
well, and the outcome of the Second Balkan War had left its
relative power reduced. Elements in the German leadership
no doubt inspired the anti-Serbian demands, which Serbia,
with the understandable backing of Russia, rejected. When
Austria mobilized against Serbia, Russia mobilized against
Austria, but it also mobilized against Germany, which may
have been a mechanical necessity in any mobilization whatever. Germany issued an ultimatum to Russia to cancel the
mobilization, which Russia ignored. Thereupon Germany
mobilized and war became certain.

It was not then credited in Germany that elements in the
German leadership encouraged Austria to be too severe with
Serbia because they wanted a war, which they were sure Germany would win. Most Germans were sure that correspond-
ing elements in Russia, France, and Britain wanted a war
which they were sure would end in German defeat.

It still is possible to make out and document a plausible
case either way. Even hindsight has not cleared away all the
contradictory factors that have made the origin of World War
I an authenticated story of righteousness by the enemies of

Germany. It is true that Sir Edward Grey called for a five-power conference to resolve the Serbian crisis which the Kaiser rejected. Had he accepted, it is conceivable that a Council of Europe might have been renewed and war might have been indefinitely postponed. Even so, Sir Edward Grey, though an open supporter of the peace faction in the British government, participated in secret arrangements for military support of France in a German war, as did Winston Churchill, who pledged the defense of the French channel coast so that the entire French fleet could be stationed in the Mediterranean. These commitments were made without the knowledge of Parliament, which, it can be argued, gave them no validity whatever. But they were indications of intent, and the absence of parliamentary approval did not bother leaders in France and Russia. Britain and France knew at least an early version of Germany's Schlieffen plan to encircle France through Belgium, having bought the information from a German staff officer. But they were confident that the British expeditionary force would hold the German drive through Belgium if it was made from that direction. They were not sure it would be, fearing that its disclosure to them might be a well-planted deception.

But it can be said with a fair degree of certainty that those in power in Russia, France, Germany, and Britain expected a war, one that either side might launch. Both sides expected that if it began in the West, the neutrality of Belgium would be violated. The Germans expected this of the French, the French and British expected it of the Germans, and it can also be said that the French expected it of themselves, if not with the same certainty as the Germans expected it under the Schlieffen plan. As the August crisis drew near, it began to be apparent to the French that the commitments made in secret with Britain might not stand up because of the obduracy of the peace faction in the British government, and it became a matter of urgency that the French should not violate Belgian neutrality first. This accounts for the stern orders issued for the withdrawal of French forces some distance from the Belgian border. Lord Esher had warned the French in 1911, "Never, no matter on what pretext, let the French commanders be led into being the first to cross the Belgian frontier." If they did, England could never be on their side. Belgian neutrality had been pledged in an international treaty in 1837. Barbara Tuchman, in *The Guns of August,* writes that by the spring of 1914 the French and British General Staffs were in complete accord as to "the last billet of every battalion, even to the places where they were to drink their coffee. The number of French railroad cars to be allotted, the assignments of interpreters, the preparation of codes and ciphers, the forage of horses was settled or expected to be consummated by July." The expeditionary force's movement, called Plan W, was prepared for in great secrecy. Half a dozen officers did all the work, down to typing it.

Actually, it did need the violation of Belgian neutrality to bring the British peace faction back into the government after it walked out for a day of protest. But for the Germans, the Treaty of 1837 certainly was not sacrosanct. They did not expect the French to observe it in a war, and they had no intention of doing so themselves. The Schlieffen plan to go through Belgium was not, however, a ruse to take France and Britain or Belgium by surprise. The Germans knew their coming by that route would be anticipated. When Chancellor von Bethmann-Hollweg called the treaty "a scrap of paper," he was not so much mistaken about its inviolability by France or Germany as he was ignorant of the sensitivity of Anglo-Saxon and American public opinion. He did not know the elementary rules of public relations. And like many a statesman suffering from the same ignorance, he was to pay dearly for it.

The world of 1914 and the years immediately preceding it was the scene of a power conflict in which preparations for a showdown were industriously and secretively conducted by both sides. The story was utterly different in 1939. Hitler wanted world dominion and told everyone he would fight for it if it were not accorded him. In 1914, candor was absent, and the certainty of victory also was much less predictable. It was an era of hesitations, circumlocutions, and deceptions.

I can write this now with the grace of hindsight. In 1914, I was both callow and overinfluenced by my German environment. With few exceptions, none of the Germans I knew wanted war, and all were afraid of the results of a conflict with Russia. I took them to be representative of the German nation. One of the exceptions was an editorial writer on the *Berliner*

Tageblatt, whose sister worked as receptionist and secretary in my office. When Germany mobilized, I found he was deeply and passionately gratified. He waved his clenched fist and thanked God. His only displeasure was that the Kaiser had waited so long. He shocked me, but not sufficiently to educate me as well. I knew that the most thoughtful persons believed that war as such was unavoidable, and even considered it to be a kind of beneficial surgical operation for improving the body of society. But as a Berlin correspondent, I should have known enough about contemporary diplomacy to have had at least an inkling of its crosscurrents and inevitable duplicity, particularly in Germany, the country I was studying. But living in Berlin, I was suspicious of Russia and not of Germany, too.

When the German government published its White Paper on the origin of the war, I was convinced by it. Here were diplomatic comments which appeared to demonstrate that Germany had tried to prevent the war. What I did not know at the time was that diplomatic papers of any contrary tenor and effect would be omitted from the White Papers, and that White Papers as such were generally to be studied with skepticism. I was not to learn more of the truth about Germany until the British issued their diplomatic papers. This education came too late to save me from writing for the *Daily News* a full report of the German version of the start of the war, without a word of sophisticated doubt. The White Paper reported that the Kaiser had tried to prevent the war. So he did, though he agreed to actions that made its prevention extremely unlikely. My article was gladly and uncritically reproduced by the Chicago *Daily News.* Chicago was a city with a large German population. I was told subsequently I had saved the *Daily News* 50,000 German subscribers. A local German patriotic society reprinted my article under the title: *How Germany Was Forced into the War,* a pamphlet still to be found in reference libraries. I have long since stopped blushing about it.

It was the day the British documents came into my hands that I made my great leap forward in diplomatic education. I ceased to trust German diplomatic documentation. But I was not to learn till later that the British and the French also omitted documents, and had engaged in the completion of secret military arrangements to assist one another in a German war. I had had my opening lesson in realizing that where national decisions are to be made by the exertion of power, half-truths by diplomats are as much implements of power as guns, and in their way quite as effective.

The German army did not like to have newspapermen "covering" the war. Their last experience with journalists at the front had been in 1870. A large element of the French army disappeared before the Battle of Sedan, and the Germans could not find it. They were to read with great astonishment in the London *Times* just where it was from the British correspondent attached to it. The information helped them win the battle and the war. But that good fortune did not soften their judgment of the effect of having war correspondents at the front. The rule was passed out in Berlin that not one of a large corps of correspondents stationed there was to be permitted to join the German armies. However, other influences were at work inside the government, though they did not at once help me and my associates in Berlin. The German embassy in Washington told Berlin quite sternly it could not ignore American opinion, which might become even more decisive a factor in the war than secrecy at the front. The first result was that a handful of American journalistic celebrities, including Richard Harding Davis, Irving Cobb, and John T. McCutcheon, was admitted to Belgium. Others were to follow.

One of the early groups included Hans von Kaltenborn, then editor of the Brooklyn *Eagle*. We met in Berlin and struck up a relationship that has remained cordial for nearly fifty years. To show how much I liked him, I lent him my fur coat to wear to the front, because he had not come warmly enough clad. These men did not witness much fighting or become acquainted with the grand strategy of the German armies. But as it turned out, they did report the brutality of German reprisals against Belgian *franc-tireurs*, so that the result of admitting them did not further the German cause as had been anticipated.

The regular foreign correspondents in Berlin at this time experienced nothing but frustration. I was a youngster and appreciated that I was not entitled to the same treatment as a Richard Harding Davis and an Irvin Cobb. Still, I felt it was my duty to report the war and if possible to get to the front to do so. The officials in the press department at the Foreign Office were sympathetic and urged me to have patience. They knew that world opinion was to be as much influenced by what we reported as by what the stars selected by the German embassy in Washington had been expected to report. What they had in prospect was not war correspondence, but visits behind the front where German successes could be attested.

The fall of Liége presented a most suitable occasion for such an excursion, for this fortress, which had been expected to withstand siege for a year, had fallen in less than two weeks, and presaged a swifter German sweep in the west than any of the French and British experts had foreseen. It was one of the turning points in the war. It put the whole concept of a Western victory over Germany in jeopardy.

The Foreign Office arranged for a group of correspondents to visit Liége, and I was included. This trip proved to be a remarkable experience. For one thing, included in our party was the German socialist Karl Liebknecht, who was to become the first leader of German Communism, and was to be murdered along with Rosa Luxemburg in 1919. Naturally I was glad to get to meet him, but I have never understood why Herr Liebknecht was taken along. The socialists in the Reichstag had voted for the war credits, but some had refused to go along, among them Liebknecht. The sensationally swift fall of Liége would hardly have reconciled Liebknecht to the war, and certainly not to the violation of Belgian neutrality, nor the brutality of the German army in Belgium. No effort was made to isolate Liebknecht from the correspondents during the trip. But he did not feel like talking freely on the train, particularly to foreigners. I had several conversations with him, but it was clear from them that he would withhold his criticisms for domestic use.

When we clambered out of the train in Liége and left the station, we saw a city here and there marked by destroyed buildings, though still carrying on its subdued wartime life. But when we were driven to the outskirts, where the forts had been, we beheld a scene of unutterable destruction. The forts at Liége had been built to resist the strongest artillery known at the time and were made of thick concrete and metal. These massive protections had been shattered as by a supernatural force. The huge pieces of the forts' sides and tops lay like piles of porcelain after a rock had crashed through a china closet. I shall not forget how it looked or how it smelled. The corpses of the Belgian garrison had not yet been removed from the ruins. The stench was not overpowering, but it was dreadfully pungent. I recall Liebknecht's expressions of horror and disgust as we climbed over the ruins.

What unprecedented force had destroyed the Liége forts? We asked the officer who escorted us on our tour, and he proved to be proudly communicative. The Germans, he said, had created siege guns the like of which had never before existed. They were Germany's secret weapon. They had reduced the forts by August 16, and it now is conceded that the Liége forts held up the Germans only two days on their sweep around the Allied western line. This remarkable achievement, as events developed, did not decide the outcome on the Western front. What it did was to prevent an early Allied victory. If the northern end of the Western front had held, the French were confident they would have crushed the center of the German front.

The great siege guns had been built by Krupp and Skoda. The Skoda guns were 305's. The Krupp guns were 420's, and the most powerful that man had made up to that time. The Krupp guns were ready by 1908. No worker was engaged on more than a detail of their manufacture, and their existence was one of the best-kept secrets of the century.

The Krupp guns were less mobile than the smaller Skodas, but were more destructive. Célestin Demblon, deputy of Liége, as reported by Mrs. Tuchman, saw one of the 420's being dragged through the city of Liége to be set up to fire at the forts. According to him, it was "a piece of artillery so colossal that we could not believe our eyes. . . . The monster advanced in two parts, pulled by 36 horses. The pavement trembled. . . . In the Parc d'Avroy it was carefully mounted and scrupulously aimed. Then came the frightful explosion; the crowd was flung back, the earth shook like an earthquake. . . ." In these days of nuclear weapons, this is almost archaic. But at that time, forts could be staunch in defense and stronger than any artillery that could be used against them.

The Krupp mortars were indeed news. The officer who told us about them certainly felt no compunction about doing so. Obviously he had not been instructed to be silent about them, and he did not pledge us to silence. We saw the havoc they had worked; we knew Liége had fallen almost immediately; and he explained to us how and why. He was not a press official, but a regular army officer. If he did fear the danger of a leak, he could reassure himself that the Berlin censorship would be able to control our dispatches, for we were not being allowed to send dispatches until our return.

We were back in Berlin the next day. I had in my possession what, in its category, certainly was the most important single military detail of the war story so far. What should I do with it? I have not hesitated to confess to being callow in diplomatic affairs. But I had resources as a reporter. My cousin Henry Mead, son of Professor Mead of Chicago, was in Berlin temporarily helping in my office, and one of his Chicago University fellow-students was leaving the next day to return to his studies. I asked this young man if he wanted to earn twenty-five dollars. How? By memorizing a news dispatch and going into the office of the Chicago *Daily News* in London and typing it off for the chief of the bureau. He agreed. I wrote the dispatch—it was about 800 words long—and date-lined it "Namur, by courier." For by the time we were back in Berlin, Namur, also an "impregnable" fortress, had been blown to bits by the great siege guns. I wrote my story as an explanation, first, of how Namur had been destroyed, and then filled in the details of the fall of Liége.

The Chicago student memorized the dispatch well and duly typed it off correctly in the London office of the Chicago *Daily News* two days later. That newspaper was to have one of the first "scoops" of the war. The Krupp guns had not by then been christened "Big Berthas," but they were the same that were used for the bombardment of Paris later in the war. Naturally my dispatch was republished around the world. I never was questioned about it by the German censorship, as I was to be about other stories sent later across the border. This may be because the censorship was not yet well organized. But it also may be because the Germans wanted the news of their great siege guns known. It made them more fearsome. It changed the forecast of the duration of the fighting on the Western front. But if that was the reason, the story would have received even wider publicity if it had been told to Richard Harding Davis, Irvin Cobb, and other notables who reached the front before I did. My own belief is that the German officer who told us about the guns had not been cautioned to keep his mouth shut. And he was as happy to tell the story as I was to hear it. I was simply lucky.

I should say at this point that my marriage did not long survive the beginning of the war. A son had been born in 1913. Another child was on the way, and my French wife, finding life in the German capital both disagreeable and the future there uncertain, returned to the United States.

Chapter 6 / A Mission to Sir Edward Grey

Among the acquaintances I made at this time was Baroness von Schroeder, wife of a *Junker* nobleman of wealth and station. She was known as "the American Baroness," though she was a native of Canada. She was tall, had sloping shoulders, an upturned nose, wide-apart bright blue eyes, a retreating chin, and a flair for politics. She was a socialite supporting the moderate von Bethmann-Hollweg against army extremists. She gave dinners to which the Chancellor and his friends were pleased to come. She repeatedly told me that von Bethmann was a moderate, opposed to any annexations after the war. I said that if that were true, he should tell me and let me repeat it to Sir Edward Grey, for the British certainly had a different view of him. And that was precisely what she brought to pass.

I was received by the Chancellor in the somber palace where his office was situated. I was invited to sit in the ample chair at the side of his huge desk, and there I was told, without any preliminary conversation, just what I was to repeat to Sir Edward Grey. Germany would not annex any Belgian territory after the war and would guarantee Belgium's independence. But he added a fateful phrase. I also was to tell Sir Edward that Germany would want an indemnity for having been forced into the war.

Herr von Bethmann-Hollweg may have noted my disappointment at hearing this. "Can I trust you?" he asked. "Not a word of this must be published in the newspapers. You understand that?" "Of course," I said. "And you are able to deliver the message to Sir Edward Grey in person, for it must go to no one else in London." I said I was confident the London office of my newspaper could assure this. "Then come back and tell me what he says." The Chancellor, a tall figure of a man, with gaunt cheeks above his short beard, rose from his desk. "I must caution you again," he said, "not a word of this in the newspapers. If it is published, I shall have to say I never said it." I repeated that I understood, and he held out his hand gravely.

My mind raced with dissociated ideas. I realized that I was in the office of Bismarck and von Bülow, where the modern German empire had been blueprinted, and that here the issue of the European war and the European peace was to be shaped. I was astonished to be there, and that I should be there undertaking to bear a message to London. I also was disconcerted by the sentence about an indemnity. I knew it made the mission to Sir Edward Grey futile.

I so confessed to Baroness von Schroeder, to whom I at once reported. "Don't be so stupid," she said. "The Chancellor was simply protecting himself. He has to do that. If the army hears he has been talking peace with Sir Edward Grey, he can point to the demand for an indemnity. After all, he has to take precautions. This is a risky step for him. Sir Edward need only say that an indemnity is out of the question, but that he is interested in the proposal about Belgium. He will be smart enough to see why the indemnity has to be mentioned."

This reassured me. That night I was on the train for Holland and a day later walked into the London office of the Chicago *Daily News*. Edward Price Bell, who was in charge, was astonished, but when I told him why I had come, he lifted the telephone and it was at once arranged that I should be received by Sir Edward Grey late that afternoon. It was faster work than would have been possible in Berlin.

I had little firsthand knowledge of the British at that time. I knew how the Germans regarded them, Sir Edward in particular. He was considered the arch-conspirator, the passionless builder of Germany's ring of enemies, and especially dangerous because of his ability to speak hypocritically about moral virtues while acting in farsighted national interest. The

Sir Edward I met was a revelation. He had the personal appearance of a shaggy ascetic. He was tall, erect, slender, with thin but untidy hair. His clothes were not well pressed. At the time, I knew nothing about Sir Edward, the naturalist, of the breed of Englishmen he represented—sensitive, shy, and complex—or that he was one of the best-educated men in the world.

I delivered my message from Herr von Bethmann-Hollweg and ended with the instructions I had received to return to him and repeat what Sir Edward had to say in reply. Sir Edward's face turned crimson when I spoke the word "indemnity." I thought of Baroness von Schroeder's explanation of it and almost blurted it out. But Sir Edward gave me no time to blurt out anything. He ignored what I said about no annexations in Belgium and Belgian independence. He struck at the word "indemnity" with a kind of high moral fury, and launched into one of the finest speeches I had heard. Did not Herr von Bethmann-Hollweg know what must come from the war? It must be a world of international law where treaties were observed, where men welcomed conferences and did not scheme for war. I was to tell Herr von Bethmann-Hollweg that his suggestion of an indemnity was an insult and that Great Britain was fighting for a new basis for foreign relations, a new international morality.

Whether I might have saved something from this interview and the efforts behind it is a question I still am not able to answer. If I had been ten years older, I should have asked Sir Edward to let me tell him a little about the political situation in Berlin, and in doing so would have explained that the mention of an indemnity had undoubtedly been a kind of escape clause for the Chancellor, in the event that the army learned that he was talking about peace with the British Foreign Secretary, through an American intermediary. I should have impressed upon Sir Edward that the message in which the Chancellor was interested was the pledge of no annexations and the guarantee of Belgian independence after the war. I should have pointed out that Sir Edward had it in his power to encourage quietly the moderates in the German government, but that a blank refusal even to give one word on the promise about Belgium might weaken, not strengthen, the very influences he must wish to see reinforced. I said none of these things and should have said all of them. But I am not sure that if I had it would have made any difference. Sir Edward's whole case for going to war rested on the German violation of the guaranteed neutrality of Belgium. A promise not to violate it further or again would not have impressed him. Sir Edward, in his memoirs, wrote that early in the war an American correspondent had come from the German Chancellor with a message that Germany would expect an indemnity for having been forced into the war, and did not even mention the promise against annexation and the guarantee of Belgian independence. That was all he remembered from my visit. If I had carried out my mission with more sophistication, perhaps he would have remembered the real purpose of it.

When I returned to Berlin, I was again received by Chancellor von Bethmann-Hollweg and repeated to him what Sir Edward Grey had said. He listened without comment, then thanked me for my report. He could not have been surprised. His government had made a public promise of no annexations with no effect on the British. I do not believe it dawned on him that everything Sir Edward had said was stirred by the sinister word "indemnity," which he himself had used. And I am sure that Baroness von Schroeder was able to solace him at the next dinner he attended at her house on the ground that my visit had demonstrated that he alone was a man of peace.

This was not my only undertaking under the aegis of Baroness von Schroeder. One of my constant complaints to her was the refusal of the German army to permit correspondents in Berlin to visit the front. She thought she could do something about this, and she did, though what she did proved improvident and short-lived.

Her scheme involved my buying an automobile and an outfit of surgical instruments. I was to enlist the co-operation of a surgeon whom she knew, then train myself to be his assistant in rendering first aid. We were to proceed to the headquarters of a commander whom she knew, the automobile and its equipment were to be donated to the army, and the surgeon and I were to be retained with it. From the front I would write dispatches to her, which she would forward to my relay man in Holland. One condition was that the plan had to be kept a secret. I could not consult my home office about it, nor tell anyone else. But if the scheme succeeded, I would be the only American correspondent actually stationed at the front. This was tempting, and I yielded to the temptation. I bought a car—and cars were expensive in those days—and the surgical equipment. I took a course in first aid and won a certificate of competence in it.

Baroness von Schroeder succeeded in obtaining permits for the car, the surgeon, and myself to proceed to the headquarters of her friend, the commander. But that was where her magic ended. We arrived at headquarters late in the afternoon. I turned the car over to the German army. The surgeon and I were invited to dine with the commander. But I was told what I must have expected, that no foreigner could be permitted to remain at the front, and I was to return, leaving the next morning.

The story, however, has its silver lining. I found th   a congenial German lieutenant and chauffeur were assigned to take me back to Berlin. The officer was provided an unlimited gasoline permit and was given no orders about what route to take on the return trip. When we set out, he told me that he, too, would like to see what Belgium looked like after its battles, and since he could draw as much gasoline as he wished, we could go pretty much where we pleased, as long as we did not take too much time about it. So, even if I was not at the front sending dispatches in my uniform as a medical corps assistant, I was riding across Belgium, seeing pretty much anything I wanted, all of which I could write up at length after returning to Berlin. This, of course, I did. And when the story about the car I had bought for the Chicago *Daily News* to present to the German army was told to the home office, I was cautioned never to spend such a sum again without permission, but was not severely reprimanded. The adventure had yielded many columns of timely copy. They may not have been first-rate war correspondence, for the only hostilities recounted were about being shot upon one night by a *franc-tireur* at a local post where we bivouacked. But at any rate, to stretch a point, I had been under fire; I had been at the front; I had seen a great deal of Belgium and had written voluminously about it. I am not now mindful that the trip through Belgium was particularly notable. We saw plenty of buildings in ruin from shells, but life was proceeding after a fashion wherever we rode. The Belgian farmers and townsfolk went about their normal occupations, now doing so under military supervision. German uniforms were everywhere. I asked some questions about the conduct of the invading troops, but because I was always escorted by the German lieutenant, the replies were laconic and uninformative. It was not much, but other Berlin correspondents had not been so fortunate.

Chapter 7 / Experiences in Turkey

It is more than a guess that the outcome of World War I—
and much more—turned on the role of Turkey. Had the crumbling Ottoman Empire, then under the rule of the Young
Turks, been an ally of Great Britain, it is easy to imagine that
Russia could have been bolstered with adequate supplies sent
through the Dardanelles and the Black Sea and sustained itself against the attack of the German army on the Eastern
front. If Russia had not collapsed, there would have been no
Bolshevik revolution, certainly not in 1917, and the rapid
growth of Communism would have been deferred and its future altered. International relations everywhere would have
been totally different today.

The Allies made two tremendous efforts to overpower
Turkey after the war had started. Both were inspired by Winston Churchill, then First Lord of the Admiralty. It is one of
the galling ironies of his history that Churchill virtually vetoed a British-Turkish alliance shortly before the war. He had
visited the Young Turks in Constantinople in 1909, and when
a Young Turk delegation went to London in 1911 to seek
a British alliance, this was turned down, largely through
Churchill's influence. The Young Turks, under Enver and
Talaat, had ceased to be an attractive social force and had de-
generated into a corrupt and decaying oligarchy, which is an
excuse for Churchill's judgment—save that history does not

excuse consequences, and the British decision was one of the most fateful made in modern times.

The Young Turks had Germany to turn to, which they knew at the time the delegation visited London. The Kaiser was obsessed with his dream of a Berlin-to-Baghdad axis, and he wanted a Turkish alliance, though he, too, knew the irresponsibility of the Enver-Talaat regime and wanted to buy his alliance at a low price and keep his commitments down. He did send a military mission to strengthen the Turkish military forces and defenses, which had been significantly improved by July, 1914. The British at the same time sent a naval mission, which had much less of an impact. In July of 1911, Turkey started talk of an alliance with Germany, to which the Germans, like the British, had previously been indifferent. On July 28 Turkey asked an offensive and defensive alliance to become operative if either party went to war with Russia. But though the Turks saw world war looming up, they were not sure Germany would win, and had their doubts about the worth of an alliance.

Once more Britain helped them make up their minds. The British had just completed the construction of two battleships on Turkish order, armed with 13.5-inch guns, for which the money had been raised by the patriotic contributions of Anatolian peasants. The British confiscated these ships with scant apologies. So it is not illogical that on August 3 Turkey should have signed a treaty of alliance with Germany. Still, the Young Turk regime was not enthusiastic about its own action. When war broke out between Germany and Russia, it did not declare war on Russia, and it toyed with the possibility of maintaining its neutrality. The sensational arrival of the German warships *Goeben* and *Breslau* in the Dardanelles was needed to stiffen the regime's militancy. This again was one of those ironic events with tremendous consequences. For the British could have disposed of the *Goeben* and the *Breslau* long before they reached Turkish waters. They failed to do so simply because it did not occur to them that the ships were heading for the Dardanelles. They thought they were bound to attempt to escape into the Atlantic. Turkey was still being tragically underestimated.

I should like to believe that Charles Dennis, managing editor of the Chicago *Daily News*, or its publisher, Victor F.

Lawson, had insight about the importance of Turkey in the war, which led them to send their Berlin correspondent to that country. But I have no reason to think so. They were assigning other men to the Berlin office—not formally, but temporarily—one of them a passionate Germanophile, Otto Schuette, the other Harry Hansen, who was later to make a name for himself as a distinguished literary editor. So I was sent on an excursion through the Balkans with instructions to end in Constantinople. Already there were rumors that the Allied fleet might attempt to force the Straits of the Dardanelles, and if there was any likelihood of this, the Chicago office wanted me to be on hand. For me, nothing could have been more appreciated than my new assignment. I already knew much of Europe firsthand, and now I was to extend my knowledge to Asia Minor. Constantinople, lying on both sides of the Bosporus, was itself a strange and new spectacle. The minarets that rose from all parts of the city and the be-fezzed men and veiled women marked it as a Moslem metropolis. Here was the Byzantine masterwork, the church of Saint Sophia, one of the loveliest of all churches. Here were the seven hills that had looked down on so much history. And here were the million and more residents whose ancient capital could change the destiny of the modern world.

I found Constantinople the scene of an unexpected and exceedingly helpful rivalry, so far as I was concerned. It was between Henry Morgenthau, United States Ambassador (and father of Franklin D. Roosevelt's Secretary of the Treasury), and Baron von Wangenheim, the German Ambassador. Though Enver Pasha had given the order permitting the entry of the *Goeben* and the *Breslau* through the straits, he had done so with utmost reluctance, for the ships were asking entry as allies and not by invitation. After their entry, he continued for a time to play at neutrality. The German warships were donated by the German government to Turkey, their names Turkified, and their German crews were capped with fezzes.

Finally the two ships made raids into the Black Sea and bombarded Sevastopol. This, of course, was the end of neutrality. The Allies declared war, and British and French interests in Constantinople were consigned to Ambassador Morgenthau, which enormously increased his importance.

There was only one other American correspondent in Constantinople when I arrived, George Schreiner, of the Associated Press, and he and I quickly formed an alliance of our own, agreeing to share everything we obtained. Schreiner was an Americanized Boer, a great hulk of a man with a thick accent, who had been an artillery captain in the Boer War. Having fought against Britain, he was understandably and ardently pro-German. But it was the warmth of his sense of fellowship, not his politics, that endeared him to me, and we became close friends.

I had arrived in Constantinople with recommendations to Baron Wangenheim from Undersecretary of State for Foreign Affairs Arthur Zimmermann and from Matthias Erzberger, the gifted and genial head of the Catholic Center party in the Reichstag, who later had much to do with bringing the war to a close, for which he was assassinated by a right-wing fanatic. So I had even better credentials at the German embassy than Schreiner, and we stood equally well with Ambassador Morgenthau. I met Enver Pasha, then thirty-eight and the military force in the government, and Talaat Bey, Minister of the Interior and the most powerful domestic political figure.

Enver was handsome and aloof, and wore upturned mustachios like the Kaiser's. I was told that he was headstrong and vain. He was responsible for the disastrous campaign against Russia in the Caucasus undertaken in October, 1914, contrary to the most emphatic advice of the German mission. Talaat Bey I found to be affable. I would not believe that such a pleasant man, with such a friendly broad face, would become answerable for the massacre of three-quarters of a million of the two million Armenians in Turkey. But he decided to rid Turkey of all Armenians by death or deportation, because he considered them a fifth column, and, heedless to the pleas of Ambassador Morgenthau, he fulfilled at least part of this plan. The racial hatred and massacre took place months after the Turkish triumph in the Dardanelles. Talaat, as I now see him, was a forerunner of Hitler in the dastardly practice of genocide.

I should also mention meeting Halide Edib, Turkey's first feminist, who was to become one of her country's outstanding writers, and at that time was celebrated both for her beauty— she was winsome, red-haired, and slender as a boy—and for her political and social courage. She openly campaigned for the equal rights of women; she had herself been divorced by her husband, and fought to obtain the same right to freedom for wives. Later she was to serve in the field as aide to Kemal Pasha in his fight for independence, and then, disillusioned by the execution of some of her closest friends for treason by Kemal, went into exile in France and Britain. I was to renew my friendship with her in London, and with her second husband, Dr. Adnan Adivar, who had been rector of the University of Constantinople. Much later, I was able to visit her for a few hours in 1955 on my way home from the Bandung conference; Dr. Adnan at that time was critically ill and later died.

As a correspondent in Constantinople, I had two primary ambitions: to go to the Dardanelles to wait for the entry of the Allied fleet, and to interview the Turkish Sultan. Both objectives were submitted to the two ambassadors. Both of them went to work on them. Both were to be realized. I became one of four correspondents—Schreiner and two Germans—permitted to go to the Dardanelles, where we were stationed for six weeks. And after witnessing the engagement of the great Allied fleet against the Turkish forts and returning to Constantinople, some of us interviewed the Sultan.

At the Dardanelles, we were housed in a small inn at Chanak Kale, a community of 30,000 on the Asiatic side of the straits. This was because the strongest Turkish fort, Hamidieh, was there, staffed by German gunners and officers and equipped with 13-inch guns that had been smuggled through Romania and Bulgaria. A Turkish officer, Fouad Bey, was assigned to us, and the five of us had, to start with, to improvise a kind of language fellowship. Wilhelm Schwedler, of the Wolff Agency, I had known in Berlin. He spoke some English. George Schreiner spoke both English and German; Ernst Grunewald, of the *Vossiche Zeitung,* spoke no English; Fouad Bey spoke French and some German. I spoke German after a fashion, and a little French. So we agreed to do all our communicating in German, a fact which finally, by the end of my stay in the Dardanelles, got me over the hump in recapturing the language. (I could not speak it grammatically, but I could express myself fluently.) While there I also read Part I of Goethe's *Faust* in German, the first German classic I ever read through in the original. Our group could take meals at a number of Chanak's restaurants, all simple and of the Greek cuisine, and we spent a great deal of time over tea, Turkish coffee, or beer, in the company of the two chief German officers in Fort Hamidieh. For three weeks this sociability was our only routine.

It was broken once by a visit by Emil Ludwig, the best-known popular biographer of his time in Germany, who was then temporarily assigned to the *Berliner Tageblatt*, and there also was a visit by Ambassador Morgenthau, who called me aside and, with his characteristic thoughtful generosity, produced a fat wallet filled with Turkish gold pounds, which he handed over to me as an emergency loan. I have never experienced more consideration from the hand of any United States ambassador.

Ludwig's visit gave me the opportunity to propose to Fouad a camel trip to the ruins of Troy, which lay on the Asiatic side of the straits, five hours' ride from the entry. Ludwig was delighted with the proposal, whereas my other colleagues had not been. Camels were duly ordered, and Ludwig and I made our long and bumpy ride.

What impressed me most about Troy was the smallness of the excavated city. It was no more spacious than a moderate-sized farmyard, and after seeing it I could well understand that the walled city itself was used only in time of siege. At other times, its residents lived in quarters outside the walls. The miniature Troy was hard to reconcile with the importance this historic site had in my mind. However, Dr. Ludwig and I scrambled about the excavations with excitement, identifying in their order the seven cities that had been excavated. Ludwig was a cultured companion, and a sentimental one, for I recall his plucking a wildflower, exclaiming volubly over its loveliness, and stowing it away in his wallet, which I confess I liked him for doing.

But the most singular happening of our visit was when we crept to the heights overlooking the water front, and there saw stationed a warship named—of all the names that might have been present there—the *Agamemnon*. It was a strange example of the depth of history.

The Allied fleet had begun serious operations against the forts at the mouth of the straits on February 19. These we could not see from Chanak Kale, but we could hear the rumbling of distant bombardment. The outer forts were not heavily armed, but the Turks had many mobile mortar batteries in the hills with which they peppered the Allied warships and mine sweepers. For the Turks this was at best delaying action. The decisive battle of the Dardanelles would be fought at the narrows—where we were stationed, and where the Turks had eleven forts with seventy-two guns. A strong Allied fleet should have been able to batter these forts into silence, quickly clear the mines, and sail on to Constantinople. Then, as Lord Kitchener is quoted as saying, it would be winning not only a battle but a war.

The outer forts at the mouth of the straits were silenced and evacuated on February 25. We did not know that the Allies had landed marines to blow up abandoned guns, smash searchlights, and wreck Turkish emplacements. Nor did we know that Turkish troops later rallied and drove the landing parties back to their ships. We were told that the Turkish howitzers hidden in the hills were proving effective against both mines sweepers and warships.

On March 3 the Allied fleet provided us with our first grand spectacle by sailing into the straits eighteen ships strong, to bombard a Turkish battery at Dardanus, five miles below the narrows. A point of land jutted out to hide the full view of the fleet, and our Turkish officer suggested that we walk the hour and a half needed to obtain a view of Dardanus from the rear. This we did and indeed came much too close to the battery for our comfort, for shells from the battleships fell not more than half a mile ahead of us, sending up geysers of dirt and showers of splinters. But we had the ships in full view and could see the great splashes in the water as the shells from the mortars in Dardanus fell around them. Our accompanying officer had one of the ships in focus in his binoculars and cried out: *"Ein Treffer!"* ("A hit!") as a vast cloud of smoke rose from the vessel. The ship withdrew and sailed out of the straits.

The bombardment lasted two and a half hours, and by the time we left, the Dardanus batteries were not firing back. We assumed they were knocked out, but we were told the next day that they had suffered no damage or casualties, and had been so skillfully concealed under cover that the British hydroplane that came over on its reconnaissance duty may not have been able to see them.

On March 5, the Allied fleet provided us a still rarer spectacle, sailing far into the straits, though keeping out of range of the forts at the narrows, and bombarding the forts at Killid Bahr, on the European side. With my colleagues, I watched this scene from the top of an ancient tower, Kale Sultanie, situated on the Asiatic side, only a little more than a mile from Killid Bahr. For a time, as I reported in the first of my Dardanelles dispatches to be published in Chicago, the shells dropped with surprising accuracy around the fort. Now and then one fell short and sent up a column of water 200 feet high, the shell bursting and scattering splinters over an area of three-quarters of a mile, which popped like rifle shots as they hit and cooled in the water. Many splinters flew over our tower.

As we looked down at the forts around Hamidieh on the Asiatic side, we could see the 13-inch guns and their crews ready for action, their massive shells hanging behind the breeches in cradles held by cranes and ready for insertion. Hamidieh was staffed by Turkish infantry in addition to the German gunners and officers. As we looked down, we could see a Mohammedan chaplain walking back and forth in a long robe, red sash, and white turban. The day before, on entering the fort, we passed a young Turkish soldier in a gray uniform kneeling on the ground with face turned upward, eyes closed, and lips moving in a silent recital of the prescribed verses of the Koran. As I wrote at the time, I had seen many soldiers of the so-called Christian nations, but I had never seen one who in broad daylight knelt down and addressed himself to God.

This bombardment had taken place on a Wednesday, and by Sunday nothing more had happened. Because the British had apparently scheduled themselves for a day of rest on previous Sundays, we expected nothing on Sunday, March 9. But we were to be surprised. At eleven o'clock the warning flag went up on Kale Sultanie, and the sound of heavy fire could be heard down the straits. We hurried to the tower and our lookout from its summit. We saw that Fort Medjidieh, just across the straits, was under bombardment. This was too close to make Kale Sultanie a safe observation post, and we descended to another shelter we had found, which lay between Kale Sultanie and Fort Hamidieh, consisting of a sandbank behind which we had dug standing room deep enough for us to protrude no more than our heads over the top for a view of the straits. Five battleships were in closer to the narrows than ever before. Two French ships were taking shots at Turkish howitzer batteries on the distant hillsides. Beside them were two British ships of the *Agamemnon* class, and on the right a ship of the *Lord Nelson* class. They were devoting themselves to Medjidieh with a din that surpassed anything I had yet heard. For a time we stood up, watching the attack. Then a shell fell in the water a few hundred yards ahead of us, sending its splinters screaming over our heads. We kept down after that.

One feature of the day was that the Turkish battle cruiser *Barbarossa Harradin* joined in the fray, taking a position in the first narrows of the Dardanelles and firing over the hills on the five Allied ships, the first time, perhaps, that a modern warship had ever engaged in indirect fire against other modern warships. The super-dreadnaught *Queen Elizabeth*, the prize of the Allied fleet, with its 15-inch guns, also tried the experiment of indirect fire, lying off the promontory behind Medjidieh and dropping shells on the fort.

But the climax of the day came when we heard sharp commands from Hamidieh, followed by a flash, another and another, and then a tremendous roar as its big guns fired at the Allied ships. I confess that we sent up a cheer. No matter how we wanted the war to end, we were ourselves imperiled by those ships down the straits and could not help identifying ourselves with the defending Turks. We rejoiced. We stood up and yelled our delight. But we had to train our glasses at once on the ships to see what the three shots had accomplished. We saw one drop plump on a warship and send up a huge column of black smoke. The other two sent up geysers in the sea close by.

The fire of the ships turned at once to Hamidieh, and the explosions around us multiplied as the sound grew more deafening. Our observation post obviously was no longer safe, and we scooted into Kale Sultanie, not to mount its ancient stairs, but to take shelter behind its thick walls. And here we remained, until I noticed that we were beside a huge pile of ammunition packing boxes. With my recollection of the havoc done at Liége when a shell had dropped into an ammunition dump, I cried my warning, and we shifted to another wall well away from this danger. There we stayed until Fouad Bey proposed going into Chanak Kale, where he knew of a teahouse on the water front with large glass windows where we could continue to watch the shelling and drink tea at the same time. It was from this more urbane vantage that we witnessed the rest of the battle. After Hamidieh had scored its hit, the Allied ships retreated to greater safety, and after a short spell, all the ships left the scene and sailed away.

We rushed into Fort Hamidieh to learn how much damage had been done. We found the German officers in the highest elation. They had waited for this day for many weeks. They had fired sixteen shells and scored—they said—three bull's-eyes. The damage to the fort was incredibly small. The earth around the forts had been messed up, but the guns were intact. Two days later I received permission to cross to the European side and see what the bombardment of Medjidieh had amounted to. The firing there had been more severe, and I expected to see much worse damage. But there, again, it was unexpectedly light. I was told that, in all, 354 shells had fallen around the forts and buildings overlooked by the ancient tower of Killid Bahr. Two shells had struck a large barracks. One had unsettled the ground adjacent to the foundation of one gun, which a pick-and-shovel crew was able to repair quickly. The old tower had been hit twice, but was not even cracked by the blows. The Allied naval guns were powerful and their shells were armor-piercing. But earth and thick masonry they could not shatter. Direct hits in gun openings of the forts could kill gunners and dislodge and even ruin guns. But these needed luck as well as science. And the forts at the narrows had luck on their side.

Nine eventless days were to pass before, on March 18, the Allied fleet made its final spectacular effort to force the straits. That is a date to take account of. On it the Allies opened the door to Constantinople and then failed to go through. They waged the greatest naval action against land fortifications in all history, and while they did not knock out Fort Hamidieh, at the Dardanelles narrows, they so depleted it of ammunition that a return on March 19 would have given entry into the Sea of Marmara, and, with some mine sweeping for a day or so, Constantinople would have lain helplessly beyond. I believe the battle of March 18, of which I was an eyewitness, was the most spectacular battle to have been seen by news correspondents in World War I. Three of us watched it from beginning to end, Schreiner, Grunewald, and myself.

We were drinking tea in a café in Chanak when the first shot fell. It struck about a quarter of a mile beyond the town. We jumped up and rushed out to see the telltale smoke. The café and surrounding shops emptied themselves instantly. Shutters rattled into place as the shops closed, and the streets filled with adults. Most of them took off for the eastern exit of the town. We went directly to Fort Hamidieh, thinking at first to take up our observation post on Kale Sultanie. The bustle we expected to find in the outer yard of the fort was absent; all personnel already had taken cover. Still, we thought that the ships were back to hammer the forts across the straits. Near the water front, directly adjoining Fort Tchemenlik, was a small, thick wall behind which we took our cover. From there we could see twelve battleships in the straits from seven to nine miles out; later, six others replaced them. Five of the first were English, the others French. They cruised in two great circles, firing rapidly. Some of the shots were going into forts across the straits, and the hillside there was soon covered by smoke, which allowed us only an occasional glimpse of the old tower of Killid Bahr. But not all the shells were falling across the straits. One dropped into the water not 200 yards in front of us. Another struck within Tchemenlik, and earth and stones showered over the ramparts. Soon a shell swished overhead and dropped into the town behind us. A house roof, rafters, boardings, and a great cloud of black earth rose before our eyes. The explosion was deafening. The time was about 11:45 A.M., and from that moment until after six in the evening, I remember only one pause of more than a few seconds in these deafening explosions. As we watched the town, another burst came, another house went into the air. A shell landed in the inner fort behind us, sending showers of earth and small stones into the yard at our feet. I saw two puppies, oblivious of any peril, rush up to the dancing stones and rollick with them. We edged toward the gateway that opened under the massive walls, and I began to think of the comparative safety of the hill beyond the town where the hospital stood. Through the gateway, the air was yellow with explosions. Repeatedly, the shells were falling within the inner yards, sending showers of small stones over the wall. Finally, the wall itself received a direct hit, and great boulders began flying to the ground immediately before us. A Turkish soldier, half unconscious, staggered into sight at the gateway, covered with yellow dust and hardly able to breathe.

We decided to lose no time in making for the hill behind the town. Darting out from the archway, we sprinted across the courtyard. We ran through its gateway onto the street just as a shell hoisted a bakery into the air not fifty yards away. It made an ugly black fountain of dirt and rafters. Tiles and stones fell around us noisily. A block farther, another explosion sent boulders leaping toward us on the street. Some of them must have been two feet in diameter. I recall seeing one of this size bouncing ponderously straight for me, and figuring whether I should be able to leap over it at the moment it reached me. Luckily, it slowed down and changed its course.

I was frightened. When a shell exploded nearby, I ducked, and an old Turkish peasant who was walking sedately along the road noticed as I overtook him. The Turk put up a quieting hand. *"Yok Kadir!"* he exclaimed, and continued his slow pace. *Yok Kadir,* I was to learn, meant something like: "Don't be frightened; trust in your fate." But I was not to be quieted by any Turkish aphorism. With Schreiner and Grunewald, I continued my run down the street, and we finally reached the hill, grateful to arrive there without injury. I did, however, appreciate that the philosophic Turkish peasant had himself in better control than I, and later I gave Sultan Mohammed V the satisfaction of hearing the anecdote.

The hospital hill was like a front seat in the balcony. Below us lay the town of Chanak. Near the water front stood out the squat and massive tower of Kale Sultanie, beyond it a series of Turkish forts. Across the narrows lay the defenses beyond the ancient tower of Killid Bahr and the little village at its feet. From our hill, the width of the straits, actually a mile, seemed not more than a few hundred yards.

Five miles down the straits to the left, behind a tongue of land, was a cloud of smoke where the Dardanus batteries lay. Still farther out, scattered smoke clouds revealed the locations and activity of numerous howitzer batteries.

But the sensation of the spectacle was the Allied fleet, sailing in two circling groups, each consisting of six great battleships. In the van were the *Queen Elizabeth, Agamemnon, Lord Nelson, Inflexible, Prince George,* and *Triumph.* This, Admiral John M. de Robeck considered his Line A, as I later learned. In Line B, about a mile to the rear, were four French battleships, *Gaulois, Charlemagne, Bouvet,* and *Suffren,* flanked by the British battleships *Majestic* and *Swiftsure.* Line C was at the mouth of the straits, consisting of six battleships, destroyers, and mine sweepers. The plan of battle was to hammer into silence the forts at the straits, a task assigned to Lines A and B, and which, when accomplished, would allow the ships at the mouth of the straits, particularly the mine sweepers, to clear the entry into the Sea of Marmara, with Constantinople lying beyond as the greatest prize of the war.

Viewed as a picture, the battle was a sight of overpowering grandeur. The skies were cloudless, the sun shone down from near the zenith on the warships, the waters were a deep clear blue, the Hellespont hills were a dark green. The picture was in many hues, the gray-white smoke of the explosions, the orange smoke of firing cannon, and the black of flying earth in eruption, all set off by the white geysers of water as they rose after the immersion of shells. The accompaniment of sound was both oppressively insistent and varied. There was the roar when guns fired, the deafening detonations of the shells when they hit, the whistle of shells in flight, the shriek of flying splinters. We were close enough on our hill site to see and hear the firing of shells and their burst almost simultaneously.

On reaching our hillside seats, we turned our binoculars first on Fort Hamidieh, knowing that its ability to withstand bombardment was the decisive factor of the battle. So long as Line A stayed out of range, the big guns in Hamidieh had to be still. But the great naval guns of the most powerful British ships in Line A were well within range of the forts on both sides of the narrows. We could see the rise of earth and water around Hamidieh and could only surmise what effect they were having. Then we watched for a time the constant shower of shells on the forts beside Killid Bahr, just across the straits, and the incessant eruption of earth into great clouds bestrewing the forts and the village. Now and again our inspection would be interrupted by a blast seemingly right at our feet in Chanak and the flight of the rafters of another building into the sky.

Then I started watching the ships. They had been under

heavy fire from the coastal batteries and received many hits on their superstructures. But a new turn was being taken in the attack by Admiral de Robeck. He sent Line B forward, and it fearlessly came within range of the guns of the forts at the narrows, fanning out to give play to the British ships behind it, and there followed the most intensive firing of the battle. It was as this took place that I began watching the ships through my binoculars. After a few minutes, I marked that the fourth ship from the left was enveloped by a vast cloud of whitish-gray smoke. It was the French ship *Bouvet*. And as I trained my glasses on it, I saw this vessel slowly turn over in the water, its stern disappear and prow protrude, and then vanish under the sea. This astonishing event lasted hardly longer than three minutes; I could see the splash of swimmers in the water, then boats rowed up to rescue the survivors, a procedure that took much longer than the swift sinking of the ship.

I thought that for a few moments the firing of the fleet ceased. But it resumed almost immediately, and the battle went on. Destroyers and mine sweepers could be seen entering the mouth of the straits to join the rescue work. But two of them paid dearly for their effort; they were sunk by howitzer fire.

We were assured by the Germans in Fort Hamidieh that the *Bouvet* was the victim of artillery fire. But the testimony of its survivors is that it struck a mine. The *Bouvet* was an old-fashioned battleship, top-heavy and not thickly armored. It sank so rapidly because it had not been possible to take in water to balance the weight of the water that rushed in at the point of the explosion. Of the crew, 639 drowned.

A diversion from the nerve-racking din of the fire was the arrival of a British hydroplane on a reconnaissance. It flew directly over us on our hillside, not much more than a thousand yards above us, coming from the direction of Killid Bahr. It was a relief to hear a variation in the firing. A shrapnel shell hissed its way skyward and burst in a pretty white ball not far from the plane. Infantry fire rattled from all sides, including the rat-tat-tat of machine guns, so that we wondered where so many soldiers had been hiding themselves during the weeks of our stay. The plane was not disturbed by this firing. It flew over Hamidieh and then back to the mouth of the straits.

From our vantage point we soon noticed another ship in distress. It was the *Irresistible*. My attention was attracted to it by a great cloud of smoke that hung over it, of lighter color than the orange which follows a broadside. It had a heavy list when my attention was first attracted to it, which was corrected as water was taken in to balance the vessel. But this operation was needed again, and then a third time. Before dark, *Irresistible* was standing in the bay behind Dardanus, where it was sunk by the 15-centimeter guns of the Dardanus batteries.

Then we noticed a third ship in distress. This was *Ocean*. I saw two columns of steam rising at the side of its funnels. It had hit a mine. Its crew was taken off by destroyers, and the fate of the ship—it sank after dark—was not known till later. When the fighting ceased, as night fell, the Turks believed the *Ocean* might have been towed to safety. And, indeed, a search for it was made after dark by Admiral R. J. B. Keyes in a cutter from the *Queen Elizabeth*. He failed to find it. It was the third battleship to have been lost that day.

When the fleet withdrew around six o'clock, we went back through shattered Chanak to Fort Hamidieh to learn the outcome of the battle. This time we found the German officers were not jubilant. The battering of the fort had not been ruinous, but their ammunition was virtually gone. There were fewer than thirty armor-piercing shells remaining. They cursed the improvidence of the German military mission in not laying in an adequate supply of heavy shells. They cursed the Romanians, who they believed had held up such a shipment. They did not too much deplore the damage done to the fort. One of the heavy guns was displaced by a nearly direct hit, the only damage of importance, but the disturbance of the earth in and around the traverses, while it was almost complete, could easily be put in order. The displaced gun could quickly be made usable again. Ammunition was all we heard about. It had cost the battle. We were assured that the Allied fleet would return in the morning, a little more resistance would be possible, but then the few remaining shells would be used up and the mine sweepers would clear the channel.

Thereupon the great Allied armada would sail into the Sea of Marmara, to become the master of Constantinople. True, in Constantinople there were the *Goeben* and the *Breslau* to be disposed of. But this time they were cornered and heavily and decisively outgunned.

We three correspondents received our orders that night. We were to be up at daybreak, packed and ready to go into the interior of Anatolia. Our inn, as it happened, was not among the countless buildings wrecked in Chanak, so we had beds to sleep in.

I wrote a dispatch that night for a courier to take into Constantinople. It told about the sinking of the *Bouvet* and the *Irresistible,* but did not mention *Ocean;* we did not know at that time it had been lost. I did not report that the Allies had won the battle and that the Turks knew it, or that I myself had been ordered to retreat into the interior of Anatolia the next morning. Judgments of that nature were military information, invaluable to the other side. The censor in Constantinople would not have passed it. The time to tell that story would come later.

But it did not come later. For the Allied fleet did not return the next day. It never did enter the Sea of Marmara and sail victoriously to the Bosporus and Constantinople. It did not again attack the forts at the narrows. The first intimation I had that it was not returning was being told that the retreat into Anatolia had been postponed. The early-morning wireless news from London reported the battle of the previous day and stated that the weather had turned bad and the fleet would not be able to resume its attack that day. The reference to the weather was a giveaway. The weather was perfect. British histories of the Dardanelles battle still repeat this prevarication, not realizing it was an invention to help conceal that the Allied command had decided to change the campaign against Turkey.

Here we have one of the anomalies of war history. The Turks knew they were beaten and that the Allies would be back the following day and inside the Sea of Marmara in another day or two. The Allies regarded the loss of three battleships as prohibitive, and due either to land-fired torpedoes or to mines plunged into the currents and too dangerous to risk a second time. They chose not to resume naval operations until they could be combined with invasion by Allied infantry. They were wrong about both land-fired torpedoes and mines sent floating into the straits currents. What they did not know was that on the night of March 8, a Turkish mine expert, Lieutenant Colonel Geehl, in a small steamer called the *Nousret*, laid a field of twenty mines in Eren Keui Bay, parallel to the Asiatic shore. I did not know, until I read Alan Moorehead's *Gallipoli*, about Lieutenant Colonel Geehl by name, nor the identity of the *Nousret*. But I had been confidentially told that the Turks at about that time had laid a new mine field in the dark of the night.

However, it is not to the point whether the Allies (or I) knew about the laying of this mine field. What is to the point is that the British airplanes which surveyed these waters for mines did not see them so that they could be removed by mine sweepers. This, I suggest, is the hinge on which history turned. If the *Bouvet* and the *Ocean* had not been struck by mines, the Allies would not have hesitated to return the next day, and, having returned, would have forced the straits and taken Constantinople. The Gallipoli landing would never have been made, Turkey would have been plucked from its German alliance, the water route to Russia would have been opened, Russia would have fed the Allies with its grain, and the Allies would have stocked Russia with their artillery and ammunition. As I have said before, there would have been no Bolshevik revolution—certainly not as early as it occurred—the United States would not have entered the war, and the history of the human race would have been vastly different.

I stress these fateful alternatives now to give importance to an examination of the causes of the Allied misjudgment at the Dardanelles. One reason certainly is the doubt some of the British leaders felt all along about the possibility of getting through the straits without a combined naval and military force. Lord Fisher was one of these, and resisted the plans for a purely naval action as advocated by Winston Churchill every inch of the way. The fleet might well have come back the second day had it not been for the pressing existence of this point of view. Sir Ian Hamilton, chosen by Lord Kitchener to command the Gallipoli invasion, shared this theory and apparently talked Admiral de Robeck out of an immediate return of the fleet to the narrows after the action of March 18. I do not suggest there is a villain in this part of the story. Sheer misjudgment is not villainy.

But there is another reason why the Allies came to make the mistakes of March 18 and lose their ships to the Turkish mines. This is a subtler and less dramatic shortcoming, but certainly significant, for it is nonetheless responsible for the fateful developments.

It is candidly admitted in Winston Churchill's *The World Crisis:* "An experiment carried out by the *Ark Royal* had led to the belief that a seaplane or airplane flying above a minefield could discern it at 18 feet depth in clear water below. We now know that the experiment of the *Ark Royal* was misleading. The seaplane could not in fact locate the regular Turkish minefields, and what they saw and reported were only mines exceptionally near the surface or submerged net buoys."

The airplane was a relatively new device in World War I. For the British navy to base its very existence on the observations of a seaplane without complete proof of its abilities is an instance of what is surely the greatest peril of the human race, its ignorance. The mine field laid on March 8 in Eren Keui Bay was considered nonexistent because it had not been seen. But for this fallacy, World War I probably would have ended differently. Here is a case where Western civilization was penalized by nothing other than an inexcusable want of scientific thoroughness.

Chapter 8 / Two Interviews in Constantinople

Not long after my return to Constantinople from the Dardanelles, I was to have two unusual experiences. I was to take a young Turkish woman rowing in the Bosporus, and I was to interview the Sultan.

The episode of the boat trip on the Bosporus did not affect my life nor that of the young woman, but it was an unexpected example of the misunderstandings that can arise when West meets East. The young woman was the sister of Fouad Bey, the officer who had been in charge of the correspondents at the Dardanelles. Fouad's family was not distinguished, but it was respectable and, I imagine, in moderate circumstances. Fouad had told us of his sister at Chanak, and I had asked if he thought it might be arranged for me to meet her when we went back to Constantinople. He promised to try. Because she was a Moslem, I had supposed that a visit would be highly stiff and formal, but an experience all the same.

Fouad did arrange it. His sister met me without a veil and with pleasing informality. She was about eighteen, tall, had smiling dark eyes. She spoke quite good English, which she had learned at school. The Fouad home was close to the Bosporus, and, for want of a better idea, I proposed that the young woman and I might go for a boat ride. She agreed, and so did Fouad Bey, so in a short time we were off by ourselves, found a boat at the quayside, and were out in the water.

The meeting was as easy and informal as if she had been a

girl from Richmond or Indianapolis. I chatted along, and when we were well out in the Bosporus, I stopped rowing to drift. I shall not pretend that the idea did not cross my mind that relations with this young woman might progress without difficulty. But I said nothing to further them. I was not going to get myself at odds with a woman of another religion and culture by being precipitate.

It was she who startled me by speaking out. "I don't understand you," she exclaimed. "I don't know why you don't tell me what lovely eyes I have and how beautiful my hair is." This forwardness, with its assault on my want of gallantry, took me completely by surprise. All I could do was to say that in my country, when a young man meets a young woman for the first time, he does not tell her right off that she has lovely hair and eyes and that he considers her beautiful. It would not be considered good form. He was supposed to wait. But Fouad's sister was not willing to wait. "Do you think I am beautiful?" she asked. "Yes," I said, stretching a point. "But let me explain," I went on. "I am a married man." Fouad's sister persisted. "I want to leave Constantinople," she said. "I want to go to America. If you think I am beautiful, why can't you arrange it?" I told her I should very much like to take her out of Constantinople and to America, but it would be impossible because of my work and the fact that I already had a wife. I do not think it occurred to me at the moment that plural marriage had been part of her culture, so that what she was hinting did not seem unreasonable or difficult to her.

I took up the oars, and we rowed back. I treated her with deference and appreciation. It is not often a young woman offers herself as a wife, and after I was over my surprise I tried to be as cordial and grateful as was becoming to the situation. Probably Fouad had talked at home about the correspondents under his charge being important men in their own countries. She knew I had asked particularly to meet her. So it was not unnatural that she had permitted herself romantic ideas. But not all of them were romantic, for Constantinople had been trembling with fear of destruction by the Allies, or, if they entered the Sea of Marmara, by the ruthless Turkish regime itself as an act of frustrating defense. Ambassador Morgenthau had been earnestly pleading with Enver Pasha and Talaat Bey to save such priceless Christian relics as Saint Sophia in their plans for destruction if the Allies got through, and he had not been meeting much success. They were dead set on ruining Constantinople themselves, rather than permit the Allies the enjoyment of doing it. It was not pleasant being an eighteen-year-old girl in that city. But I was not to relieve her fears or fulfill her romance. We parted politely at her doorway, and I did not attempt to see her again.

The interview with the Sultan had been asked for and promised before I went to the Dardanelles. Here the rival influences of Ambassador Morgenthau and Ambassador Wangenheim had collaborated to produce what we wanted. I shall admit that the importance of the interview loomed up much greater to me at that time than it does in retrospect. Sultan Mohammed V, who had been made caliph by the Young Turks after they had overthrown his brother Abdul-Hamid II, a capable if ruthless ruler, was at that time seventy-three and of no political weight. But no Sultan of the Ottoman Empire had ever been interviewed by an American newspaper correspondent in all its history, and I was living in a time when newspaper "firsts" came ahead of events of greater historic significance.

George Schreiner, Emil Ludwig, and I were the three chosen for the interview. Schreiner and I had the prestige of having witnessed the great battle of March 18; Ludwig was a distinguished writer of Turkey's ally Germany.

The Sultan's palace had been built in 1853 and looked like an opulent Italian villa, partly hidden by trees in a handsome garden on a slope above the Bosporus. The view from it over Constantinople is one of the sights of the Middle East. The palace was decorated in full oriental luxury. Its rooms were high-ceilinged; it was furnished with richly colored divans, seats, and rugs. It contained the throne room of the Caliph, then head of the Mohammedan church as well as Ottoman emperor; the residential quarters of the men in the Sultan's suite; a section where the crown prince lived with his family; and a fourth occupied by the women of officials of the Sultan's staff. We came into the palace after driving through the gates and the handsome park and climbing the long marble steps to the palace entrance. We were met by the Sultan's aide, Salih Pasha, who escorted us to a handsomely decorated waiting room. There he offered us the longest cigarettes I ever had seen. They measured seven inches, with gold tips two inches long. We had heard about them. They were the celebrated palace cigarettes and were made of the finest obtainable Turkish tobacco. We also were served Turkish coffee in delicate porcelain cups. We talked for a time, then an orderly informed Salih Pasha that the Sultan was ready.

We were led through a long corridor and then up a staircase with a gilded balustrade, and into the small room where the Sultan was sitting. He was a short, gray-bearded man, somewhat stooped, more like a bishop than the head of the Ottoman Empire. He wore European clothes, but with a fez. My recollection may be at fault, but I believe the interview was in English. Each of us was introduced, and the Sultan's face lighted when he was told that two of us were Americans who had witnessed the battle of the Dardanelles. The conversation was brief. The Sultan expressed his certainty that the Allies, who had now landed at Gallipoli, would never be able to force the straits. He spoke with great appreciation of the Germans who had fought at the Dardanelles, and, at Dr. Ludwig's prompting, of the Germans fighting on the European fronts. Dr. Ludwig assured him that the Kaiser was not ill, as had been reported, for he had recently seen him and found him in excellent health.

The Sultan asked about our experiences at the Dardanelles, which gave me the chance to tell him about the peasant in the Chanak street during the bombardment who had quieted me with his exhortation of *"Yok Kadir."* Dr. Ludwig broke in to say that German soldiers had taken up use of the word *kismet.* And this gave the Sultan a chance to instruct us on the difference between *kismet* and *kadir. Kismet,* he said, applied to superficial things. *Kadir* dealt with deep destiny in which a man's own effort also was involved. When we ended the interview and walked to the door, the elderly ruler put his arm around my shoulder, as though to express appreciation of my anecdote.

The interview as such was of no news value other than of being given. It made page one in the Chicago *Daily News,* whereas my long account of the battle of the Dardanelles, which I sent by mail, was used to fill page six. And even my first and cabled report of the battle of March 18, in which I described the sinking of the *Bouvet,* only made page two.

Chapter 9 / Encounter with a Spy

It was after the interview with the Sultan that I was to have my first encounter with a spy. I did not know for some time that he was a spy. He was the son of a Midwestern American theologian, and because my father was a theologian and knew his father, I knew about the father and that he was a man of distinguished scholarship. The son was a British spy, and I acquired and still have strong objections to him because he exploited his relationship with me to do his intelligence service and thereby risked my life along with his own. He did this without giving me any choice in the matter. However, I now realize that that is what a man in Intelligence would do in time of war, if he had no alternative, and that from his point of view, he was serving the Allied cause in using me. No doubt he thought it was a cause that I, too, would be glad to serve.

I first heard about him when I came back to my hotel one afternoon and some colleagues told me that another Chicago *Daily News* correspondent had shown up, and he was asking how to find me. My work in Turkey and at the Dardanelles had been both fortunate and successful, and I could not believe the Chicago office was displacing me. But I was not suspicious about the new correspondent. I was simply puzzled.

He found me toward the end of the evening and asked if he could go with me to my room for a talk. There he produced a letter to me from Edward Price Bell, head of the London bureau, introducing him and saying that Mr. Bell had given

81

him credentials from the Chicago *Daily News* as a favor to his great friend the editor of the London *Chronicle*. Actually, according to Mr. Bell, Mr. Longford (to give him a pseudonym) was representing the *Chronicle*, which wanted to get some firsthand correspondence from Turkey. The letter from Bell was genuine, and the explanation that the correspondent he introduced was representing the *Chronicle* was plausible. Anyhow, I believed it. But I did not like it, and I said so. Mr. Longford was sympathetic. He said he was sorry to put me in a false position, and all he wanted from me was that if I was interrogated by the Turkish officials, I would say that a letter he brought me from Bell was genuine and that he carried credentials from the Chicago *Daily News*. As I sized up the situation, I had no choice but to agree, for the other alternative was to tell the Turkish authorities the truth, which in Turkey might well have meant the end of his existence.

I was of two minds about young Mr. Longford. I was angry at his having appeared, and yet I liked him. And I argued with myself that my anger was at Mr. Bell and not Mr. Longford. For a *Chronicle* correspondent to risk so much for a few stories out of Turkey was, I thought, harebrained but in a way admirable. The muddy ethics of putting me in danger belonged to Mr. Bell and the editor of the *Chronicle*. So I decided to be cordial to Mr. Longford. I introduced him to such of my colleagues as he had not met and said that he was backstopping for me, for I might have to leave Constantinople at any time, which happened to be true. The next morning I was visited by a police official, who inquired about Mr. Longford. I told a half-truth, saying that he had come with a letter from the head of my London bureau, who also was head of the Chicago *Daily News* foreign service, and that he bore credentials from the paper.

The next day the activities of Mr. Longford in Constantinople suddenly terminated. A friendly colleague came to me and told me the police were highly suspicious of him and were about to arrest him. I do not know how they found out about him. I saw Mr. Longford only minutes later and gave him this information. He thanked me, packed his bag, and was off to the station to catch a train to Bulgaria. I did not know whether he made his train. He simply dropped out of sight.

A few days later, I was ordered by my paper to leave Turkey for Bucharest, where I was to wait for instructions. I was loath to leave Turkey. The Allied landing at Gallipoli had been made, and Turkey seemed to me as good a place for a correspondent to be as any. It occurred to me that Mr. Bell may have needed to do his friend on the *Chronicle* a favor by according Longford some real status and making him the acting correspondent in Constantinople. But that was only a passing thought. Anyway, Mr. Bell would find out soon enough that Longford had fled from Turkey.

In due course I was in Bucharest, waiting for instructions. It was not my first visit to the city, and I had a few acquaintances and one good friend, the American Minister, Charles Vopicka.

He is worth a diversionary description because he was the most unusual diplomat I ever encountered in the service of the United States. He was a Chicago Czech businessman who had risen to political power in that city by controlling the Czech vote, and had thrown all his considerable influence behind William Jennings Bryan in the convention which nominated Wilson. Bryan became Secretary of State and rewarded his loyal follower. I imagine he did so by asking first what would be the least important United States legation in Europe, and being told it would be Bucharest, Sofia, and Belgrade—then a triple assignment—named his adherent to that post. That was before Mr. Bryan and many others in the United States had any premonition that war in Europe was imminent, and that Bucharest, Sofia, and Belgrade might be capitals of unusual importance.

Mr. Vopicka was an uneducated immigrant and a ward politician, not a diplomat. He was plain and unpolished. His wife was like him. He called her "Ma" in the presence of visitors. And though she lived in a legation well staffed by servants, she cooked for her husband as she had done in Chicago. "Stick around for lunch," the Minister would say to me. "Ma has cooked something good." I am telling this not to disparage the Minister. If an American citizen got into trouble in Romania, Bulgaria, or Serbia, Mr. Vopicka would not rest until he had pried him out of jail, if that was where he was, or sent him to a hospital, if it was medical attention he needed, or lent him money, if he was out of funds. His idea of being American minister was to take care of every American in his jurisdiction. Later he was to become responsible for many thousands of Allied prisoners, and won a reputation for excellent administration in his care of them. Mr. Vopicka had nothing to do with my spy, beyond being in Bucharest while I was there.

I spent some time at the American legation during this stay, but also read a good deal in my hotel room, awaiting the expected instructions. The Bucharest bookstores naturally did not stock American books. But one of them carried a number of the German Tauchnitz editions, which included Shakespeare's works in English. I bought these two or three at a time, and had the privilege of reading a Shakespeare play each night in my bedroom. In this way I came to read such delightful works as *Antony and Cleopatra* and *Coriolanus* for the first time. Reading them for pleasure in a Romanian hotel room was quite different from reading them as classwork for a college English course, and I came to appreciate Shakespeare with growing wonder.

It was while I was immersed in a Shakespeare drama one evening that someone knocked at my door, and who should bound in excitedly but Mr. Longford. He was full of his escape from Turkey, which had been by a hair's breadth. And now that he had found me again, he was bursting with ideas for undertakings we might tackle together. I was lonely and had not developed any hesitancy about accepting the fellowship of Mr. Longford. If he was the correspondent for the London *Chronicle,* we could collaborate, I thought, without impropriety or even much danger.

The idea he came up with that interested me most was an excursion to the Banat, adjoining Transilvania, because there had been rumors of a possible German invasion through this region. We might go there to look for signs that the Germans were coming. The undertaking involved a long train trip to Szeged, but I decided it was better than hanging around in Bucharest and agreed to go.

Near the end of the train ride, we crossed a river just before reaching Szeged, where our American passports were carefully scrutinized by German officials at the border. I noticed that Longford left the negotiations to me, as though he knew no German. Longford carried a small camera, and, as if he were a tourist, he asked the passport officer if he would do him a favor and take a snapshot of the two of us on the bridge at the border. He said he wanted a souvenir of our trip. The officer agreed, and in my innocence I did, too.

We spent a few hours in the afternoon wandering around Szeged and did not see any signs of military activity or preparations. When night fell, Longford said he wanted to go out again, and I said I would rest and read. We had not been able to book separate bedrooms, for which I was later to thank my lucky stars, and I was asleep when he came in again. But I was aroused enough to see him take a revolver out of his pocket and lay it on the night table beside his bed. This woke me completely. I pretended to be sleepy, however, when I asked what he was doing. "I put it there," he said, "to make sure that if I am to be killed, somebody will be killed along with me." I showed no alarm at this astounding assertion, and again feigned sleep. I lay still until I heard Longford breathing heavily. Then I got out of bed stealthily, put on my clothes, packed, and tiptoed out of the room. I went downstairs, paid my bill, and asked for a cab. In a few moments I was at the railway station. I inquired when the next train was leaving for Bucharest. Luckily, it was due to depart in a few minutes. I boarded it, and after another halt at the border, where again I passed inspection, I was on my way to safety.

I had not been back in Bucharest for more than two days when my hotel porter told me that a Mr. Longford was asking for me. I said that he was to be sent up. He came into the room, bubbling over with greetings and good humor, and again crying out about his narrow escape. I froze him as quickly as I could. "I want you to admit the truth," I said. "You are working for British Intelligence. The *Chronicle* was just a cover-up, and a dirty one. You took me into the Banat to shield you in your work. You didn't give a damn about my life." I was furious, and he knew it. And he became at once humble. "You don't understand," he said. "This trip has been of utmost importance. Yes, I am working for Intelligence. Six men have been sent into the Banat. I am the first of them who has returned. You have helped save my life and helped the Allied cause."

I refused to be mollified. I was particularly angry with him for having the snapshot of the two of us taken at the border crossing. "Where is the camera?" I asked. "Sorry," he said, "they got that." "With the film of the two of us?" "Yes," he said. I have a temper, and I gave him a piece of it. What sense had there been in having that photo taken? How did that help his work? All it did was to identify me as a fellow-member of British Intelligence. I sputtered and fumed. Longford continued humble and contrite. "Now," I ended, "get out of this room and out of my life. I am going to the German Minister and explain about you and that photo, for when I cross any frontier where Germans are in charge, they will have that photo and will be looking for me. They will be looking for you, too, so you now are on your own." And I parted from him. I did go to the German Minister, who assured me that my status as a neutral correspondent would not be impaired.

The story of Longford does not end here. Years after the war, when I was head of the Philadelphia *Public Ledger* and New York *Evening Post* bureau in London, he showed up in my office again, ostentatiously agreeable, and obviously hoping to find me forgiving and friendly. I asked what he was doing. He said he was running a news service out of the Soviet Union and had his office in Edinburgh. He was in a position to supply me unusual information from the Soviet Union, he said. He looked a bit run down and much older. I was sure that he was still in the service of British Intelligence and that this news bureau was his latest cover-up. I told him with what dignity I could muster that I had not forgotten how he had risked my life, and I wanted nothing to do with him. I said I did not want to be unfeeling or unreasonable, but I believed it best that we make no effort to re-establish a relationship. He looked crestfallen, but he departed. He did leave me alone, and I never saw him again.

Chapter 10 / A Visit to the Gallipoli Front

The instructions which ultimately reached me from Chicago were to return to Turkey for a short stay and try to get to the Gallipoli front. This suited me down to the ground. I was sanguine that a trip to the front could be managed. I decided to stop over in Sofia on my way back and profited greatly by doing so, because I obtained an interview with the Bulgarian Premier in which he strongly affirmed the intention of his country to remain neutral. Bulgaria was reported to be in receipt of an offer from the Western Allies to join them in return for rectifications of the boundary resulting from the Second Balkan War and for giving them Kavalla and Thasos. Premier Vasil Radoslavov denied the story. He talked frankly and in detail about Bulgaria's position and affirmed that the ethnic division of Macedonia which his country wanted above everything might be given by either side without Bulgaria having to fight.

Back in Constantinople, I found George Schreiner, and he was willing again to pool our influence to get a trip to the Gallipoli front. Again we succeeded, and it was arranged that we were to visit the headquarters of Otto Liman von Sanders, the German in command of the Turkish defense, and be allowed into the front trenches. The Turkish aide of Enver Pasha who brought us this news ended by saying that we should sleep at army headquarters that night and be up at seven in the morning, when our horses would be ready for the nine-mile ride to Liman von Sanders's headquarters.

The mention of horses and a nine-mile ride filled me with the liveliest apprehension. The only horses I ever had ridden were the broad-beamed horses on the farm outside Oberlin the summer I worked there, and I had never advanced on them at a faster pace than a walk. The horses of the Turkish army were spirited and undoubtedly capricious animals. I confessed my plight to Schreiner. I asked him whether I should try to make the trip. He said, with all his Boer vehemence, that I should. He would teach me to ride a horse. He knew all about it. He promised he could tell me enough so that I could stay on my horse the next day. So that evening he instructed me about sitting upright, holding the reins in my left hand, gripping the horse by my knees to keep my seat in the saddle. He told me how to stop the horse by reining in sharply. We slept that night in a tent at headquarters. Schreiner practiced his autosuggestion on me late into the night, and I fell asleep almost convinced that I could manage the excursion.

We were up early, had our breakfast, and were called for by a competent-looking Turkish officer. He took us to our horses. A party of six was making the trip. Schreiner was shown his horse, and though he was a massive person of well over 220 pounds, he threw his leg over it and settled in his seat easily. My horse was pointed out to me. It was a gray Arab stallion. I must have gasped on seeing it, but I had determined to follow the experience through without a word. An officer held my stirrup, and I mounted. As I had been taught, I sat bolt upright, gripped the horse with my knees, and held the reins in my left hand.

The next thing that happened came about quite unexpectedly and noisily. A motorcycle messenger zoomed toward us down the road, his engine popping like a machine gun. My stallion had been on the road, but he made an agile leap across the ditch bounding it, and stopped nervously to survey the scene. I do not know why I was not thrown by this sudden leap, but I still was in the saddle. And then the command came to go forward. The horses started down the road, and my stallion once more jumped the ditch. Once more, by incomprehensible good fortune, I stayed in the saddle. And then we began a trot. Schreiner had told me that if I wanted to stop the horse, all I needed to do was to give the reins a sharp tug. I did not enjoy the trotting, and thought that I would feel more self-confidence if I could demonstrate that my stallion would obey my signal with the rein. So I gave it. I signaled it to stop. But there was some misunderstanding between us. Instead of stopping, or even slowing down, he rushed forward in a canter and quickly passed the other horses. The others then galloped behind us. I was in a panic. I knew I could not keep my saddle on a galloping Arab stallion, and, true enough, my feet slipped out of the stirrups. I fell forward, grasping the horse around the neck.

Fortunately, the Turkish officer who was leading the expedition saw my plight, dashed ahead of me, grasped the reins on my stallion at the bit, and brought him and his own horse to a standstill. I ingloriously worked myself into an upright position and found my stirrups again. Thereafter, the Turkish officer proceeded at a walking pace, and all of us walked the rest of the way to the Gallipoli headquarters.

A nine-mile walk on horseback is not an ordeal, but it is an undertaking, and I was glad when we arrived at Liman von Sanders's headquarters. Here we went through the formalities of introductions and partook of refreshments, but with the lesser lights. We were not to meet the Commander till lunch. Then we were taken into the trenches.

Both sides were thoroughly dug in by this time. It was like the stalemate on the Western front. The trenches were well built, deep, and adequately protected. The Turks, we were told, made admirable soldiers, a fact which is now universally known. But before the Gallipoli landing, it had not been known or acknowledged, and to a certain extent had not been true. The Liman von Sanders mission arrived well before the war, and though, as I was to learn, he was not a sociable man, he was a great organizer and trainer of troops. He had zealous support from Enver and Kemal, and the Turkish army was soon to be the equal of any in the kind of warfare that had developed.

We walked for a couple of hours in the trenches, being permitted to come to the point closest to the Allied trenches, the precise distance of which was not a stone's throw away from the Anzacs. If I had shouted over to them from the top of the trench, they would have heard me. We had come on a quiet day. No gunfire went off while we were in the trenches and no grenades were thrown. Now and again, a single plane overhead dropped a few bombs, apparently on Liman von Sanders's headquarters. The soldiers we passed were grimy, and for the greater part were taking their ease, lying on their blankets or leaning against the trench side.

The lunch with General von Sanders and his staff was not informative. The General was terse and reticent. He did not like strangers about. I am sure he did not like Americans. But he did speak his praise for his Turkish troops and said he had no doubt that the Allies would not be able to get through. If they had landed a few days before March 18, he said, they would have found only light forces below the narrows and no heavy ones above them. The story then would have been different. But he had been given time to bring up reinforcements and prepare his positions.

Our visit was made after a heavy and costly Turkish attack on May 18 and a remarkable armistice arranged after it to allow the gathering of the wounded and the burial of the dead on both sides. I do not now recall that this unusual event and the great battle were even mentioned at the meal. We were told little more than that General von Sanders was sure that the Allies could not get through, which proved to be true.

Soon after lunch, we were ordered to make ready for the return trip. The officer in charge of us told us that we would not be able to use the route by which we had come; part of that road was under heavy artillery fire. Our route would take us up and down and be long and steep. It proved to be heavily wooded, with no pathway through it. First we went down, and at a sharp grade. Part of George Schreiner's instructions in horseback riding had prepared me for such a contingency. I was to allow my horse to go as he pleased, find his own footing, and take his own pace. My Arab stallion did just this. And when we finally reached the gully between the two high slopes, he started his steep climb upward. This proved to be a less happy experience. I could not believe any horse could keep his footing on the steep ascent, and I expected him to slip and fall at any moment. As for me, I leaned forward and did my best to keep my feet in the stirrups. This was a long vale. I had little expectation that we would come safely to the top. Schreiner had told me to trust my horse, that horses on hillsides could perform wonders.

Mine did. More than once I was heavily brushed by branches, but my horse did not slip, and after what seemed an interminable time we were at the top and I could assume my upright posture again. Another long ride followed, which mercifully was taken at a walk, and finally we were back at our starting point at headquarters, where I could dismount.

I shall not boast about my horsemanship. Still, the fact remains that I had ridden eighteen miles on the back of a nervous Arab stallion and had not been unseated once. But I was not elated. I was utterly exhausted, and I resolved that this beginning in horseback riding would also be the end of it, which I may say it has been.

Chapter 11 / I Encounter the E-11

The visit to the front was to be one of two; the second was to follow in a few days and to end in an indefinite stay. The trip down the Sea of Marmara to the straits was to be made at night in a Turkish torpedo boat. A larger group of correspondents had now gathered in Constantinople, and most of them were to take part.

The evening before, we all were told that a small Turkish transport was to leave Galata pier, on the Constantinople water front, the next afternoon, to take a physician from the German hospital to Liman von Sanders, who was indisposed, and some medicines and supplies. We were offered our choice —to go in the little transport with the doctor or in the torpedo boat. I alone chose the transport. I did this because I judged it would be safer. I had heard reports of a British submarine being in the Sea of Marmara. The story had been going about that it had sailed right up the Bosporus the day before, had surfaced, and the crew had hoisted the British flag and sung "God Save the King." Like so many of the Constantinople tales, this was not true, but the submarine was inside the Dardanelles, and I thought that a small transport would be less likely to attract its attention than a torpedo boat.

I was well fitted out for this second visit to Gallipoli. I wore a uniform similar to that used by a German officer, minus the shoulder straps, and was provided a white arm band inscribed in Arabic to designate my status as correspondent. I wore boots and leather gaiters, like an officer, and I had stocked a goodly supply of canned goods in a long canvas bag. I also had a sleeping bag, and, of course, my portable typewriter. With these, I was driven to Galata pier, and to the 600-ton freighter *Nagara*. I went on board, found the captain (who was, in fact, a naval lieutenant), and presented my Turkish credentials. The lieutenant spoke a little English, which he said he had learned on a vacation at Ostend. He ordered a sailor to take me to a small cabin down in the hold and carry my gear aboard. One look at the cabin convinced me I would spend my night better in my sleeping bag on deck. So I brought up my belongings, and then examined the vessel. The *Nagara* had a commodious open space amidships, and there, under a tarpaulin, I saw a long naval gun, which I learned was an eight-inch gun from the *Goeben* being taken to Gallipoli to fire into the Allied positions. I also saw several boxes of what I took to be shells for the gun, and in addition some boxes of groceries, no doubt containing delicacies for Liman von Sanders and his staff. The gun and the ammunition marked the *Nagara* as a Turkish supply ship, and I realized it was a legitimate target for a British submarine, if such was about.

I was soon joined by the only other passenger, a Dr. Seiler, a little rotund Bavarian with a round face and ruddy coloring. He was head of a Constantinople hospital and told me scornfully that he had been summoned from his busy post by Liman von Sanders, who, he thought, probably had nothing more severe than a cold. He was annoyed and did not hide the fact. But I was glad to have company, and the doctor and I soon were engrossed in conversation about Munich, the opera, and our Wagnerian favorites.

In a lull in the talk, I asked him if he had heard anything about the submarine. "What submarine?" he replied, with round eyes. I told him the rumors. "If that is so," he said, "I shall move my things to the saloon and sleep there," and he gave orders to have his baggage moved. He also wanted to interrogate the lieutenant in command, who, however, spoke no German. So, in English, I asked the lieutenant, at the doctor's behest, if there were any danger. "There is a little danger," the lieutenant asserted—but did not elaborate.

It was with this evaluation that we began the night. The dark came swiftly. Orders were given that there should be no smoking; the ship's lights were kept off, and life belts were distributed—not a gesture of reassurance. But Dr. Seiler went to the saloon and I to my sleeping bag on the upper deck without admitting any concern to each other.

I had, however, picked out a good life belt and noted carefully the position of the two lifeboats, which were in their davits, ready for immediate launching. In fact, the place I had chosen to stretch out my sleeping bag was beside one of them. As the *Nagara* slipped quietly down the Sea of Marmara, I stood for a time at the rail, looking at the lights of Constantinople as they waned behind us, and then at the blackness of the water. Soon I kicked my way inside my sleeping bag and tried to go to sleep. But it was too early for that. I had to ponder submarines first. I wished I knew their habits, knew more about torpedoes, knew whether a single explosion would be enough to blow me out of my sleeping bag and into the sky, knew whether one could hear it coming. Safety, I decided, depended on the swiftness with which I could get into my life belt and to the side rail. It was pitch-dark, and there was no one to observe me, so I decided to hold a private submarine drill. I buttoned myself into my sleeping bag, and then on a self-given signal emerged, donned life belt, and rushed to the rail. I found this operation took between ten and eleven seconds. This satisfied and reassured me. I kicked my way again into the sleeping bag, instructed my subconscious mind to arouse me instantly at any cause for alarm, and went to sleep.

I slept deeply for several hours until my subconscious mind, like an alarm clock, shocked me into full wakefulness. I was out of the bag in a trice and at the rail, with my life belt on. What had wakened me was the sound of signal bells from the bridge to the engine room. The *Nagara* was slowing down to a standstill. The sky was overcast and the night was quite dark. I stared at the black water of the sea and was thoroughly alarmed. But nothing was happening and every sound was stilled. Were we about to be torpedoed? Must I wait there simply to find out? I decided not to.

I felt my way to the steps leading to the bridge and mounted. When I reached the bridge, I found the lieutenant and asked why we had stopped. He answered almost casually, "We are just making soundings. It's all right." He said it with so much assurance that I felt abashed at my alarm, went down to the deck, climbed into the sleeping bag again, and went to sleep.

I was awakened by sunshine on my face. It was past 8:15, and I jumped up to look about me. We were well off the European coast, which was barely visible. No other land was in sight, nor any vessel. The Sea of Marmara was quiet. I opened a tin and was having my breakfast when Dr. Seiler joined me and accepted some of my food. He said he had slept well, but had been awakened when the ship stopped. I told him about my night visit to the bridge and what the lieutenant had said. "Go ask him again," he suggested. I mounted to the bridge. The lieutenant was cordial, but this time he told a different story. A submarine had been sighted at ten in the evening and again at two in the morning. It apparently had followed us all night, but with the coming of daylight had submerged. "Now we are safe," he declared.

I went down to Dr. Seiler, who was leaning against the rail, and I translated the information. I reached the words "Now we are safe" when, a few hundred yards away—directly behind his head, in the water—there emerged a great, black, massive, diabolic thing. One could not have conjured up a more formidable and frightening monster. I pointed to it and screamed: "There it is!" I made a dash to my life belt and took up my station beside the lifeboat I had selected. It seemed that everybody else on board was scampering about. I heard a "ping," a sound like a shot, but much too miniature for a naval gun. I heard it again. I tried to imagine what it could be. A further "ping" followed, then another.

I looked out to see if the submarine was in sight. It was by now fully in view, with at least five men crowding the ship's tower. It bore on its side the mark "E-11." But I did not stay to watch it. Along with the crew, I huddled under the bridge at the foredeck for what seemed like an endless time. "Now we are going to be torpedoed," I said to Dr. Seiler, a comment for which he later reproached me. "If we were going to be torpedoed," he chided me, "saying so wouldn't improve matters; and if we weren't, you simply made them worse." He added, "You were as white as a sheet," and asked, "Was I pale?" In fact, he was too ruddy to be pale, but the blood had gone out of his face, as I told him. I noticed, too, that the Turkish sailors also were pale. It did not occur to me that the fact that the submarine had surfaced was an omen of safety. If we were going to be torpedoed, it would have been from a submerged position. But I thought we were about to be blown up, and I was terribly frightened. The suspense was insupportable. I could now see the submarine bearing down on us. A man was bent over a large wheel, which he was cranking. Beside him was a man in a white sweater with a rifle. That explained the "pings" we had heard. He had been firing to bring us to a halt. And in this he succeeded, for the engine bells sounded, we slowed speed, and the *Nagara* stopped.

Then the tension was broken for me by noticing the Turkish sailors pointing at me and then pointing up to the bridge. I looked up. The lieutenant was leaning over and calling to me. "You speak!" he shouted. I realized that he was turning negotiations over to me because I could conduct them in English. I ran to the rail, enormously relieved to have something to do. I saw that one of the men on the submarine was shouting at us through a megaphone. I tried to make out what he was saying. It sounded as though he were an Englishman trying to talk Turkish. I put my hands to my mouth and shouted: "Speak English! Speak English!"

Something confused came back through the megaphone. I decided to take the initiative. "Will you give us time to get into the boats?" I shouted. Then came back a reply that seemed to me the most welcome I should ever hear in my life—"Yes, and be dom quick about it!" The "dom" was like Irish brogue— and the man with the megaphone, as I was to learn later on, was Irish.

As though Irish brogue were a universal language, the message had been understood by everyone on the *Nagara,* and a rush began to the boats. Dozens of the sailors did not even stop to enter the boats, but plunged overboard. The boat I had chosen was already out of sight, so I seized one of its ropes and started sliding down. Before I had gone halfway, I looked to see what I was heading for, and under me I saw the boat—but it was brimming with water, and a single sailor alongside it was trying to bail it out with his fez. I climbed up the rope hand over hand. I do not know how I managed this —I had never done it in school—but I came up that rope like a gymnast and reached the deck.

The *Nagara* had three lifeboats in all. One was gone, and, as I saw, it was already filled with sailors. The second was swamped. The third had not even been hung from the davits. It lay unready on the top deck. Five sailors remained on board and were tugging at it to bring it to the davits. The operation of launching it was going to take some time.

"Wait a minute," I shouted to the submarine, and waved my arms like a brakeman signaling his engineer. The submarine commander returned this signal, so I joined the sailors and worked with them a time. But it was taking too long, and I ran back to the rail. "Can you give us a minute?" I called. By now the submarine was not twenty yards away, and the commander did not have to shout his reply. "Yes," he said quietly, "I will give you time." Then he asked me: "Who are you?"

I supposed he wanted to know who *I* was. He might have thought me something of an anomaly. I wore a German officer's uniform and had a white arm band, was in the middle of the Sea of Marmara on a Turkish transport, and I spoke English. So I answered, "I am Raymond Swing of the Chicago *Daily News*." The submarine commander—young, tall, towheaded, and broad-shouldered like an American football captain—bowed with mock politeness. "I am glad to meet you, Mr. Swing, but what is the name of your ship?"

This colloquy, to say the least, is funny, and the humor of it was not to die. Rudyard Kipling, writing a series of articles on British submarines during the war, read the log of the E-11 and came upon the report of this dialogue. According to his version, I said I was "Silas Q. Swing of the *Chicago Sun*," which made it even funnier. The story was to become a favorite in naval messes in England. I was told that everybody in England knew it, and if I had any idea of going to work in London after the war, I had better give it up.

But I was not aware at that time of having made myself ridiculous. I told the commander the name of the ship was the *Nagara*. "Where bound?" he asked. "Chanak Kalessi," I replied. "What is your cargo?" I was not going to tell him about the eight-inch gun from the *Goeben*. "I am a newspaper correspondent," I said, "and I don't ask about such things." "What is your crew, commercial or naval?" This time I lied. "Oh, I think it is just an ordinary freighter's crew," I said. "Can you find me a line?" he asked.

This request I should have thought the easiest in the world to fulfill. On any ship there always is rope; it is everywhere. So I started out to find rope. I searched and I searched. I swear there wasn't any rope on the *Nagara*.

"Better see to your boat or that will be swamped, too," the submarine commander finally said. I looked to see that it was indeed ready for launching. But I continued to look for rope. "Never mind the line," the commander said. "Your boat is launched. Better get in." I saluted the submarine commander and thanked him. He returned the salute. I had one last look around. I was not unaware that I was the last person to be leaving the ship and that in nautical values the significance of this was worthy. I slid down the rope and dropped into the lifeboat. The sailors made room for me in the stern, as though I were the officer in charge, and we rowed away from the *Nagara*.

The view of things changed in a rowboat. I saw that at least a dozen sailors were in the water, one of them, his life belt caught under his neck, floundering and bellowing like a calf, though it was plain that he was in no danger. The lieutenant who commanded the *Nagara* was in the one boat which was crowded. The one that had been swamped was by now pretty clear of water and was picking up sailors, and we went to work to pick up the rest. I pointed to man after man to be picked up, leaving the bellowing one to the last.

Among the first I helped get out of the water was Dr. Seiler. It took some pulling to get his round carcass aboard. Once in safety, he began imprecating the British and submarines in general, including the man who invented them. I told him he had died a short while before in New York. "Glad he is dead," he growled.

We saw that an officer from the submarine had boarded the *Nagara* and was looking about. He was in good spirits, for he waved to me, and I waved back. In a brief time, he boarded the submarine again, and it slowly backed off until it was 200 yards or so from the *Nagara*. We rowed for a time and then, as the submarine stopped, we stopped and watched. By intuition, we all knew what was going to happen, as did those in the other two lifeboats, for they stopped to watch, too. And as we looked, the *Nagara* burst open like a flower, sending a great cloud of black smoke far upward, interlaced by orange flames. The sound of the explosion followed, somewhat muffled. Burning timbers showered into the water. The ship began sinking rapidly. The prow suddenly turned up and then slipped under the water, and the *Nagara* disappeared. The E-11 also began slipping under the water, and soon disappeared, leaving the three lifeboats alone under a great cloud of orange smoke. In the distance, a line of black smoke was to be seen, obviously of an oncoming Turkish destroyer. This might have induced the submarine commander to submerge so suddenly.

"What a wonderful picture!" I exclaimed. Dr. Seiler retorted: "Damn your wonderful pictures!" He went on grumbling: "Think of all my medicines poisoning the water! Think of my razors that now will rust on the bottom of the sea!" I let him prattle on. He spoke at first in German to me, then in bad French to the sailors, who could not understand him. I did say something about how lucky we were to be allowed to get away alive. "Phew!" the Doctor snorted. "You didn't even get wet." I did not know at the time that the commander of the E-11 was consistently considerate in carrying out his mission of destruction in the Sea of Marmara, in contrast to the commander of a preceding British submarine, which sank everything at sight.

We were six miles from shore, and it took us two hours to reach it. We were greeted on land by a crowd of villagers from Kum Bal who evidently had watched the drama of the *Nagara*. But before any sociability was permitted, the lieutenant commanding the *Nagara*—again in command—lined up his men and counted them. Not one was missing. The mayor was there and took us to his commodious but sparsely furnished house. There, with the help of neighbors, dry clothes and towels were supplied for those still wet. And then we were gathered into the living room, where we were supplied with that unchanging symbol of Turkish hospitality, coffee. The mayor arranged for six barrel-shaped and ox-drawn wagons to transport us to the next town, Rodosto. Dr. Seiler, again in dry clothes, repaid the hospitality by giving the mayor's crippled grandson a medical examination. Townsmen were doling out hand-rolled cigarettes.

As we left the house, we were confronted by the entire membership of the village school, lined up in unprepossessing apparel, who, at a signal from the schoolmaster, broke into the singing of the Turkish national anthem. They sang it lustily, fervently, and well. The leader's face was tense with feeling. A small, cross-eyed boy at the end of the line sang with particular enthusiasm, so that at the end of the song I made sure to give him a pat on the back. We all were moved. Some of the emotion aroused was patriotism, which did not touch me. But some was brotherhood and human kindness, and to find these on the shore of the Sea of Marmara was a good experience.

The ride into Rodosto was over roads so primitive that we expressed a preference for submarines. But even bad roads have to end, and in Rodosto we were again warmly welcomed. A Turkish military group was stationed there, and the commander and the mayor joined in providing us food. The lieutenant and his crew from the *Nagara* were under orders, and they had to wait for instructions from Constantinople. But Dr. Seiler and I were not under orders, and we begged the commandant and mayor to help us get back to the capital. They provided us carriages, and we were driven the fourteen miles to the nearest railway station. There, in due course, we were able to take seats in a third-class passenger carriage attached to a freight train, and sixteen hours later we arrived in Constantinople.

I sat down to write the story of my adventure for the Chicago *Daily News*. I must confess I sent my account by mail. This put the *Daily News* to the embarrassment of carrying the first detailed story of my encounter with the E-11 from London, at the time Lieutenant Commander M. E. D. Nasmith of the E-11 was awarded the Victoria Cross for sinking vessels in the Sea of Marmara. A member of the crew told of the encounter with the "Yankee" correspondent aboard the *Nagara*, who had been asked, "Who are you?" and who had answered, "I am Raymond Swing of the Chicago *Daily News*." My own account did not arrive till more than two weeks later. I had my own reason for thus treating the experience. It had to do with my concept of my function as a newspaper correspondent, which I considered to be to report facts and not to recount his own personal adventures. I was not employed to risk my life in the Sea of Marmara so that I could help the *Daily News* sell papers. I quite consciously did not relish the idea of dying for the Chicago *Daily News*. However, if in the line of duty as a correspondent I ran into dangers, that was the price of duty, and I was willing to pay it. But I was not willing to put the dangers ahead of the duty. So the Chicago *Daily News* had to wait more than two weeks after the E-11 had returned to London and received its honors before publishing my own story of the submarine in the Sea of Marmara.

The narrative about the E-11 apparently delighted the editors of an Italian newspaper, for it published this version of the affair. Under the heading "Frankness Rewarded," the newspaper described the colloquy between me and the officers of the English submarine in the Sea of Marmara:

"Who are you?"

"Who are we?"

"Yes, who are you? And hurry up, we haven't time to lose."

"I am an American journalist, correspondent of the *Chicago Daily News*, and have come here to see the war."

"Ah, I am much pleased. But I wish to know the name of the ship that hosts you."

"The name of the ship that is hosting me?"

"Yes, and be quick, because I must—"

"The Turkish transport *Nagara*."

"Then, my friend, descend at once and save yourself. I must—"

The correspondent of the *Chicago Daily News* descended precipitously and with him descended the equipage of *The Nagara*, to whom Mr. E-11 had made a death declaration that did not admit reply or attenuation. And shortly afterward *The Nagara* was a cadaver at the bottom of the Marmara.

I did go to London after the war to work as a correspondent, and though the story of my landlubber's mistake in answering the question "Who are you?" seemed to be known by everyone I met, it did not prove an obstacle in my work.

For some curious reason, I had never heard the name of Lieutenant Commander Nasmith until long after my arrival in London, where I discovered it through reading a passage quoted in a Sunday newspaper from a book on British submarines in the war which repeated the "Who are you?" story. The British still found it funny ten years later. By that time the submarine commander was a rear admiral and in command of all the submarines of the British navy, with headquarters at Portsmouth.

I immediately sat down and wrote him. I told him that in

1915 in the Sea of Marmara, we were having a conversation which had been interrupted by events beyond my control. It was a conversation I should like to resume at his convenience. I signed my own name, and put the name "Silas Q. Swing" under it, in parentheses. I posted it to his headquarters in Portsmouth.

But I did not get a reply, not in the next days, as was to be expected from a British official, nor the next week. Six weeks later, when I had given up hope of hearing from him, I received a note saying that he had been in the Mediterranean on a tour of duty and had just received my letter. Would I be so good as to lunch with him at the Army and Navy Club the following Tuesday. He added that he would see if he could get Captain d'Oiley Hughes, of the battleship *Tiger,* to join us. He believed he was in England at that time, and he had been his second-in-command on the E-11. Captain Hughes, as it turned out, was beyond reach, but I had lunch with Admiral Nasmith and so was given my first opportunity to thank him for saving my life.

One thing I learned from him was that Rudyard Kipling had not invented the name "Silas Q. Swing." That had been done by Captain Hughes, the Irishman who had said, ". . . be dom quick about it." The Admiral gave me the briefest rundown of his own experiences in the Sea of Marmara, but I had to pry most of it from him by questions. He was a genial but a modest host. Hughes, he told me, had brought my big canvas bag of food and my typewriter back to the E-11. It was he who had boarded the *Nagara* and planted the explosive to sink her.

Captain Hughes later was to become commander of the aircraft carrier *Ark Royal,* and lost his life when it was torpedoed and sunk by the Germans off the coast of Norway early in World War II. His widow later came to work in the British embassy at Washington, and I had the privilege of taking her to lunch. We met almost like old acquaintances. Her husband had spoken of me often, and he had been pleased that the Raymond Swing who gave the weekly American commentary for the British Broadcasting Corporation before and during World War II was the same "Silas Q. Swing" he had inscribed in the log of the E-11. She told me that he had carried my typewriter with him wherever he went, and that it had gone down with him in the *Ark Royal.*

Chapter 12 / More about Submarines

I could not be aware while I was in Turkey of the extent to which the submarine was changing the nature of the war between Allies and Turks. The E-11, on its way out of the Sea of Marmara and the Dardanelles, crossed paths with an incoming German U-boat, the U-21, under Lieutenant Commander Otto Hersing, which had just performed the formidable feat of dispersing the Allied fleet supporting the landed Anzacs by sinking two battleships, the *Triumph* and the *Majestic*. Hersing was on his way to Constantinople to refuel and receive his deserved acclaim. His first victim, the *Triumph*, was skillfully torpedoed at noon through an encircling ring of destroyers. This led to the immediate retirement of the rest of the fleet, excepting only the *Majestic*, which was left behind as a symbol of encouragement and power for the troops. The soldiers in their dugouts, however, were dismayed and wondered if the *Majestic* would manage to survive. She did live through the night by retiring to the harbor of Imbros. The British command, not relishing the ending of all naval support for the men on shore, ordered the *Majestic* back to her post off Cape Helles, where for a second day she upheld the concept of British naval power. However, the men aboard her had little faith in it, for they consumed what was left of her stock of champagne and port on the ground that it would be a pity to have it go to the bottom. The following day, the *Majestic* returned once more, but that was her fatal day. She was torpedoed early in the morning and sank after part of the crew was rescued.

I have told the submarine story unchronologically, for the E-11 and the U-21 were not the first submarines to be active in this war theater. The pioneer had been the E-14, which entered the Sea of Marmara on the day of the Allied landing, April 24. She sank a White Star liner that was transporting 6,000 Turkish troops to Gallipoli, which was her major exploit. Otherwise, she destroyed much small merchant shipping and was responsible for the rising panic in Constantinople. When she had to return to Malta for fuel, she was replaced by the E-11.

Lieutenant Commander Nasmith's first victim in the E-11 was a Turkish gunboat. His second was a sizable Turkish freighter, the *Stamboul*, which was anchored off the Constantinople arsenal. The *Nagara* came soon after. Then he sank one merchant ship after another as they entered the Golden Horn, which gave rise to the report that several submarines were involved. The Turks ordered that no vessel of any size was to leave port without an escort of destroyers and gunboats, and these repeatedly tried to ram the E-11 whenever it rose to the surface. Ultimately, the submarine's supply of torpedoes was down to two, and since the main port motor had developed a defect, Commander Nasmith decided to cruise back to Malta. He was in the narrows on the way out when he turned impulsively back to find some way to use his last two torpedoes. He espied a large transport anchored off Nagara and sank it. Then he made his way through the narrows again.

The arrival of the German U-boat Commander Otto Hersing in Constantinople changed the atmosphere in that city, as it had changed British spirits on Gallipoli, though in an opposite way. The dispersal of the Allied fleet was like an admission of coming defeat, and the Turks in Constantinople so viewed it, though not yet with solid justification.

Commander Hersing was world news, and George Schreiner and I managed to corral him for ourselves for his first interview, thanks to the help of the German embassy. He told a first-rate story. Schreiner and I, in accordance with our long-standing agreement of sharing everything equally, arranged to meet in the hotel lobby after writing our dispatches, and then go to the cable office to file them at the same time, which we did. It is not to my credit that for some inexplicable reason my cable reached Chicago three days before Schreiner's reached the New York office of the Associated Press. The "scoop" is still a greatly treasured factor of newspaper life. My office gained kudos from this scoop, and for years I had to explain to colleagues that I did not do a thing to merit credit for it.

I shall add only one footnote to my estimate of the part that submarines played in the war in Turkey. Two British submarines came after the departure of the E-11, and then in due course the E-11 itself returned, with Lieutenant Commander Nasmith again in command. Her first feat was to sink the Turkish battleship *Barbarossa Harradin,* which she encountered at the top of the narrows, escorted by two destroyers. Nasmith then went on to Constantinople, arriving just as a collier from the Black Sea berthed herself beside the Haidar Pasha Railway Station. Coal at that time was in dire scarcity in Constantinople, since everything depended on it—factories, ships, railways, the city's light and water supply. Alan Moorehead relates in his *Gallipoli* that a committee of officials was standing on the wharf, discussing how the coal should be apportioned, when the E-11 blew it up before their eyes. The E-11 then turned to the Gulf of Ismid, where the Constantinople-Baghdad Railway ran over a viaduct. There d'Oiley Hughes, the first officer, swam ashore and blew up the railway line. He was half dead when he was picked up in the water again. General Liman von Sanders wrote after the war that had the British pressed their submarine campaign, they could have starved out the Turks on Gallipoli. The statement adds to the list of ironies in the relations of the Allies with Turkey. They fought there with utmost bravery. But obviously it also takes judgment and vision to win, and, I might stress, good fortune. I must say, too, that the British fought with modesty. In my luncheon with Admiral Nasmith long after the war, he did not tell me any of his feats in the Sea of Marmara and the Bosporus. And even Mrs. d'Oiley Hughes did not tell me of the audacious blowing up of the railway viaduct by her intrepid husband, which was one of the most spectacular acts of courage in the war.

Chapter 13 / Back and Forth to America

My stay in Turkey was the high point of World War I for me. I did not immediately resume work in Germany after leaving Turkey, but paid a brief visit to the United States. The voyage home produced two episodes that still seem incredible and bizarre to me. I met two young American brokers on the ship with whom I spent virtually all my time. They were alert and congenial, and they were more than interested in what I had to tell them of the war. Before the end of the crossing, one of them gave me $1,000 as an outright gift and the other offered to buy the Toledo *Times* for me.

The gift was more than welcome, because my family could use more than I had been able to allow them. The broker who gave it explained that he had just made a killing on the market and it literally did not mean much to him to give it to me. He felt flush and friendly. He assured me that no obligation was involved. I cannot imagine a present being made more easy to accept, so I accepted it.

The offer to buy me the Toledo *Times* was serious. The broker was a Toledoan; he knew he could buy the paper for a relatively small sum; and, while it was not making money, he thought good management and editing could put it on its feet. This was a proposition I had to weigh before accepting or declining it. I was twenty-nine; by then, I had cut my eye-teeth in journalism. It was time that I plan for the future. Did I want to be a foreign correspondent all my life, or would I like to have a hand in building a middle-sized American community, influencing its policies and politics? These were interesting questions. I asked time to think about them before making up my mind.

I tell this incident as though my career was something I always did or could plan, which is far from the truth. As this narrative of my life will show, most of the important developments in it came about without my willing or foreseeing them, through actions beyond my generation or control. But, in due course, I did turn down the opportunity to publish the Toledo *Times*, and this decision did have something to do with shaping my life, even if only negatively. That is assuming that my broker friend would have been able to buy the paper and would have let me run it, and that it would have made money. As American newspapers have changed with the times, a city of the size of Toledo could not have supported two dailies. The paper it did support was the *Blade*, of which my friend and sponsor Grove Patterson was editor. So in saying no-thank-you-very-much to my broker, I now presume I was simply avoiding a failure. But it was pleasant to think, when I went back to Berlin, that I was working there in preference to publishing a newspaper back in Ohio.

When I did get back to my post in Berlin, there were to be no such experiences as I had gone through in Turkey. The work was still limited by the obstinate refusal of the Germans to allow correspondents at the front. At best, there were brief excursions. I recall two in 1916, one to Düsseldorf to make a study of German industrial production, and, following it, a trip to the Eastern front.

I made the junket to Düsseldorf, but at the last minute was forbidden to go to the Eastern front. I was told I had violated German censorship on the Düsseldorf excursion. I knew quite well the basis of the accusation, but it was unjustified.

It is not much of a story, but it did prove one could get a cable out of Germany if one tried. The subject of the cable was a statement made to me as one of a party of journalists on the trip by a German steel manufacturer. It was over the luncheon table, and the Foreign Office representative in charge of us was at the other end of the table, out of hearing. The manufacturer was talking, possibly at my instigation, about Germany's war aims. I am not sure I led him into the subject. Very likely he would have spoken as he did without prompting from me. What he wanted me to understand was that on one side of the frontier between Germany and France lay coal mines in the Ruhr Basin. These were in Germany. On the other side were iron mines in the Briey Basin. These were in France. German industry in the Ruhr and the remainder of highly industrialized western Germany lived from both the iron and the coal, and to have them divided by national frontiers was an absurdity. It was this absurdity Germany was fighting the war to end. Germany had to have the iron along with the coal. He said this simply and with conviction.

The catch I could see at once in his proposition was that it was completely contrary to the war aims Germany had proclaimed, which explicitly renounced the annexation of any territory belonging to another country. However, I did not say this to the German industrialist. The official war aims, I knew, were propaganda. What the industrialist had said was sincere. So I did not dispute with him or even argue about what he said. I drank it in. I knew I had a story, if I could only manage to get it out of the country.

I did manage, and that is why I was not permitted to go to Poland on the coming tour. I did not resort to trickery. I simply used common sense.

The Düsseldorf industrialist had spoken so frankly and simply about the union of the Briey and Ruhr Basins that I assumed that his view must be shared by virtually everyone in that region. Of course there was a post office of major dimensions in Düsseldorf, and I was sure it had its own censor of outgoing telegraph messages. I also felt sure this censor was a local man and would share the opinions of the region. He would agree with the industrialist with whom I had talked. So the way to get the news out was to send it from Düsseldorf and not wait until the return to Berlin. That meant sending it in German, and I went to the post office, obtained telegraph blanks, and composed the telegram in German. My mastery of the language was somewhat skimpy. But it was sufficient for me to tell my story so that the Düsseldorf censor—if there was one—would understand it and so would stamp it, for forwarding to my relay correspondent in Amsterdam.

I came to the telegraph window and handed the message in. The official looked at the address of the relay man in Amsterdam and grunted. Then he called in a colleague. This was the local censor. He was an elderly retired army captain, no doubt recruited by the post office because of manpower shortage. The retired captain took the message and succeeded in reading it easily enough. He agreed with it. As I quoted the Düsseldorf industrialist, he nodded his head approvingly. And when he had finished reading the dispatch, he produced his rubber stamp and smacked it down. I then paid for the telegram and slipped out to rejoin my colleagues.

The dispatch reached Chicago and within two days appeared in the London *Daily Telegraph*, and no doubt many other Allied newspapers. Here was an unequivocal statement about what Germany was fighting for. If it had been written by someone in England or France, it would not have attracted attention. But it was written by an American and filed from Düsseldorf. I was right; it had been news.

A summons to the Foreign Office followed within a day or two. The press officer said he had called me in to inform me that I would not be included on the coming visit to the Eastern front. Probably I would be expelled from Germany, he said. Why? Because I had been guilty of evading censorship. I denied this forthrightly. The press officer quietly held to his point. Where had I evaded censorship? I asked. In Düsseldorf, he told me. I warned him not to make charges that he could not prove. I denied having evaded censorship in Düsseldorf or anywhere else. He became testy. A dispatch of mine, he said, quoting a Düsseldorf industrialist, had appeared in foreign papers. It could only have reached them if I had evaded the censorship. I told him again he must be sure of his facts before making such serious charges. I admitted I had written such a dispatch. "Have you not seen the original of it?" I asked him. He looked taken aback. No, he had not seen it. "Then see it, and see if it bears the censor's stamp," I said. How could he see it, he asked, if I had smuggled it across the border? I said I had not smuggled it across the border; I had filed it in the usual manner in Düsseldorf. I saw the press officer gulp. He would not take anything back until he had learned if I was telling the truth and had the dispatch before him. He said I was to come back in two days. That meant missing the junket to the Eastern front, which left the next morning, but I would not be expelled from the country, for the time being. I knew I could not be after my dispatch had been examined.

I confess I felt sorry for the old army captain at the Düsseldorf post office. He would be the one to pay for my cable. But I consoled myself by thinking that if he believed in making war to conquer French territory, he had an unpleasantry coming to him.

Two days later, I was called back to the press office. A sour and somber press chief told me that no action would be taken against me on account of the Düsseldorf cable. Hereafter, however, all correspondents taking trips under the aegis of the Foreign Office would be forbidden to file any message till after their return to Berlin and would do it then in their regular manner.

I am sure the press officer would have been delighted to expel me. I already was branded in Berlin as anti-German. My having served as unofficial envoy from Chancellor von Bethmann-Hollweg to Sir Edward Grey had not assured me a place of favor; so far as I knew, it may even have hurt me. I had enjoyed good if formal relations with Foreign Minister Gottlieb von Jagow, and quite cordial ones with his Undersecretary, Herr Zimmermann. Herr von Jagow I had found not very communicative, but he had been accessible, and I paid numerous visits to him. He was in the Prussian tradition, austere and on the taciturn side. Herr Zimmermann—the same one who later wrote the ridiculous note to Mexico urging it to attack the United States—was not ridiculous in my contacts with him. He was a big, sandy-colored man with a bluff kind of congeniality, and did not mind talking with engaging candor. But my connections with them would not have saved me if I had been caught red-handed in a flagrant evasion of the censorship. The time of popularity for Americans was already over. The sharpening duel between President Wilson and the German government over submarine warfare was reaching a climax. German tensions had risen, too, as the war in the west settled into an unbreakable stalemate. The ebullience of 1914 was gone. The far-seeing already were sure the United States would ultimately be in the war. There was no reason why Americans should be popular.

The time from my return from Turkey until the break with Germany, to be followed later by America's entry into the war,

does not stand out in my memory as being anything but unpleasant in a rising degree but with outstanding exceptions.
The heavy casualties of the war had long set in, and I knew
hardly any German families that had not been depleted. My
relations with these families were bound to be affected, even
though American neutrality was still a formal fact. Some of
my colleagues were pro-German with unmistakable sincerity,
and they could have cordial relations with German families.
The exceptions in my case were mostly Jewish artists, who,
while themselves loyal to the German cause, were more generous to foreigners. I went to two Jewish homes almost every
alternate Sunday for musical receptions. One was of the
sculptor Fritz Oppler, not a world genius, but a man of rare
sensitivity and understanding of the arts. His brother Hans was
a celebrated painter. Frau Oppler was a woman of unusual
culture and charm. They knew intimately many of the outstanding musical performers of the time, and always were able
to produce one to play or sing at one of their Sunday functions.

A member of the other family became a world celebrity,
Wanda Landowska. Her husband, Lew, was a writer on musical subjects. When I first knew her she was known as Lew-Lan-
dowska.

Food was beginning to be scarce in Germany, and the feat
of supplying refreshments for large roomfuls of visitors was a
problem that Lew solved through methods into which I never
inquired too closely. He had sources in the countryside, and
he must have known his black market. Everyone was glad to
go to the Lew-Landowskas because of the good pastries and
the genuine coffee. It is a sign of the times in Germany that I
should mention refreshments ahead of the delight in hearing
Madame Landowska perform at the piano, which she did on
each of these occasions. I do not believe she possessed a harp-
sichord at the time, and I did not hear her play one until she
concertized in England after the war. Lew, who was killed in
a streetcar accident before the end of the war, and Madame
Landowska came to the train to see me off when I finally left
Germany, bringing a box of their celebrated pastries. In those
days, greater friendliness could hardly be imagined.

After my return to Germany from Turkey, what I felt most,
after the change of warmth in relations with the Germans, was

the hunger. The British blockade was having a marked effect on the German food supply. Rationing had been decreed, and the amount of rationed food was skimpy. The black market did a meager business and could not supply middle-class families and restaurants with their normal supplies. I felt hungry a good part of the time, not ravenously so, but still hungry enough to be aware of it.

I had a privilege denied to Germans. I could go to Holland at regular intervals and eat myself full. And this I did. I would take a train overnight on Friday and return Sunday night, which gave me all of Saturday and most of Sunday in Holland. I did this every few weeks.

Chapter 14 / Did Britain Plan to Invade Holland?

Among my friends in Holland was an American naval architect employed by the Dutch government in the construction of submarines. He and his wife often opened their home to me when I came to Holland. This close relationship led to one of my most unusual experiences in the war. It remains remarkable to me because up to this time I have never been able to establish the facts involved, which, so far as I know, may not have been facts at all.

I had been coming to my friends in Holland for months when, on my arrival one day in 1916, I found them unusually excited. My host said he must tell me something of utmost importance. The day before, a Dutch torpedo boat had come upon a line of markers of some sort that ended at the island of Flushing, and, when followed, led back to a British naval port which appeared to be crowded with transports. Obviously, he said, the British were going to invade Holland, and it was my duty to obtain the facts, publish them throughout the world, and save Holland from the disaster of war. He said that on discovering the markers, Hendrik Colijn, head of the Royal Dutch Oil Company, had gone to England to protest to the British authorities. He was the businessman having closest relations with England. He was back by now, my host said, and wished to see me. He helped me arrange an appointment. My host was highly excited. He wanted Holland to be kept out of the war. He was sure I could help save it.

The war on the Western front at that time was in a stage of stalemate, and a breakthrough by either side seemed impossible. A British landing in Holland would place Allied troops behind the German lines and force a German retreat. I admit that I had never heard anyone mention the possibility of a British landing in Holland. World opinion had become convinced that the British were sincere in their defense of Belgian neutrality. A British violation of Dutch neutrality would have been rejected by the British public and by the friends Britian had won by its dedication to the cause of Belgium.

I am not now saying that the British were preparing an invasion of Holland, for I do not know the facts. I can only relate what happened, and that was ominous enough. I did go to see Mr. Colijn and told him I had come to ask about what he had learned in England. Mr. Colijn looked at me gravely. For several moments he remained silent, then he rose and took me to a map that hung on the wall. He pointed out Flushing. "You see it is an island," he said. "It connects with the mainland by this one railroad line. Nothing would be easier than to cut that line. The island is small." He ran his finger around it. "We could not put more than 5,000 men on the island to defend it. They would be cut off and useless. It would be only the most formal kind of resistance. Once in Flushing," he went on, "a foreign army could pour into Holland and we could do nothing to prevent it."

"Would the Dutch resist?" I asked.

"Her Majesty's government," he replied, "is determined on that score. It would. But what use would resistance be? Look at the geography of Flushing."

"Then what is to prevent a landing at Flushing?" I asked. His hand pointed to the German frontier at the south of Holland. "If an army were to be ready here, one that could march into Holland at the moment of a landing in Flushing, the landing might not be made. If it had to face only the resistance of Dutch troops, that would not stop them. But if the British knew they had to face an invading German army, that would be another matter."

"And you found the British were actually preparing for a landing in Holland?" I asked.

Mr. Colijn did not answer directly. His face darkened. He almost growled, "Churchill is a gentleman but sometimes forgets it. Lloyd George is a cad and never forgets it." Then he said to me, "You have good connections with the Germans, I am told." I said I had. "It is a terrible position, terrible for Holland," he said, almost as though speaking to himself. And with these words, he rose and the interview came to an end.

I went back to the home of my host and repeated what had been said. He was passionately earnest. "You will go to Ambassador von Rosen?" he said, not as a question, but almost as an appeal. "I don't know," I answered. "I have to think it over."

It was clear to me that Mr. Colijn wished me to pass on to the German Ambassador what he had told me. But why could not the Dutch government do it? I no sooner asked myself that question than I realized it could not appeal in advance to the German government for help. That would prejudice its neutral position. The only way to stop the British landing—if it was planned—was through unofficial communication of the facts to the Germans.

I did not like bearing messages. If I could publish what I had been told, it might be enough to prevent a landing. But again, it might not. My story would be denied, certainly, by the British government, almost as certainly by Mr. Colijn. The Germans might not have moved troops to the border. It was not publicity Mr. Colijn wanted, but a discreet communication to the German Ambassador. I was not interested in saving the Germans on the Western front, but I did care about Holland. I might add that I also cared for the British cause of upholding neutrality. I wanted it to be sustained. But it was the Dutch I was principally concerned about. I liked them and the way they ran their affairs. I did not want to see them endure the depredations of war experienced by the Belgians. I now had to consider if it might possibly depend on my action whether they did so or not.

I did call on the German Ambassador after making a telephone appointment. I was promptly received, and I repeated what I knew in about the words I have written. The Ambassador looked very serious. When I had finished, he asked me: "Have I your permission to report this information to my government?" It was a stupid question under the circumstances, but I assume it was meant to be courteous. "Of course," I said. "And may I say from whom it has come?" "Why not?" I replied. "Then let me say a final word," he went on, after thanking me. "A great newspaper correspondent is great for what he writes, but also for what *he does not write*. Take my word for it."

So I was being advised not to publish the report about the British, which was my one valid reason as a newspaper correspondent to be involved in this episode at all.

A few days later, I was in Berlin and heard there were troop movements on the Dutch frontier. Undersecretary Zimmermann, the next time I saw him, remarked guardedly that he appreciated some help I had been able to render Germany. I did not correct him to say it was not Germany I had sought to help. And that was all I heard about the story for a long time. The British transports at the end of the markers leading to Flushing—if they ever existed—did not move. The war in the west continued to be a stalemate. Holland continued to be neutral and free. And there, except for two strange postludes, the story comes to an end.

One of these was a hearing by a Reichstag committee after the peace on the conduct of the war, which brought out the fact that two army divisions had been moved from the hard-pressed Western front to the Dutch frontier at the time of this incident. This had been done at the insistence of the Foreign Office, and it was cited as an instance of the unwarranted interference of the civil authorities in military affairs. Nothing was said at the hearing, so far as was published, about the reason for this troop movement, or what it might have accomplished. If Herr Zimmermann, who was under investigation, believed he had prevented the invasion of Holland by the British, he did not say so, or at any rate his saying so was not published in the newspapers. It may be that the Weimar Republic needed the support and friendship of Britain after the war, and that the full story, which would have discredited Great Britain, was deliberately suppressed. It also may have been that the Foreign Office's insistence was considered to have been based on insufficient evidence, so no reason for it could be published.

There is a further possible explanation of the incident. The British may have conjured up the threat of invading Holland for the precise purpose of inducing the Germans to move troops from the Western front to the Dutch frontier. They may have thought the whole plot through, known from their secret service that I was making one of my regular visits to Holland and that I had the desired connections with the German embassy and Foreign Office. They may have taken Mr. Colijn into their confidence, and he may have connived with them to deceive me and to induce me to give untrue information to the Germans; after all, his business interests were closely linked with the British. I have thought about this possibility. I do not believe my friend the naval architect was involved in any such elaborate conspiracy. He was genuinely disturbed about the possibility of Holland being invaded.

The British secret service has some sensational coups to its credit, and if this is one of them, it can be expected that in due course the information will be published, as that of the other coups has been. But arguing against this theory is that the Western front was not weakened by the withdrawal of German troops enough to have affected the stalemate. That is, the coup, if such it was, while it appears to have succeeded, failed in its real purpose.

The second postlude to this story does not prove anything, though I must also say that it does not disprove anything. Mr. Colijn went to Geneva after the war as head of the Netherlands delegation to the League of Nations. I covered this session for the Philadelphia *Public Ledger*, and when I learned that Mr. Colijn was there, I was elated. I had a newspaperman's faith that any secret I had suppressed for reasons of policy or expediency would one day become usable. Here I thought that the debt which fortune owed me was going to be paid off. The war was over; Mr. Colijn did not need to be discreet; the invasion of Holland was not at stake. So I asked him to receive me, which he did in his hotel suite. After greeting him, I said: "Meijnheer Colijn, I have come to remind you of the remarkable conversation we had in your office during the war when you showed me the map of the Netherlands and explained how vulnerable Flushing was to British invasion. You had just come back from England. I should like to know what happened after that visit." The Dutch oil executive looked at me blankly. "I don't know what you are talking about," he said. "I have never seen you before in my life."

There was no argument to this, and I left. And that brings the unusual story to an end, so far as I am concerned. I know only a few facts of what happened in Holland in 1916. I know

I was told that a Dutch torpedo boat came upon markers that made it appear that the British might be preparing to invade Holland. I know I was sent for by the head of the Royal Dutch Oil Company to communicate this information to the Germans, which I did. And Herr Zimmermann obtained the transfer of strong forces from the Western front to the Dutch border, for which he was interrogated after the war by a committee of the Reichstag. I cannot be sure why Mr. Colijn repudiated me after the war. It may be because he participated in the British stratagem, which had worked, and this was his way out. It also may be that he did not want the story published because it would embarrass the British government at a time when the Netherlands government needed good relations with it.

Whatever the truth of the matter, Britain did not invade Holland, tempting as such a possibility must have been. Holland did not suffer the depredations of World War I. Whether the British ever were tempted to the point of near-action and were deterred by the appearance of the German divisions on the Dutch border, or by internal political opposition to the concept, can be left to historians to discover. They are likely to do so if anything is in the records. What I know is what Mr. Colijn told me in 1916 and that he later denied ever having seen me before. It is a good mystery story. It may be simply a secret-service story.

Chapter 15 / Farewell to Germany

The effectiveness of submarine warfare was not better understood in the great European war than in Turkey, or at least not more promptly so. The Germans, under the prodding of Admiral Alfred von Tirpitz, went in for unrestricted submarine warfare, and then under the pressure of President Woodrow Wilson, backed away from it. Finally they resumed it, and so brought America into the war. But the effect of the submarine war on Britain was unmistakable. Had this attack been begun earlier and been pursued with greater intensity, Britain would have been reduced to a fateful shortage of food and materials. This would have come to pass just at the time Britain was preparing to take the place of France as the mainstay on the Continent of the war against Germany. It had recruited a million soldiers and was working overtime to equip them with armaments. France had come to the bottom of the bin. It had strong forces in the field but could not replace them.

The argument pro and con as to the risk of bringing the United States into the war preoccupied the circles around the Kaiser. It certainly dominated all conversation between Germans and Americans in Germany. The Germans saw that the ultimate outcome of the war was at stake, for if Britain could not be curbed, the war in the west could not be won. They shrank from the accusation of "frightfulness," but feared they had to accept it if they were not going to be beaten. It was no easy decision to make. In World War II, similar decisions had to be made in regard to the bombing and burning of cities, and ultimately as to the use of the V-2 and the atom bomb. Scruples by that time had lost still more of their ruggedness. The frightfulnesses of World War II were unspeakably greater than those of World War I; the casualties among soldiers were much fewer. In other words, World War II represented a shift from the greater death of soldiers to the greater death of civilians. This had its beginning in unrestricted submarine warfare in World War I, but the end of what was beginning was not foreseen, not by the Germans or by those who so soundly and indignantly berated them.

As the Tirpitz policy prevailed, at the end of 1916, the American newspapermen working in Berlin had to decide what they would do if diplomatic relations were broken. We talked about this among ourselves at length. Some of the news-agency representatives felt it was a duty to stay on in Germany as long as they were permitted to do their work. I knew what I would do: I would go out on the Ambassador's train. We soon learned that the Foreign Office was ready to guarantee the freedom of movement of any American newsmen who stayed at their posts and would permit them to continue their work. Several chose to accept this offer. They justified themselves on the ground that their news duties had to be fulfilled, war or no war. But those who were going to stay were personally pro-German, while those of us who were leaving were not. As it turned out, the German government did not keep its promise of freedom of movement. It found itself under the pressure of public opinion after America entered the war, and while it did not put the American newsmen into concentration camps, it kept them under rigid surveillance.

Early in February, diplomatic relations were broken, and the departure from Berlin took place. Among the correspondents to go was Carl Ackerman, of the United Press, who was later to make a name for himself as dean of the Columbia School of Journalism. I need to say a word about my relations with him. At this time I had broken off a long-standing friendship with him, and in hindsight I have come to see I had done so unjustly. I had known Ackerman intimately long before he came to Berlin; he had been the Earlham College representative of the Richmond *Evening Item* when I was its city editor. He met his wife through my sister. I was in

Berlin when he was first appointed as representative in that capital by the United Press. He had just married, and I greeted him and his wife with warmest possible delight, helped them find an apartment, and made it my business to show Acker- man the way around and aid him in performing his duties as correspondent. He was without any experience in Germany and little if any outside the United States. I was greatly pleased to be of use to him. We worked side by side on the closest terms, and this intimacy was to continue until the time when Ambassador James Gerard made a public statement warning the American public that the reports of the American correspondents in Berlin were not reliable. He said that they were not to be trusted because the newsmen worked under restrictions of the German government which prohibited them from telling the truth. Obviously we were under censorship, but so were correspondents in all the Allied countries. I knew from my own experience that Mr. Gerard did not know of any occasion in which I had been kept from reporting responsibly. I was well acquainted with the Ambassador. I had the im- pression that, in making his statement, he was playing politics, that he wished to arouse anti-German feeling in the United States and thus hasten the abandonment of the official policy of neutrality still in effect. There was nothing reprehensible in this. But he went too far, I felt, in impugning the integrity of American news reporting. The corps of American newspaper correspondents met to discuss his statement and draft a reply to it, Ackerman alone not attending. Censorship was not the point. The impression we thought Mr. Gerard wanted to give was that the American correspondents in Berlin were under some additional restrictions, and this was not the case. All of us signed the reply except Ackerman, and it was duly pub- lished in the United States.

I strongly reproached Ackerman for siding with the Am- bassador and going back on his colleagues and his profession. I felt his action all the more keenly because of our long and intimate friendship. He argued that he must not cut himself off from the embassy if he were to fulfill his functions as United Press correspondent. At the time, I thought he was currying favor with the Ambassador at the cost of loyalty to his colleagues and his profession. He admitted he knew of no instance when, more than other censorships, the German government had made his dispatches irresponsible. But the embassy was the organism of the United States government in Berlin, and he chose not to be estranged from it. I now think he was not wrong. I believe he probably could have signed the statement of the correspondents without losing status at the embassy. But I can see that as a press-association representative, he had reason to avoid doing anything he believed might injure his position there.

We did not become friends again, which I admit was my fault, not his, and I regret it. I was being emotional.

For the remaining months in Berlin, Ackerman, naturally, became the Ambassador's favorite, and Mr. Gerard's influence subsequently helped him to be named head of a newly established European service of the Philadelphia *Public Ledger* and New York *Evening Post*. The Ambassador had close relations with the Curtis Publishing Company, which owned them, and wrote his memoirs as ambassador for the *Saturday Evening Post*. But I must say that he never showed me any hostility while we were still in Berlin, or on the ambassadorial train to Paris, or on subsequent meetings, of which there were many.

When the diplomatic break with Germany finally came, I was asked—I do not now recall by whom—if I would take the responsibility of caring for an American music student in the Leipzig Conservatory and deliver her to her mother in New York. She was something of a child prodigy, a brilliant pianist, and came to my office, her hair on her shoulders like an Alice in Wonderland. She was fifteen, and in another year was due to receive her diploma at Leipzig. She was to become my sister-in-law after the war, marrying my brother Dolf after he became a professional singer. On the long trip back to America via Spain, I found her prim and shy. But on the ship that took us to New York, there was a good piano, so I had the reward of hearing some first-rate piano-playing.

Chapter 16 / A Mission for Colonel House

I came away from Germany with a belief that the Germans were ready, or certainly on the way to being ready, to negotiate a moderate peace. I had this assurance from Matthias Erzberger and other Reichstag leaders of the center and left. So when I arrived in the United States, I wanted to have the opportunity to present their views to President Wilson. I did succeed in presenting them to Colonel E. M. House. But the word that I got back from the White House was that the President did not want to hear anything about moderate Germans. He was angry with the Germans and did not believe that any of them, or enough of them, were moderate. Colonel House told me he hoped the President would let me tell him later on about my conversations with Reichstag leaders in Germany, but Mr. Wilson was not in the mood for it then, and a meeting never came about. In fact, I never met President Wilson, much to my regret.

My contact with Colonel House, however, led to results which greatly excited me, and were to cause me great trouble. He asked me to go back to France as his representative and interview French left-of-center politicians to inform and persuade them of the value and importance of President Wilson's program for a moderate peace—the Fourteen Points—which was to include such features as self-determination and disarmament. He wanted the liberals and radicals to be primed to support the Wilson program against the expected opposition of Premier Georges Clemenceau when the time came to proclaim it. And Colonel House set a condition that was extremely awkward to meet. I was not to tell the Chicago *Daily News* or anyone else about my mission. I was simply to go back to France as a Chicago *Daily News* representative and fulfill it. While there, he said, if I heard any news that I thought he ought to know, I was to take it to a certain high diplomatic officer at the United States embassy, who would be instructed to forward it to him.

This presented me with a quandary. Colonel House was not paying me anything, so the Chicago *Daily News* would have to go on supporting me, for I had no means of my own. To do this without the sanction of the publisher or editor certainly would be unethical. But not to serve Colonel House, and the President through him, in time of war, seemed to me to be just as unethical. I told Colonel House that I really should tell my editor what I was doing. But he was positive about it; he said I must not. He told me I need not be worried about the problem, in due time he would explain it to Victor Lawson, and there would be no difficulty for me. Naturally, I wanted to go. My work in Germany had come to an end, and I had no idea how or where the *Daily News* intended to make use of me. So I agreed, booked passage on the next steamer to France, and took off. I do not deny that I was entranced with the idea of being used by Colonel House and that it gave me a feeling of importance I could not easily resist.

Back in Paris, I saw Paul Scott Mowrer, of the Chicago *Daily News*. I pledged him to secrecy and told him how I came to be there. He appreciated the conflict of duties and interests which beset me and wrote the Chicago office that I was there, and, while he could not explain why I had returned to Paris, he knew the reason and considered it a sufficient one.

The French politician Colonel House most wanted me to interest in President Wilson's peace program was Jean Longwy, leader of the extreme left in the French Chamber of Deputies. As an envoy of Colonel House, I had no difficulty in meeting him, and I found him exceedingly interested in the Wilson program and outspokenly in favor of it. He gave me the names of other men of the left to see, and these I also found friendly and favorable. This I wrote to Colonel House, and he replied appreciatively.

Among the new acquaintances I made in Paris was a Pole named Joseph R. Rettinger, who was the representative of the undercover nationalists of Poland working for the independence of their country and who became an important figure in the political life of his country after it was reconstituted. We had friends in common, and he accepted me as someone worthy of his confidence.

One day he told me he had grave news to report. Serious mutinies had broken out in fifteen French army corps, and the government was exceedingly anxious over the situation. This was at a time when French losses had been cruelly great and the stalemate in the West was dispiriting to both the French troops and the people. I had the impression that Rettinger gave me this information in the hope of spurring on the Washington administration to greater haste in sending American troops to the Western front, but that it was trustworthy. He knew of my association with Colonel House and expected me to report the mutinies to him.

This was the first dispatch I had thought important enough to ask Colonel House's confidant at the embassy to transmit to him. I had no doubt that I ought to send it. So I wrote out all that I had learned from Mr. Rettinger and took it to the embassy. The diplomatic officer received me without delay. I told him I had been promised by Colonel House that he would forward any news I considered merited his attention, which he said was so. The official read my dispatch.

"If you will allow me to offer my advice," he said, "I do not think you should send this to Colonel House." "Why not?" I asked. "Because what you say is not true. I am in closest touch with the Ministry of War, and I would know about such mutinies if they had taken place."

"Colonel House," I retorted, "did not instruct me to ask your opinion as to the merit of the information I wished to send him. He simply said you would forward anything I brought to you."

"If you put it that way," the official replied, "I shall send your dispatch." So, in the chilly atmosphere, I thanked him and departed.

This message turned out to be a personal catastrophe for me. The mutinies in the French army are a historical fact. Indeed, the news of them, when it ultimately reached Washington, did spur the administration into expediting the dispatch of the first token American troops to France to raise French morale. But my message had no part in this. It took some time for the news to become known and even believed. Several of the early histories of the war omitted it altogether, and the credit for publishing it first belongs to Winston Churchill, in *The World Crisis*, Part I, written in 1927, ten years later. "The demoralization of the French army was proceeding apace," he wrote. "Want of confidence in their leaders, cruel losses and an active defeatist propaganda had produced an intense spasm throughout its ranks. Mutinies of a very dangerous kind occurred in sixteen separate Army Corps. Some of the finest troops were involved. Divisions elected councils. Whole regiments set out for Paris to demand a peace by negotiation and more home leave." A later historian, C. R. M. F. Cruttwell, writing in 1934, gives greater details of the mutinies in *A History of the Great War, 1914-1918.* In 1963, an entire volume, *Dare Call It Treason,* by Richard M. Watt, was devoted to the mutinies.

It is a coincidence that Herbert Brougham, one of the editors of the Philadelphia *Ledger*, a close friend of mine, was sitting with Colonel House on the veranda of his New England residence when my cable from Paris came in. Colonel House, he later told me, read the message, then remarked: "Too bad, we can't use Swing any more," and tossed the cable to Brougham to read. The diplomatic officer in Paris had added a footnote to my story of the mutinies, saying that I was known to be associating with untrustworthy elements of the left, and that the news of the mutinies simply was not true.

I did not learn this till later. All I knew was that the correspondence I had been receiving from Colonel House ceased. And after a silence of several weeks, I realized that I had been dropped. There was nothing I could do about it. I did not know the reason, and I went back to America, a puzzled and dispirited young man. I sent my resignation to the Chicago *Daily News* as the least I could do in acknowledgment of my peculiar behavior in sailing for France without explanations or orders. I had hoped the resignation might be rejected, but it was simply acknowledged, which, under the circumstances, was not to be wondered at. I also wrote to Colonel House for an explanation, but received no reply.

I can make two addenda to this story. After the war, I received a letter from Colonel House, handsomely apologizing for his action in leaving me stranded in France. He said he had later learned he had made a mistake and was very sorry for it. The other addendum is a letter I received from the diplomat in Paris, after I had become a broadcaster. The Colonel House story had been told in an article about me in the *Saturday Evening Post*, and the diplomat wrote me to assure me that his footnote to my dispatch about the mutiny in the French army had not been as my friend described it. He had not done more than question the reliability of my information, he said, and had not criticized me for associating with irresponsible people of the left. It is conceivable that the contents of the footnote were not repeated to me with precise accuracy. Mr. Brougham, who had been with Colonel House when the cable arrived, was one of a number of other writers, including William C. Bullitt (later to be ambassador to Moscow), and Lincoln Colcord, who had formed an informal association, to which I belonged, to explore the possibility of finding an "angel" to buy a New York newspaper which we were to publish. The "angel" we had in view was Bernard Baruch; the newspaper we wanted was the New York *Tribune*. The plan had been born before I went back to France for Colonel House. The upshot of this episode was that it left me without a job, which was a state I was to endure for several months.

However, the project of buying the New York *Tribune* was very much alive, and I had high hopes for it. It had been agreed that Bullitt, Colcord, Brougham, and I were to conduct the policy of the paper—if we succeeded in buying it— as a board. I had been informally designated as managing editor, the others were to be in charge of the editorial policy. We talked several times with Mr. Baruch, and he gave us to understand that he was with us all the way. He did, however, want some business facts to go on. He needed to know what the earnings of the *Tribune* had been from advertising and circulation and what the probabilities were of increasing them. He had to have these facts to know what to offer for the property. I was the one with free time, so I was assigned to make a study of the *Tribune*, and I devoted many weeks to it. I assembled my data, and on the basis of them, it was agreed what the offering price would be.

But it was never actually offered. There had been soundings of Whitelaw Reid, and we were told he might be willing to sell at the right figure. But before matters could proceed further, President Wilson appointed Bernard Baruch chairman of the War Production Board. Right away he told us that the newspaper deal was off. Obviously he could not be a newspaper owner and work for the administration in a high official capacity at the same time. So I folded up my sheets of data about the *Tribune*. I assume that if anyone had suggested to Mr. Baruch that it would be appropriate for him to pay me a nominal sum for the time I had devoted to the study of the *Tribune* property, he would have done so ungrudgingly, but nobody did. Certainly it did not occur to him. He owed me nothing and he paid me nothing. The idea of buying the *Tribune* had not been his; it had been ours.

I might say that being unemployed worked to my benefit, for during this time I went through a season of severe self-examination, and at the close of the period, I had learned better how to face up to the truth about myself and the problems of living. I have said earlier that I am not writing my confessions, and would not undertake to tell how I came to be the person that I am. All I am inclined to say now is that this period was to be of enormous value to me. I suffered and pondered and somehow gained insight and strength, an experience for which I have ever since been profoundly grateful.

In this time, I made the acquaintance of Frank Walsh, who was appointed chairman of the War Labor Board set up early in 1918, and he employed me as an examiner, so I went to work again. The War Labor Board was the pioneer organ of the federal government in adjudicating disputes between management and labor in industries affecting war production. It had little authority and had to rely for success on public opinion, effectiveness, and persuasiveness. The full legal recognition of the right of collective bargaining was not introduced until the Wagner Act, passed in the presidency of Franklin D. Roosevelt.

My duties as examiner were to inquire into labor differences, ascertain the facts, and report confidentially to the Board, which then held hearings and tried to bring national influence to bear. I consider my service for the Board an invaluable part of my education. I came to know both employers and employees in many parts of the country, and learned to listen patiently to both sides of an industrial dispute. I also learned to recognize that there were trustworthy and untrustworthy men on both sides, and that hostilities were often too bitter to ameliorate completely through outside action. Frank Walsh was an able chairman and made a valuable contribution to the progress that has by now developed in labor-management relations.

I did not wait for the Board to go out of existence at the end of the war to resign as examiner, because I was employed by the *Nation* for the winter months of 1918 and 1919. I wrote editorials, editorial paragraphs, and a couple of full-length articles—one on the Lawrence, Massachusetts, textile strike, which won me special commendation from Oswald Garrison Villard, the publisher.

Chapter 17 / Back in Berlin

There was no question in my mind that I wanted to return to Europe, and it was at this moment that my friend from Orrville, Ohio, days, Heber Blankenhorn, became of providential help to me. He was city editor of the New York *Herald*, recently purchased by Frank Munsey. Mr. Munsey was considering the creation of a foreign service, and Blankenhorn persuaded him that I would make a good Berlin correspondent. Mr. Munsey sent for me and asked some questions about my experiences at the War Labor Board and the *Nation*—which he did not like—but ended by saying that he saw no reason why my views on labor should make me unsuitable to represent the New York *Herald* in Europe.

I took my brother Dolf back to Berlin with me. He was a student in Oberlin and had a remarkably good baritone voice. My father had by then retired and was living with my mother in Coconut Grove, Florida. I asked them if they would be willing to have me take Dolf to Berlin, where he could obtain first-rate voice training, as well as a rich musical education. My oldest brother Harold had been killed in an automobile accident a few weeks after the death of my sister, Betsy, in 1915, so the prospect of Dolf as well as myself living abroad for perhaps years was of concern to them. Dolf at the time was twenty-one, and my mother was particularly devoted to him. However, they gave their consent, and in due course we arrived in Berlin and rented a furnished apartment.

Berlin under the Weimar Republic was much more friendly than under Wilhelm II. Its rigid Prussian posture had been relaxed. Defeat in the war did not have a depressing effect; on the contrary, the spirit of the capital responded to the liberation the country was experiencing under the Weimar Republic.

What was exciting and unexpected was that the arts suddenly flowered as by a miracle. I can speak of the theater, opera, and painting from firsthand contact with the persons engaged in them.

My brother Dolf was taking voice lessons with Herr Paul Knuepfer, one of the great basses in the Prussian State Opera, and being coached by Artur Ruebling, who was *Chorrepetitor* at the State Opera. Ruebling was an enthusiastic devotee of Richard Strauss, then coming into his own as the outstanding German composer, and played for us all the Strauss operas that had then been published.

On my return to Berlin, I consorted occasionally with Germans of monarchist dedication, but my happier impressions of the Germans were derived from those in political power, the Catholic center, labor, and socialist elements that had brought about the abdication of the Kaiser and now hoped to build a free nation. In affability, the contrast between the Germans I had known, even before the war, with those now dominating the country was striking.

The history of the Weimar Republic, the beginning of which I was to record as a correspondent, came ultimately to a shocking denouement: the rise of Hitler and the Nazis. But it was preceded by years of troubled efforts to reach an accord with the Allies, which were rendered difficult by the stubborn punitiveness of the French as much as by secret nationalist activities in Germany. The assessment of reparations was looming up as the basic issue, with the French insisting on staggering sums which Germany clearly was unable to pay, and with the United States serving ultimately as an advocate of common sense and realizable figures, at first in the Dawes Plan and later in the Young Plan.

My first year, journalistically, for the New York *Herald* was not dramatic. The eyes of the world were focused on Versailles, and developments in Germany did not make much first-page news. I had to find my way around again, build up new connections in the government, and familiarize myself with the social and economic problems of the Republic.

I renewed my association with Herr Erzberger, Philip Scheidemann, the Socialist leader, and Friedrich Ebert, later to become president. My best friend among the new leaders was Rudolph Breitscheid, head of the Independent Socialists, a tall, narrow-shouldered man, a little stooped, who to me personified the hopes and virtues latent in the Weimar Republic.

It is next to impossible for me to revive in their true perspective the memories of the new factor in world affairs I encountered in postwar Germany, the rise of the Soviet republic. Communism at that time was chiefly an important movement in Russia, with secondary importance in Germany. People generally had not yet adopted fixed reactions to it. The Soviet republic was weak and impoverished; it had had to sign the Brest Litovsk peace treaty as the only way to buy the freedom to begin establishing the new Marxist state in Russia. The beginnings had been made by the time I got back to Germany in 1920, but they were exceedingly flimsy, and Soviet power, as it now exists, was something undreamed of by most of the outside world.

Among the individuals I met in the new Germany were German Communists and representatives from the Soviet Union. The Communist revolution in Russia, as I came to know more about it and meet more of its participants, seemed to me fanatical and almost incomprehensibly doctrinaire. I was unschooled in the baffling rhetoric of dialectical materialism, though I hastily read Marx's *Das Kapital* in the hope of understanding it. I was sympathetic with the overthrow of Czarism and the objective of raising the political and economic level of the Russian peasantry, but that was not what most Communists talked about in my hearing.

Among the Russians of importance I met was Iurii Vladimirovich Lomonosov, who was a transportation official and had what surely was one of the most intractable tasks in postwar Russia. The railroads had been paralyzed by the war, many of the lines were torn up, and the rolling stock was virtually ruined by neglect or destruction. Lomonosov was in Germany to arrange for the repair and purchase of locomotives and freight cars. He had little money to pay for anything.

The new Germany was under the shadow of the coming reparations bill from the Allies and so was not able to lend. Lomonosov himself was an engaging and cultured man. He was not a professional Communist, and, as it turned out, he did not last long as a member of the Communist hierarchy. He was a technician who wanted to believe the best of the Bolshevik revolution, but he was not a veteran Marxist.

I had to thank him for giving me my first insight into the economic difficulties of the revolutionary regime in Moscow. A burly figure of a man, with a heavy brown beard, he was like a character out of the Russian fiction I had read. But he was kindly to me, and I saw him frequently.

Another Russian I met in Germany, and one who was to play a fateful role in Soviet history, was Karl Radek. He was the opposite of Lomonosov, a fully seasoned conspiratorial Communist who had served a brief prison term in Germany for Communist activities. Radek was a sharp-faced, bespectacled journalist and had a profound interest in what was happening everywhere. He had the talent I have encountered in one or two other Soviet journalists of being able to construct the news behind the news. He could read a communiqué and tell from the language that was used, or from what was said or omitted, just which faction or person in the Foreign Office of a government had prevailed over some other faction or individual. He may have been able to do this because Communist agents reporting on the differences between elements in government offices had supplied the background information. But he remembered it, and used it. It was a kind of scrutiny which I do not believe many United States diplomatic representatives applied to official statements in foreign countries. This faculty of Radek's greatly impressed me.

Later, when I returned to the United States and made the acquaintance of one or two Soviet journalists there, I discovered that their insight into American affairs that I happened to know about was sadly distorted by their Marxist doctrinal prejudices. So now I have become doubtful of the accuracy of the judgments of Karl Radek and other Soviet experts whom I wondered at in Europe. But one thing was sure: they took their journalism quite seriously. They knew that knowledge, if it was not of itself power, was essential to obtaining it. They also did not keep themselves aloof in those days, and a newspaper correspondent whom they liked could receive information unavailable from normal sources. Relationships of that sort did not exist later on, when the hostility between the Soviet Union and the Allies was further developed. But at this time, the gravity and import of the Bolshevik revolution were not generally understood in Allied countries. The revolution was still romantic, and many liberal political observers believed that on balance it was beneficent.

Chapter 18 / A View of the Russian Famine

It was in 1921 that the Soviet Union, after excluding all foreign correspondents for a period of six months, decided to admit three of them to tell the world about the great famine of that year. It was clear that Moscow had concluded it needed foreign relief, and the journalistic report was expected to expedite it.

Floyd Gibbons, of the Chicago *Tribune,* who wore a black patch over an eye blinded at Château-Thierry, John Graudenz, of the Berlin office of the United Press, and I were the ones chosen to go.

Gibbons was to become widely known on the radio as the person who could rattle off the most words in a minute, in a highly emotional style. I found him a good traveling companion. We virtually camped out on our visit of the famine country, and he always cheerfully did his share or more than his share of our labors.

I welcomed the assignment as adding a country to my newspaper experience, and as a chance to see Russia for the first time. I knew it would be dismal, dilapidated, and ragged, but I was reconciled to witness these deprivations because I would be seeing for the first time the land and people with whom I had become acquainted through reading Russian literature. I am sure the thought did not cross my mind that within my lifetime the Soviet Union would grow to be the chief rival of the United States for world power and on the way to becoming its equal in industrial production.

Our stay in Russia was to last six weeks, starting with a few days in Moscow, followed by a trip down the Volga and into the heart of the famine area. After that we were to return to Moscow and then go back to Berlin. We entered the Soviet Union by train from Helsinki; we went to the Volga port of Samara (now Kuibyshev) by train, then overnight down the river on a filthy and vermin-infested river boat. We did not fly a single mile. In fact, I did not see a passenger plane all the time I was in the country.

Moscow looked worse than I had been told to expect. The people on the street were not in rags, but their clothing was drab. They looked excessively impoverished. The houses had not been painted for years and were cracking with old age. The Kremlin, to be sure, was an exception, with its onion-towered Byzantine churches and their highly colored tiles. About this cluster of buildings there was an air of historic magnificence. But most of the city and the people on the street were like the setting and the actors in a drama about Asiatic poverty.

Our hotel was superannuated and dingy. It had the proportions of a handsome French structure of a century earlier. Some of its furniture dated from that time. The plumbing did not function. Our meals were ample, simple, but no more stylish than those of peasants.

Samara was even more desolate than Moscow. Before boarding our boat, we visited the market, where, under the so-called New Economic Policy recently adopted by Lenin, we watched the peasants selling food for their personal profit, food they had grown on their small private garden plots. But the peasants had little food to sell, and they themselves were haggard and undernourished. We bought some black bread and goat cheese to eat on the boat.

I have never seen a more harrowing sight than people starving to death. After an overnight ride from Samara, we stopped at an encampment of refugees, several hundred of them, who had come to the river from the interior in the hope of being taken away by the government to regions where they could obtain food and lodging. They had built shelters of leafless branches, but they had little to eat but grass. The state had done nothing to save them. When we arrived at the encampment, it was obvious that the refugees thought we constituted an expedition of rescue. They were greatly excited and swarmed about us with pitiful expressions of delight. But these passed when our interpreter explained who we were, and that rescue, while it might later become possible, was a long time away.

This group of refugees had a leader, an old, gaunt, tall, and white-bearded figure right out of a Tolstoi novel. He told us how long they had been waiting there on the banks of the Volga, and how many had died waiting. He took us to the adjoining field where the dead were buried, each tomb decently identified with some primitive wooden marker. About as many in that community had died as now survived, and the death rate was increasing. In a short time all would be dead. The children were the most heart-rending, with their pallid faces and swollen bellies. It needed no expert eye to know that they were doomed to die. The adults were little more vigorous. The old white-bearded patriarch with whom we talked stood erect and carried himself with dignity, but he did it from spiritual, not physical, stamina. All in all, it was a terrible spectacle, the like of which I expect never to see again.

What made the plight of these people both tragic and—if I may use the word—beautiful was the fact that in a field within plain view of the little community was a great mound of sacks filled with grain and guarded by a single soldier, who marched back and forth with a rifle at his shoulder. This was seed grain for the spring. I asked the patriarch why he and his hungry people did not overpower the soldier and bring their fast to an end. He replied, "That is seed grain. We do not steal from the future." I was profoundly moved by his answer. These might be the most wretched peasants to be seen anywhere in the world. But they had a sense of right for which, as they themselves knew, they might have to die, and would do so without question.

We went back to the boat, got the bread and cheese we had purchased at the Samara market, and handed them over to the patriarch. The courtesy with which he thanked us was exemplary. His refugees started stampeding him, and he ordered them back with a word. Mothers kneeled to express their blessing to us. It was almost unbearable, for the amount of food we gave them was negligible; it would not change the death rate by a fraction. We gave it out of a sentimental feeling of frustration, not being able to bear doing nothing. Our interpreter assured the patriarch that Moscow was striving to the utmost to send boats and relief and they must not lose heart. But he was exaggerating. Moscow was unable to do anything to organize relief on a scale that could have saved this little dying community and the scores like it that lined the river and filled the famine region. Nothing substantial could be done until the following year, when the Hoover Relief Mission brought in supplies and distributed them. All that our Volga trip had contributed was to prepare foreign public opinion for that mission.

Back in Moscow, I set out to learn what I could about the social plans of the new Soviet republic. I wrote a series of eight articles about it for the New York *Herald,* deluding myself that my editors would consider information from a country, a former great power which had been shut off from the outside world for so many months, to be news. I talked with many leaders in many departments. They seemed to me to answer my questions freely, and I thought that my articles, while perhaps on the superficial side, were objective and informative. I had some trouble in finding a common language with the Soviet officials I interviewed and the Communists with whom I talked. I do not mean a common speech, because, of course, I had the use of an interpreter. But the Russians talked about themselves and the rest of the world in the rhetoric of Marxism, and it was as though they spoke something two languages removed from me. The Russian could be interpreted into English. But there remained a second language, Marxism, that needed to be translated into American, and this the interpreter was unable to do. I wanted in my articles to discuss Soviet problems in terms familiar to those who dealt with similar American problems. I fear that I failed in this, and that my series of articles could not have been much good on that account. But they were not loaded with Communist clichés, for I kept those out.

Many months later, on searching the files of the New York *Herald* in my Berlin office, I came to realize that the articles had not appeared. I was sure the material was newsworthy because of the concern of the rest of the world about the Russian revolution, so I decided to try to place the articles with some magazine. Carelessly, I had not saved a copy of them, and when I wrote to the New York office, asking for the return of my original manuscript, I was told that the articles not only had not been used, but they had been thrown away. Subsequently, a friend in the office told me that the managing editor had said that the only articles he would run from Bolshevik Russia would be about Lenin and Trotsky cutting their throats.

Karl Radek at this time had returned to Moscow and was a member of the presidium of the Communist International, with residence in the Kremlin. I sent word to him that I was there and would like to see him. He invited me to his quarters one evening. I found him in a room lined with bookcases jammed with volumes, and many others lying untidily on the floor. He was dressed in Soviet-style clothes, wearing high leather boots and a blue, high-collared shirt. We at once engaged in a lively conversation in German, and he held forth while pacing the room with excited strides. In the course of this talk, he referred repeatedly to the individuals who had led the French revolution, and I had the strong impression that as these Frenchmen, in Radek's mind, were walking the pages of the history of the French revolution, so he, Radek, would walk the pages of the history of the Soviet revolution. Neither of us dreamed at that time what his role in that history would be, and that he would be sent to prison as a victim of a Stalin purge.

While I was in Moscow, an international congress was in session. I no longer remember what it was; it may have been the Comintern. But I saw many of its delegates, most of them Asians, all of them dressed poorly, and few of them having the alert and intelligent faces I would have expected from future world leaders. I suppose nearly everyone is marked by the snobbishness of his own country. Looking at these international Communists, who were dedicated to conquer the world, I had the certainty that countries like the United States were in no danger from them, and I came away from the Soviet Union oblivious to what the future might bring in my lifetime. I did not foresee the swift industrialization that was to follow on electrification, nor imagine that Soviet education and technology could pull abreast of our own. The Soviet Union I saw seemed hopelessly behind by many decades.

When the time came to return to Berlin, I was not much

wiser about the Russians, but I had some vivid memories: Radek, already striding through the pages of history; the impressive old Tolstoian villager, dying on the bank of the Volga; Moscow, in its dilapidated, unpainted, unrepaired drabness. But one was dear to me, the recollection of a night service I attended in St. Basil's Cathedral, in Red Square adjoining the Kremlin. The church was lit only by candles, and the air was spiced with incense. The service was ritualistic in the extreme, with priests and other clergy garbed in lavishly colored vestments. This lavishness, however, was not what most impressed me—it was the singing, and, in the singing, the remarkably deep sonority of the basses. Anyone brought up to enjoy church music, as I had been, is bound to be uplifted and even startled by the vigor and richness of Russian church choral singing, and in particular by the basses. They sing lower and with greater power than any basses anywhere in the world. They filled the church with a C two octaves below middle C. I found the Byzantine service florid, as most Russian art is florid. But the deep, ringing tone of those basses was rich and unforgettable.

in Financial Journalism

Frank Munsey came to Europe that year, and I received notice that I was to visit him at one of the west German medical-bath centers, at ten o'clock in the morning. The chief reason I recall this visit was the greeting I received from my publisher. To keep my appointment, I had had to arrive the night before, which he knew. Mr. Munsey was having breakfast in his room when I joined him. His first question to me was pitched in a professionally hearty tone: "What have you learned this morning?" I did not understand. So he explained. I had been in the village all morning, and he expected me, as his representative, to have rustled around that morning and picked up some news. The question showed that Mr. Munsey did not have much idea about the duties of a foreign correspondent. I did not argue with him or try to instruct him. I listened to what he had to say. He asked no intelligent questions about the international situation or about German developments. He was not interested in anything I had seen in the Soviet Union. He simply wanted to impress me, as my "boss," that I was expected to be out and scrambling for news, even in a far-away German medical resort, at eight o'clock in the morning. Mr. Munsey had been in the magazine field before entering the newspaper world, and had been exceedingly successful there. I was sure he was an able administrator. But I also was sure he did not have the faintest idea how his foreign service had to function.

Not long after this, another publisher, Clarence W. Barron,

of the *Wall Street Journal,* entered my life as a strong contrast to Mr. Munsey. My Berlin office was on the second floor of a small street behind Unter den Linden, in the Dorotheenstrasse, and one day Mr. Barron came puffing up the stairs and announced himself. I say "puffing up the stairs" advisedly. Mr. Barron must have weighed close to 300 pounds. But his heaviness and girth were not the first impression he made. He was the incarnation of a parlor Santa Claus. He had a handsomely trimmed white beard, sparkling eyes, and an open, happy countenance. He was most pleasing to meet. He was a distinguished man and looked it.

He introduced himself and said he had come to ask me some questions about German reparations, in particular how much I thought Germany would be able to pay. This was the prime issue before the Allies and Germany at this time. The Allies, France in particular, were hoping for something like the equivalent of one to two billion dollars a year. I expected Mr. Barron, as publisher of the *Wall Street Journal,* to show annoyance when I answered promptly that I thought Germany could not pay in excess of 125 million dollars a year. Instead, his face brightened, and he asked me to analyze the economic situation in Germany and justify this figure. I gave him my explanation at length, and a long discussion about economic conditions in Germany followed. I do not lay claim to any expert knowledge of finance and economics, but I believe I have been blessed with an ability to write about these subjects in a way that laymen can grasp, an ability that was to stand me in good stead for the rest of my professional career. Mr. Barron was no layman, and he asked me some questions to which I did not know the answers. But I had done my homework on German reparations and held up my end of the conversation. When the time came for him to leave, he said I should be hearing from him again. "I am always on the lookout," he said, "for newspapermen who have an understanding of economics and finance, and when I find one, he ends up sooner or later on the *Wall Street Journal.* You belong in this category." Naturally, I was flattered, but did not take his prediction seriously. I was quite sure at that time that I did not want to be a financial journalist.

I was to encounter Mr. Barron again at the Genoa conference of 1922. By then, I had married Betty Gram, who was with me in Genoa. She was an Oregonian from Portland, daughter of Danish parents, and an active feminist. She had served her prison term and had hunger-struck for the vote for women. And I shall make a diversion at this point to say that she also was on the verge of being a "Lucy Stoner," that is, a feminist who retains her own name after marriage. She was studying singing in Berlin when I met her, and when we were married, she raised the issue of keeping her own name. I considered myself a good feminist. I came from a family of able and independent women. Oberlin had taught me to believe in the equality of women. I liked the fact that Betty Gram was a suffragette and had been a hunger-striker. But to live with her in Germany as Miss Betty Gram presented practical difficulties. My work required travel to all parts of the country, as well as abroad. For my wife to register at hotels as Betty Gram while I registered as Raymond Swing, and for us to be assigned to the same room, called for somewhat embarrassing explanations. I did not fancy having to make them. So I came up with a compromise. I told my wife that if she would take my name, I would take hers. To this she agreed, and I at once asked the New York *Herald* to sign my dispatches Raymond Gram Swing, which it did without question.

The sequel to this arrangement is that when, after twenty-two years, the marriage came to an end, I no longer was entitled to the "Gram" in my name, and asked my radio network to omit it, which it did. But I learned a lesson from this experience. To this day, only my friends omit the "Gram." It is used especially in England, where I was called "Gram Swing" without the given name. I discovered that a person's name is not a possession of his own, with which he can do what he pleases, but belongs to those who use it—something that Lucy Stone, perhaps, had not realized.

It happened that at the time of the Genoa conference I was annoyed with the New York *Herald*. The story of Genoa shortly turned into the story of Rapallo, where the Germans unexpectedly held a meeting with the Russians to sign a treaty of co-operation which shook the Allied world. The *Herald* assigned another man to cover the Russians at Rapallo, a man I thought had no special distinction as a foreign correspondent. It issued no instructions as to how we were to collaborate. As the *Herald*'s staff man on the job, I should have had at least nominal direction of the operation, even though the new man was much older than I. The German in the Rapallo negotiations, Walther Rathenau, I knew quite well; I had first met him during the war, when he was in charge of mobilizing economic resources inside the Reich, and I had seen him often after returning to Berlin. I also had my experience in Moscow to prepare me to interpret Russian policy. I felt affronted. Either the New York office did not trust my ability to report objectively the significance of the German-Soviet development, or it did not want it reported objectively, for the additional correspondent was strongly anti-Bolshevik. I may have been quite wrong about the reason. It may simply have been that this other man was a friend of the managing editor, had turned up and asked for an assignment and been given it. But the effect was pronounced. I decided to call on Mr. Barron and ask him if he still wished me on the staff of the *Wall Street Journal.*

Mr. Barron, without a moment's hesitation, said he did. I asked him in what capacity. He asked me what capacity I desired. I said frankly I should like to be in charge of the paper's foreign service, with headquarters in London. He said at once that this was agreeable to him. I asked him what my salary would be. Mr. Barron said he would start by paying me what I was receiving from the *Herald.* He added that I should plan to go back to New York with him at the conclusion of the conference, bringing my wife along at his expense. We were expecting our first child, and Mr. Barron said he would put my wife up at his seaside residence at Cohasset, Massachusetts, while I was working in the New York office.

This was not only satisfactory but also pleasing, as all my relations with Mr. Barron were to be until my resignation two years later. I liked him enormously. He had a prodigiously active mind, he was a generous and thoughtful friend and host, and he knew the profession of financial journalism to its last detail. He also fascinated me because he was a Swedenborgian, the only one I had ever met, and he talked freely about his faith and the remarkable man who had founded it.

I was willing to join the *Wall Street Journal* not because I anticipated a career as a financial reporter and correspondent, but because I thought it would add to my understanding of the economic structure of the United States and Europe, which underlay all the news and needed understanding if the news was to be adequately treated. I knew I was not the *Wall Street Journal* type, and I felt sure that my appointment would not be popular in the home office. The men in the home office considered Mr. Barron an eccentric, and I was at once labeled as one of his eccentricities. But I reasoned that if I could work for the *Wall Street Journal* in Europe for two or three years, I would have rounded out my education as a foreign correspondent.

I have said that my appointment was not popular with the home staff, not that I myself was not, for I was treated with cordiality and developed some genuinely friendly associations in the office. But the European appointment was a plum, and in all good reason it should have gone to someone in the home office as a reward, and not to an outsider who did not have the faintest inkling of financial reporting in New York. While it is true that I did not know the first thing about New York financial reporting, I was, however, better equipped to have the chief responsibility for the foreign service of the paper, for the two were utterly different.

In New York, as I discovered, the skill lay in developing connections inside the big corporations and knowing in advance what the state of corporation returns was going to be, or what actions were to be taken, so that their effect on the market value of the corporation's shares could be intelligently discussed. This called for both good personal relationships and an expert knowledge of the businesses.

The high standards Mr. Barron expounded for financial journalism were not always lived up to, as he well knew. It was no secret to him that the man who was on the inside in regard to a corporation would exploit his foreknowledge to play the market, and that the difference between financial and ordinary reporting was measurable in the extra money the reporter could make out of his beat. That is why Mr. Barron so persistently preached high standards. He hoped that he might bolster the ethics of his staff by persuasion. Probably there was no other way to go about it. He could not discipline his men by dismissals, because the vacancies would have to be filled by others who in time also would exploit what they knew. The best he could hope for was that men who made money on the market out of their knowledge would not try to mislead investors by what they wrote, and I had the impression that they did not, and most of them certainly had consciences of their own that kept them in check and in some instances kept them from playing the market at all.

The view of the inside of the *Wall Street Journal* was novel and instructive. I learned a great deal about what the newspaper needed from its offices abroad, which in the first place was judgment about the financial and economic decisions being made in Europe. To obtain this judgment, I would have to be able to tap the wisdom of dependable experts in a number of countries. I should have to do it first of all in London, still the financial center of the world. My chief work would be in London and Berlin. The *Journal* already had a seasoned Paris correspondent. Some of my material was to appear in *Barron's Weekly*. Most of what I sent the *Wall Street Journal* would go by mail.

I went back to Europe fully aware of my inexperience with the great financial and economic problems then engaging world attention, but I do not remember being frightened by it. I set out in London to establish connections, and I can look back with special gratitude to the *Economist*, which invited me to take part in its weekly editorial conference with invited experts. I was designated to be the American representative in these discussions. Here I first met Walter Layton, editor of the *Economist*, who later, as Sir Walter, was editor and chairman of the *News Chronicle*, Sir Josiah Stamp, and a dozen other men of standing and ability in the "City." Their weekly talks, well-informed, well-weighed, were a wonder and a delight to me, as well as an education. I met many economic and financial leaders from the Continent in much the same informal way, always being cordially received. The rise of United States influence set in after World War I, and the accessibility of the outstanding national leaders to American journalists was just beginning. I was fortunate to be able to take advantage of it.

There were no signs of friction with the home office during my first two years. My material was published. Mr. Barron cabled many suggestions and questions, which were helpful. But I knew perfectly well that my lease on life on the paper was limited. Someone in the home office, I did not know precisely who, would make it his business to have me dismissed so that the head of the foreign service would no longer be an outsider.

Quite punctually at the end of two years, the trouble started that was to end my services. It was over an article I had written about the French budget. Mr. Barron, I might say, was about as pro-French as he was pro-Swedenborg. My article had translated the figures of the current French budget into prewar dollars, to give Americans a realistic sense of what they meant. These showed that France was spending much more on military outlays than on education. If I had used the current depreciated French francs in my compilation, the discrepancy between expenditure on education and defense would not have been striking. Mr. Barron cabled me to do just this. I cabled back that it would be more honest to give the figures in prewar dollars, which was true. We often had discussed the obligation of the writer to present his facts in the most honest way possible, and I was appealing to his own standards in making my reply. It did not matter to me that my story represented France as neglecting its public education. But it mattered to Mr. Barron, and he cabled the terse command that I was to obey his instructions. That, as I saw it, left me no choice but to cable my resignation, which he said in reply was accepted.

One of Mr. Barron's best London friends was H. Gordon Selfridge, who had given London its first example of a great American department store. It was a thriving business in a handsome edifice on Oxford Street, and Mr. Selfridge, then a man of wealth, lived in Lansdowne House, formerly the residence of Lord Lansdowne. Mr. Barron gave me a note of introduction to Mr. Selfridge, and I was most cordially received there, met his gracious mother, and his son and daughters, and started a friendship with the son, Gordon, which continues on close terms to this day.

One of the first acts of Mr. Selfridge was to invite me to a men's dinner at Lansdowne House. This was to give me one of the most embarrassing, if trivial, social experiences of my life. I knew the dinner was formal, so I had to dress in evening wear. But it was a men's dinner, and according to the etiquette I had learned, tails and white ties were worn only when ladies were to be present. So I donned my tuxedo and black tie. When I arrived at the dinner party, to which some thirty guests had been invited, I was startled to discover that all of them were wearing tails and white ties. I am a shy person, so that my black tie, in my imagination, began growing and growing until it overpowered the reception room.

The story is worth telling for what then happened. I was rescued, not by Mr. Selfridge or his son, but by one of his guests, Sir Thomas Lipton. He saw my embarrassment, came over to me with a twinkle in his eye, introduced himself, and engaged me in a lively conversation on all kinds of subjects. He learned, among other things, that my father and mother were in London on a visit at the time, and he invited them to come with me to his country estate for tea on the following afternoon. His car would call for them at their hotel. This came to pass, and the Swings had a delightful tea party on the veranda of the Lipton estate, served by Ceylonese servants in their traditional Ceylonese hairdress and costumes. In a world in which thoughtful kindness is exceptional, this was an event of unusual generosity, and I hope that Sir Thomas derived a fraction of the pleasure from it that he gave.

Chapter 20 / I Join the *Public Ledger*

I had had my two years' course in European economics and finance on top of my other experience as a newspaper correspondent, and in theory I should have had no trouble finding a good position in foreign journalism. But I soon discovered that in this profession it was not true that there always is room at the top. Few American newspapers maintained foreign services, and in none of these did there happen to be a vacancy among bureau chiefs. I should have liked to be a correspondent in London or on the Continent for the New York *Times*, but I learned that this newspaper did not employ outsiders; it promoted its own staff men. If, added to my other experience, I had served in the New York or Washington offices of the *Times*, I might have aspired to a top bureau position abroad. I might even have been wedged into a second position for early promotion if there had happened to be such a vacancy, but there was none.

I went back to the United States to meet the executives of papers with foreign services. I found there were no vacancies where the salary approximated what I had been paid by the New York *Herald* and the *Wall Street Journal*. Robert Smiley, editor of the Philadelphia *Public Ledger*, proved to be the one most interested in me, but he could make no offer above that of second-string man in the London bureau, with the promise of the next bureau-chief vacancy that occurred. He thought one might be open in either Berlin or Paris before long, and he made it a condition of appointing me that I study French diligently. The step-down in salary in London was drastic, around forty dollars a week, and since I had four children from my two marriages to support and educate, the reduction, if it did not mean actual hardship, would call for the most economical management. But I accepted the job because there was nothing else to do.

I was glad to go back to London, where I already had connections and a good understanding of the political situation. I liked London, excepting its climate, and had come to realize that the earlier prejudices against the British I had acquired on the Continent represented the dislike the Continentals felt for Britain because it was powerful. Much later I was to see the same dislike in Europe for the United States, and to learn that the strong, even when generous, are almost automatically disliked politically. At this time, however, the general tone of British sentiment was sympathetic toward America. I had begun making real friends in London, something that I am sure takes no less than two years even to begin to do, for the British are shy and reserved. So I was pleased to be resuming work in London despite financial limitations. And I had Mr. Smiley's assurance that I could count on getting a bureau post of my own in the not too distant future.

The chief of the London bureau, whom I shall call Johnson, was an affable Southerner with long news experience at home and an insatiable thirst. I soon found that my duties were to do virtually all the work in the office. I wrote most of the lead stories, and they went to the Philadelphia office bearing Johnson's signature and appeared in print under his by-line. This was not what I had bargained for, and as the months went on I found myself growing more and more resentful. I recall that after one period, I counted up the first-page stories from London which I had written and which had been published under Johnson's name, and they came to twenty-three in a matter of months. Only two or three signed by Johnson had actually been written by him. This was no way for me to get ahead, for Mr. Smiley had no means of knowing that I was doing most of the work. I became so indignant over the situation that I finally warned Johnson that unless he sobered up and did his share of the work in the office, I would not hold my tongue. He promised, but the situation did not change.

It was in the heat I was feeling about Johnson's conduct that I received word from Mr. Smiley that he had appointed Dorothy Thompson to be head of the Berlin bureau. For her it was a promotion from being Vienna correspondent, and for her sake I was delighted. She was a good, even a dear, friend, and already one of the best American journalists. Her appointment made her the first woman to be given a foreign bureau in the history of American journalism, which also pleased me mightily. All the same, I had been promised the first bureau vacancy, and I keenly felt the unfairness of my having been passed over, particularly in view of the unhappiness to which I was subjected in London.

I wrote Mr. Smiley, congratulating him on his courage in naming a woman to head a foreign bureau and expressing my pleasure in Dorothy Thompson's success. But I also reminded him that he had promised me the next bureau vacancy, and added that if I had known what the work in the London office would be like, I would not have accepted the job in the first place.

Mr. Smiley at once replied, asking me to explain the sentence about the work in the London office. Thereupon I was confronted by the same kind of problem I had experienced when I was excluded from the Berlin Press Association in 1913 on the ground that I had conspired to take another man's job away from him. What should I now say to Mr. Smiley? If I had not gone through the experience of that false charge in Berlin, I might have felt compelled to tell him precisely what it meant to be second-stringer to Mr. Johnson in the London bureau. I had no doubt that if I told him, he would dismiss Johnson and put me in his place. But I had, by a kind of inexplicable preview, received advance instruction on the ethics of this problem. I had learned that a colleague should not take action, however justifiable, to deprive another colleague of his job. I had not done this in Berlin, but I had been taught the law all the same. Now I must apply it in London, as though that was what the Berlin experience had been about.

I will not deny that I had the greatest difficulty in doing so. I wrote letter after letter to Mr. Smiley, answering his question about the conditions of work in London. I tore them up one after the other. I paced the floor for hours. I argued to the empty air that Mr. Smiley was my employer, and he was entitled to know from me the true situation in the London bureau. I wrote more letters, and then tore them up.

Finally I capitulated and accepted the law as presented to me in Berlin. I wrote Mr. Smiley a brief letter, expressing regret that I had mentioned the conditions of work in London and withdrawing what I had said. Peace then descended on my spirit. The struggle within myself had kept up at least three days.

The next act of this drama, which I had not foreseen, was notification from Philadelphia that Miss Thompson was returning to the home office for a month before going to her new post, and that I was to go to Berlin forthwith as her substitute. I was glad to be getting out of the London office and to be seeing old friends and associates in Berlin.

When the month was up, Miss Thompson returned and I went back to London. But something unforeseen had happened in this month. In the entire time, not a single London cable had appeared in the *Public Ledger* from Mr. Johnson! Mr. Smiley cabled me to find out why none had been sent and to report promptly. I knew the reason, but I was not going to reveal it. I went to see Mrs. Johnson and asked what she wanted me to tell Mr. Smiley. She said she wished me to say her husband had been ill. I cabled Mr. Smiley that this was what Mrs. Johnson had asked me to say.

Mr. Smiley at once ordered Mr. Johnson to come home and appointed me head of the bureau. I cannot say that I was jubilant. But I was gratified by the way the appointment had come about. Mr. Smiley later explained to me that he had not given me the Berlin post because he felt fairly sure he soon would be appointing me to head the London bureau.

I spent, all told, nearly twelve years as a correspondent in London. London, prior to World War II, was still the capital of the world. It also was the most seasoned of the capitals, politically. The House of Commons was the best debating club in existence. British foreign policy was better articulated than that of any other country. British finance was conducted with greater wisdom. British superiority continued despite the political crises attending two defeats of the Conservative party and the first experiments with Labour rule.

As I look back on my ten years with the *Public Ledger* in London, I realize that my view of Britain had been too close to allow me much perspective. Though the years 1924 to 1934 were journalistically lively, they were not greatly to the credit of British statesmanship. They were unpleasant years. Business everywhere was bad. Unemployment rose, and, with it, unrest. The British had to adjust themselves to a lesser importance in the world than they had enjoyed. This is a painful experience for any country. World War I had weakened them woefully. It had killed a substantial portion of their ablest young men. It had eaten away their resources and sapped the vitality of the Empire. The years after my departure in 1934 up to World War II were no better. Britain ceased to play the role of stabilizing leadership it had so rewardingly played in the nineteenth century in world affairs. In retrospect, Ramsay MacDonald, Stanley Baldwin, and Neville Chamberlain, the big men of the time between the wars, were not of heroic stature. True, they were beset by well-nigh insoluble problems, economic and political, and they did far better than the Germans and even a little better than the French. But these were not glorious years for Western Europe.

My reporting of this time began with the German reparations crisis and the adoption of the Dawes Plan. It went on through massive unemployment problems, strikes by railwaymen, transport workers, miners, and finally the abortive general strike of 1926. The nine-month rule of the first Labour Prime Minister in 1924 was followed by years of varying political patterns, Baldwin having five years from 1924 to 1929, Labour coming back to give MacDonald another two years as prime minister but still in the minority, with the National government to follow under MacDonald from 1931 to 1935. This turbulence and improvisation made news, and my work in consequence was interesting as never before. The experience I had gained with the *Wall Street Journal* stood me in good stead, for economics, even more than politics, dominated events, and I had by then good news connections in both fields. In the early 1930's the first and second round-table conferences met in London to discuss the demand of Indian leaders for independence, and I had the rare experience of interviewing Mahatma Gandhi. I also could report on the conferment of dominion status on part of the Empire in 1931, which was to permit the establishment of the British Commonwealth.

Of the United States ambassadors during this period, Alanson B. Houghton, the Corning Glass magnate, was certainly the ablest. He had served in Germany and knew European problems firsthand. Andrew W. Mellon served during the unhappy days following the Depression; I remember calling on him in 1933 and his assuring me, with his slender white hands trembling slightly, that the crisis had passed.

The elder Robert W. Bingham, publisher of the Louisville *Courier-Journal*—nothing like as worldly-wise as his distinguished son Barry—found himself in a capital in which socialists had been in office and most likely would be there again. Labour leaders had never been invited to the embassy, so a luncheon was arranged, at which Major Clement Attlee, the party leader, sat next to the Ambassador. Mr. Bingham was more at home with the grouse-shooting British aristocrats than with a socialist, and apparently did not know how to start a conversation. So he turned and asked: "Do you shoot?" Major Attlee, for whom shooting was a class symbol, replied coldly that he had not shot since he had shot Germans in the war, a retort that did not make the luncheon much of a success.

I look back on these years as notable for several personal reasons: the formation of some of the dearest friendships of my life, the development of my children, and my own start at creative writing. The best of the friends made in England, and by now the friendship of longest duration, was John Gunther. He came off a cattle boat to London to escape from being a reporter on the Chicago *Daily News* and to find a future for himself as a writer about world affairs. He came to see me as a *Daily News* alumnus, and in that first week of our acquaintance, we walked the streets every night, talking with a candor and excitement that adults seldom achieve with each other. The result is that we came to know each other exceedingly well. This was before any of the "Inside" books, but not before his first novel, *Red Pavilion*, which I had read before I met him and found bristling with promise. He served first as substitute correspondent of the *Daily News* in London, did a longer service in Vienna, came back as London correspondent, and then graduated from daily journalism to write his books.

My first close British friend was Mrs. John St. Loe Strachey, widow of the editor of the *Spectator*, whom I had known be-

fore his death. His widow was in need of a kind of fellowship I
was able to offer her. I lived for a time not far from her home
in Surrey, and she became a generous patroness of my family.
She was a tall and outwardly somewhat severe old lady. What
she loved was to converse on politics and books, as she had
done with her husband, and which she did with great judgment. Through her I became a friend of her son, John, later the
distinguished Labour Secretary of State for War, and her
daughter, Amabel, who wrote novels and other books and
was married to England's foremost town-planner, Clough
Williams-Ellis.

I am not going to call the roll of my British friends, though
I should mention Ellen Wilkinson, who was to become Labour's second woman cabinet member, and whom I had found
to be a witty and candid guide to Labour party policy long
before she reached this eminence.

I also must register a fairly close acquaintance with
Bertrand Russell, not attributable to his interest in me, but to
his having established an experimental progressive school with
his wife at that time, Dora. We wanted a progressive school
for our children, being somewhat alarmed by what we knew
about discipline in the so-called public schools in Britain. On
inquiry we found that the Russell school was to use the
country home in Hampshire of Bertrand's brother, the Earl of
Russell, and that part of the house was available to us to rent
as a home. This simultaneous solution of the two problems of
residence and school was irresistible, and we moved in. As
tenants of Lord Russell, we soon were on cordial terms with
him and enjoyed many a rewarding conversation with him.

Bertrand Russell was only a part-time schoolmaster, giving
some attention to the older children, none of whom was beyond primary-school age. He was a fascinating instructor, as
our own children testified. But the responsibility for the school
lay with Mrs. Russell and two young women teachers. The
school was conducted according to themes of freedom, which
Mr. and Mrs. Russell ardently believed in. It was a small
boarding school, with day students from the district, and was
attended by children from intellectual homes, but it did not
last beyond its first year.

Naturally, I was impressed by the privilege of knowing
Bertrand Russell, already recognized as one of the great intel-

lects of his era. I dutifully read everything of his I could understand, and I am sure I always showed him the highest respect.
I cannot, however, say that he had the slightest respect for
me, not, I believe, on account of my personality, but simply
because I was an American. The anti-Americanism prevalent
in Britain in recent years had not set in. Bertrand Russell's
anti-Americanism was his own. I might say he did not so
much dislike Americans as scorn them. He made an exception
of my wife, to whom he always showed gallantry, but I had
no benefit from that. He never concealed his arrogance from
me. Later Bertrand Russell was to spend years in the United
States. He was to marry a young and beautiful American after
divorcing Dora Russell. He was to receive appreciative honors
from American intellectuals, and a generous stipend for his
lecturing services. But I am not aware that these mitigated the
scorn he felt for Americans.

I do not mean to disparage Bertrand Russell's greatness.
Most men whom the world regards as great have had their
strong likes and dislikes, their weaknesses along with their
strengths. I do not even call it a shortcoming for a man
of Bertrand Russell's stature to have so much disliked Americans. There were excusable reasons for such a dislike.

After the Russell school closed, two of my children, Peter
and Sally, went to Dartington Hall, another progressive
school. This was in Devonshire and had been founded by Mr.
and Mrs. Willard Straight, whose money also founded the
New Republic. Mrs. Straight was an American. She and her
husband had many interests. Dartington Hall was not only the
seat of a first-rate progressive school, but an experiment in progressive agriculture.

I had many residences in and around London, but enjoyed
none more than a tiny flat at the top of a corner tower in
Lincoln's Inn, the sequestered quadrangle near the Temple,
and the office and living quarters of many barristers. Here my
youngest son, John, was born, and if environment has any influence on the future of a baby, it certainly influenced him,
for he was to graduate from Yale Law School and practice in
Connecticut before becoming administrative director of the
Council on Foreign Relations in New York. My daughter Sally
also is engaged in international affairs, being one of the top

UNESCO officials stationed at the United Nations in New York. Perhaps the genes of heredity helped determine both their careers.

Incidentally, my oldest son, Albert, is now a United States official serving in Pakistan. My daughter Elizabeth Françoise, Albert's sister, after taking her master's degree in social service, became the wife of a Hartford, Connecticut, surgeon, Dr. Gerald Greene. In that city she has been long absorbed in cultural affairs and is now, I believe, the only woman belonging to the national boards of both the Symphony Orchestra League and the Community Arts Centers.

A foreign correspondent makes almost innumerable acquaintances because of his work. Some of these become friends in the true sense of the word. Friendships with colleagues were the most natural to form, and I had close relations with Negley Farson while he was Chicago *Daily News* bureau chief, and with Ferdinand Kuhn, Jr., then with the New York *Times*.

The friendship with Ferdinand and Delia Kuhn was to ripen. He worked for a time on the editorial page of the *Times* when I had become a broadcaster, and at the beginning of World War II, I do not believe a day passed without our discussing the frightening events in Europe. Later the Kuhns moved to Washington, as I did during the war, and they have been neighbors and close and treasured friends to this day.

I was blessed by two admirable assistants in London, César Saerchinger and Morris Gilbert. Gilbert later worked with me for a while after I had begun broadcasting, then left to join the Office of War Information at the outbreak of the war, and at this writing is with the New York *Times*. César Saerchinger was European correspondent of the *Musical Courier* when I first met him in Germany. He kept the connection when he joined me in the *Public Ledger* bureau in London. Later he was made the first head of the Columbia Broadcasting System European service, and, after returning to America, wrote the standard biography of his close friend Artur Schnabel. For years he gave a weekly broadcast for the National Broadcasting Company, sponsored by the American Historical Association, called "Behind the News." He is a man for whom I formed a great affection.

Chapter 21 / I Do Some Amateur Creation

I wish to say something at this juncture about my own creative work. In volume it is small, and if I say that its importance is altogether personal to me, I mean just that. I believe that to be a creative artist is the highest achievement a person can attain. Even in this day and age, I would rather be a poet or a musician than a mathematician or physicist. The privilege of artistic self-expression I consider to be the most precious one accorded to human beings, and self-expression in creative art I think is of similar value to self-expression in procreation.

I do not say how good any of my creative work is. That is not for me to judge. I should be delighted if, sometime, a few of my poems might be read with enjoyment. Any man should be grateful if he creates a few beautiful poems.

I have written two satirical plays, somewhat in the style of the German Frank Wedekind. The first foresaw the problem of automation long before it had reached its present importance, along with Communism and fascism. It was written in 1934. The second, called *Mister Man,* is a dramatization of the decision of apes to become men, the first "man" having discovered fire. This is a satire on the atomic age, and is in the style of a morality play. I wrote it in 1958.

The text of this play was to become a libretto for an opera composed by a young woman in Waco, Texas—Miss Shirley Mackie. She obtained a copy from a mutual friend in Waco to whom I had sent it, and after mulling over it for two years sat down to compose the opera—quite without my knowledge—on March 25, 1963, which by coincidence was my seventy-sixth birthday. She had been a pupil of Nadia Boulanger in Fontainebleau, and of Darius Milhaud at Aspen, Colorado, and had an M.A. in music from Louisiana State University. When she later played it for me, I was struck by its stark, rythmic modernity, and came to the conclusion that the text was more suitable as a libretto than as a drama.

There is no satire whatever in my poems. They suffer, if that is the word, from being out of step with contemporary poetry. They are subjective, with a few exceptions; many of them are romantic in content and style; while others are metaphysical. The poets I love most—Hopkins, Donne, Keats, Blake—no doubt influenced me most. Poems like mine are not now in fashion. But since fashions change, they may be read at another time. If I were to make a judgment about myself as an artist, it would be that a few of the poems are better than the plays or such music as I have composed.

As I already have noted, I did not know at eighteen whether I wished more to be a writer than a composer, and the doubt was settled by my dismissal from Oberlin, which hurtled me into newspaper work. At Oberlin Conservatory, I had taken four terms of harmony, some piano and organ. I did not progress to counterpoint or receive instruction in composition. However, I subsequently wrote a little music. The output was exceedingly slender, a dozen or so songs, a sonata for violin and piano, and a setting for voice and piano of Keats's *La Belle Dame sans Merci*. These last two, however, were given nationwide radio performances in America. *La Belle Dame* was sung over a nationwide broadcast with the piano accompaniment orchestrated by Robert Russell Bennett and sung over the Blue Network by my brother Dolf. This was after the violin sonata had had a second nationwide broadcast. Both compositions were written in England; in fact, all the music I ever wrote was composed there, as was most of my poetry.

I wrote the introduction to the second movement of the violin sonata to be played by my son Peter on the cello. He was musically precocious, and I wrote this lyrical section for him to learn as part of his study as an eight-year-old. It was too difficult for him at the time, and I put it aside. I accumulated some thematic notes for a longer composition, which I decided to make into a violin sonata, writing first of all the second movement. I composed at the piano with no facility whatever, and the sonata took some months of my free time to put on paper. When it was finished, I copied it and laid it away. My daughter Sally had a violin teacher, and I did ask her to try reading it, which she was unable to do. I did not show it to anyone else until I was back in America. There, one night, Martha Thompson, the young girl I had brought out of Germany in 1917, came as a visitor to our house. Her marriage to my brother Dolf had been consummated and ended, but she visited us occasionally and always played for us. On this occasion, she asked me if I did not have any old manuscripts to show her. I recalled the violin sonata and placed it on the piano before her. She played it and expressed interest in it. At the time, she was director of a group of WPA musicians in New York, and she said there was a violinist in her group who, she thought, could play the sonata. Would I let her borrow the manuscript?

This was fourteen years after I had written it. I had never heard it played. I might say that the piano part was far beyond my own capacity as a performer. I gratefully turned the sonata over to her, and in due course I was supervising rehearsals of the sonata, which she and Walter Eisenberg later performed at a WPA concert at the New York Public Library.

By this time, I was broadcasting for WOR, and word about the sonata reached the station. Alfred Wallenstein, then in charge of music for Mutual and WOR, asked to see the manuscript, and approved the sonata for a nationwide performance.

In 1942, a second performance was played over a network by the same violinist and a different pianist. Later, when I was broadcasting from Washington for the Blue Network, Major Philip Cook, military attaché in the Canadian embassy and a musical enthusiast, arranged for a concert at which the violin sonata was played by Erno Valasek, an excellent Czech violinist, and Jorge Bolet, the now famous Cuban pianist, at a Red Cross benefit in the Shoreham Hotel. They gave it a wonderful performance. This led to another nationwide broadcast and eventually to the publication of the sonata. The next year it was given an admirable performance over the Canadian Broadcasting System by Alexander Brott and Helmut Blume.

To finish the story of this sonata, it was rerecorded in 1962 by Jerome Wigler and George Reeves, both of Philadelphia and friends of my son Peter, who by then had become chairman of the music department at Swarthmore College. This recording was issued, along with excerpts from half a dozen of my wartime broadcasts, in recognition of my seventy-fifth birthday. The suggestion for such a recording came from a colleague at the Voice of America, Harold Courlander, himself an authority on folk songs, author of books about them, and editor of recordings of them. He proposed the recording to Folkways, whose proprietor, Moses Asch, agreed to issue it.

I have gone into such detail about the sonata to point out that at no time did I take any initiative to get it performed or ask anyone to play or even to see it. The New York *Times,* commenting on the recording, called it "an attractive work in a conservative vein," saying that it recalled the late works of Fauré, though nothing like as suave in writing or well-integrated formally. It spoke of a definite if limited lyric gift, but said that the work on the whole lacked direction and that I fell back too easily on obvious developmental devices.

A more favorable critique of the sonata was written by Thomas Archer, music critic of the Montreal *Gazette.* He recognized that composing as an avocation is rare, and that all creative work ultimately springs, as he said, from a common source. "Call it psychic energy, if you like," he wrote. "Winston Churchill, for all his tempestuous political life, has found time to be a gifted painter and an eminent author. And I have not the slightest hesitation in saying that much that is basically distinguished in Swing the journalist and news analyst will be found in Swing the musician. Character will come out." Mr. Archer proceeds generously:

Take this sonata. It is bold and sure in form. Mr. Swing knows the technique of composition a good deal better than some of his contemporaries who devote their whole time to composing. . . . Above all the feeling is intense. Those familiar with Mr. Swing's quiet, deliberative analyses of news events are likely to be amazed at the depth of the intensity displayed in this music, by turns stormy and passionate, meditative and brooding, quasi-mystical in places. They will admire especially the successful construction of the first movement, the sustained lyrical feeling of the introspective slow movement, the bold contrasts set forth in what corresponds to the scherzo, the broadly conceived finale with its wide-spaced melody. This finale is quite an achievement in a semi-improvised style. Such rhapsodic music is often hardest to mould into a form that is acceptable and convincing.

What amateur would not be grateful for such a comment? I have my own opinion of the work: that it was only semi-modern at the time it was written, more than thirty years ago, and that it is actually antimodern in being determinedly romantic, and is saturated with Schubert, Brahms, César Franck, Moussorgsky, whose works I loved. What I want to emphasize is that I considered myself only an amateur, and I have some thoughts to utter on behalf of amateurism as such.

First, the amateur artist—and I now refer not to the performer, but the author or composer—not only has the pleasure of expressing himself, but he also gains through the experience of writing a far greater appreciation of the works of the masters. He becomes a better judge of musical worth. He reads or listens with mind aware of his own standards and capacities. He knows whether what he encounters is something he would like to have created himself. This holds good for music and poetry and, not in the same way, for prose.

A second point I wish to make is that modern life—unless it goes into restless turmoil—is coming into an era of abundant leisure, and the sturdiness of civilization depends in no small degree on the use made of this leisure. I believe that educators, who naturally want individuals to live the richest possible lives, should encourage the development of artistic creativeness, and should do so deliberately with an accent on amateurs rather than, as now, exclusively on professionals. The aim should be for the individual to express himself rather than to impress or influence others. In our present society, a considerable proportion of the creative artists, it seems to me, is seeking status and recognition instead of beauty and its articulation. With good teaching, the amateur can learn his techniques (which I did not do thoroughly before writing my own music) and find delight in writing well. But it should be done for his own happiness, not for the praise of his fellow-men.

In modern America, the growth of musical interest has been phenomenal. The number of professional and semi-professional symphony orchestras is in the hundreds, and this is something of superlative value. But I have something additional in mind in pleading the case of the amateur musician who should be trained to create for his own gratification.

If we come into a time when men and women have, say, double the leisure they now enjoy, how shall they spend it? I imagine that they will play more games, but competitive games, of themselves, are not profoundly satisfying. People, having greater leisure, will indulge in more social life, which has its undoubted rewards. In the Elizabethan era, leisure was spent by neighbors gathering to perform together music written for the recorder and to sing madrigals. This was more civilized than the bridge-playing and cocktail-drinking of many Americans today. People with leisure will read more, and they will watch television, which one day may become still more rewarding, even if it is not self-expression. But the life of leisure to which we seem surely to be heading will be richest if its outranking occupation is self-expression for the sake of self-expression. On that foundation can be built appreciation for the art of the masters, and the amateur can learn to make for himself utterances of truth and beauty.

Chapter 22 / Experiences in London

In my years in London, I recall in particular three professional experiences. One was accompanying Prime Minister MacDonald on his visit to President Hoover in the United States in 1929. This mission was preliminary to and prerequisite for the naval-disarmament agreement reached in the following year. The visit was made before prime ministers and presidents flew over the ocean often and easily. This trip was made by passenger liner. In addition to his diplomatic staff, Mr. MacDonald was accompanied by his daughter, Ishbel, and the event of the voyage for me was trouble I caused Miss MacDonald with her father. Ishbel was a pleasant, solid girl. I had made her acquaintance and that of her brother, Malcolm, in London and was glad I would have the opportunity of getting to know her better. I had had many journalistic dealings with her father, so I felt at ease with the MacDonalds on this voyage. The consequence was that I spent several evenings in the improvised ballroom with Ishbel, and we danced together. I am not a proficient dancer, and I might say that neither was Ishbel. We both had practiced it a little, just enough to take part in it with enjoyment. I presume that our pleasure on these evenings derived from opposite reasons. I obviously was glad to be associating with the Prime Minister's daughter; she probably enjoyed what she assumed to be a brief escape from the responsibilities of that role. But that was her mistake. For we danced on a Sunday night, and some newsman on the voyage radioed that Ishbel MacDonald had danced on board on a Sunday. The result was that word reached the Prime Minister that some Midwestern church organizations had criticized Ishbel for dancing on the Sabbath. With a dark, solemn mien, Mr. MacDonald called her to his stateroom, reproved her, and forbade her to do any more dancing. "He was quite upset," Ishbel told me, and so was she to have been accused of being of discredit to her father. The incident did not affect my relations with either Mr. MacDonald or his daughter. However, since the New York *Evening Post* assigned a woman reporter to cover Ishbel throughout her stay in America, I did not get to see much of her on this trip.

The second professional incident was another minor tragedy, but of an entirely different nature. In 1931 Britain was in economic difficulties which led me to believe it would not be able to stay on the gold standard. This judgment was not unique with me. It was slyly referred to in public by many financiers and businessmen. Winston Churchill had returned to the gold standard when he was the Conservative government's Chancellor of the Exchequer in 1925. The intention was praiseworthy. It was to elevate British currency to its supreme position among the currencies of the world. Many economists believed that the decision was taken too soon, and that sterling pegged at its prewar value was too high. The Bank of England had trouble curbing the outflow of gold. And the depression in the United States created echoing difficulties in Britain.

I decided to make a thorough study of the problem and write a series of articles on it. The New York *Evening Post,* published jointly with the Philadelphia *Ledger* by the Curtis Publishing Company, was not another *Wall Street Journal,* but it concentrated more on news for the financial and business world than any other newspaper in New York. The series was intended primarily for the *Evening Post.*

My previous *Wall Street Journal* connections were of inestimable value to me in preparing this series. I talked with some of the most authoritative British economic leaders, including Sir Josiah Stamp, then a director of the Bank of England. Sir Josiah did not tell me outright that Britain would not be able to stay on the gold standard. The way he put it was to say that he did not see how it could manage to do so. "Swing," he told me, "I read in bed every night the history of British economy. And I have come to the conclusion that if we managed to get through the crisis of the 1830's, we may manage to get through this one."

Most of the others I talked to were equally gloomy. So I foretold the departure from the gold standard in my articles, and backed up my judgment with a careful analysis of Britain's economic difficulties. I had some help in gathering material for my articles from a young Philadelphia investment banker, William Stix Wasserman, who came to London to advise the Bank of Manhattan on whether the bank should invest some of its funds in selling sterling short in anticipation of the abandonment of the gold standard. He hungrily read my articles and my background material. He was convinced that England would have to go off the gold standard and urged me to get into the market myself and sell sterling short. I did not have much money. My total capital at the time was about $10,000 in investments left by my father, from which I was to enjoy the income during my lifetime, while the capital was to go to my children at my death. Wasserman assured me that I could treble this sum in a few weeks, and naturally I was sorely tempted to do so. But my first reaction was that there was impropriety in a journalist playing the market on the basis of information he obtained as a journalist. I did believe I had the right to reinvest the capital from my father, if I so chose.

The decision of the Bank of England was believed to be a week away. And in this week, Wasserman continued to urge me to sell sterling short, and I continued to be intrigued by the idea. Inside me warred two factions, one wishing to uphold the purity of journalism, one wishing to make a justified profit from having studied the financial situation. The "don't-do-it" faction still was stronger than the "do-it" faction, but the "don't-do-it" faction was getting weaker. The temptation of turning my $10,000 into $30,000 was not easy to resist. The arguments in favor of it were highly respectable and even ethical: I had my family to take care of, and my knowledge was my only asset; I should exploit it.

As the week began, I was clear in my determination not to go into the market. By the middle of the week, I was wavering. By the end of the week, temptation had floored me. I placed an order on Saturday with a broker to sell sterling short on Monday morning.

If such a sale was a sin, I was saved from it by the Bank of England. On Sunday night, it announced that the gold standard was being abandoned with the start of Monday.

I have often thought of the values involved in this issue of playing the market and selling sterling short. I think my original decision not to do so was more right—shall I say—than a decision the other way. But as things turned out, I did the right thing—or the more right thing—not through virtue, but solely through the timing of the Bank of England's decision. I shall never be able to boast about my high journalistic standards in this instance. And if the mortification of pride is the most useful occupation of the sincere spirit, I came out of this experience without pride—and without $20,000 in profit.

In the meantime, my articles went off to New York, and I had been thoroughly pleased with them. They had cost me a great deal of work, they represented the best judgment obtainable in London, and I expected appreciation for them. Julian Mason, editor of the *Evening Post*, shattered these expectations by writing me that the articles would not be published. Cyrus Curtis's son-in-law, John C. Martin, who had immediate charge of administration of both the *Ledger* and the *Evening Post*, was heavily involved in the stock market. My articles, he thought, would have a depressive effect on prices, and he ordered that they not be used. Mr. Mason did, however, have copies made and sent them out to a number of eminent Americans, including Colonel House, and some leading bankers. He made it a practice to circulate to such men private information from the foreign service. Unfortunately, my articles were to be private.

I have lost the letter he wrote me with the names of those to whom he sent the articles. He also sent me their replies. Colonel House answered that he had long feared the decline of British power, but he had not foreseen that it would come about so soon or through economic weakness. However, he did not dispute my prediction about the abandonment of the gold standard. Without exception, the bankers did. One of them even asked, "What is the personality of the writer?"

I received Mr. Mason's letter enclosing these replies on the Saturday before the Monday Britain went off the gold standard. On Monday Mr. Mason cabled me: "Hail thou most sapient prophet," and with him, at any rate, my stock was high. But professionally, it was a great frustration for me that the articles were not published. More than once I found myself complaining about my lot. My day-to-day duties for the *Ledger* bureau were easy and a much less experienced man would have done them as well as I. My work simply did not make what I considered full use of my capabilities. My interests in world affairs were greater than those of the American news services.

I mention this because in a few years, when I became a broadcaster, and the world, including my own country, was at war, and national life and death were at issue, I found that I needed far more insight, experience, and judgment than I possessed. In this work I did not have wisdom equal to my responsibilities.

The third experience I wish to record is meeting Miss Mary Somerville, then in charge of broadcasting to the schools for the British Broadcasting Corporation. I made her acquaintance socially and do not believe that at that time the thought had crossed my mind that I might become a broadcaster. But we naturally talked a great deal about broadcasting. My own enthusiasm for it was demonstrated by my purchase of a primitive short-wave set with which I tried to pick up American stations. I sat up till all hours, and the set squeaked and squawked and tried the patience of my household, which condescendingly called my radio set "Papa's electric train." Now and then I managed to hear an American broadcast and was thrilled. Mostly, I failed.

Miss Somerville's educational broadcasts interested me, though at that time I was not imaginative enough to appreciate their potentialities. Miss Somerville had wide blue eyes, and spoke with a precise articulation and perfect English in a way to make her at once charming and formidable. She invited me to give a talk to the schools about an American subject, and then repeated the invitation a number of times. Through her I came to know Charles Siepmann, director of talks for the BBC, and Sir John Reith (to become Lord Reith), the director general, who was to give me a major assist in launching my broadcasting career. Siepmann was a man of unusual intellectual vigor. He imaginatively saw the potentialities of radio, believing that the right kind of programs could result in swifter and sounder social progress than Britain had ever experienced. He considered radio as the greatest instrument ever put at the service of downing ignorance and prejudice. This, of course, branded him as a somewhat dangerous radical, and the BBC's Board of Directors quietly dropped him. Harvard then invited him to be a guest professor, and he later became head of the department of communications of New York University.

Actually, my own first broadcast over the BBC was a discussion program with S. K. Ratcliffe, a well-known liberal journalist and the leading lecturer in the United States on British affairs. I also was invited by William Hard to broadcast from Geneva a news report for NBC. And César Saerchinger, then head of CBS's European service, and I made radio history with the first transatlantic interview. It was on the British election in 1932, Saerchinger speaking from New York and I from London. But I owe my start as a professional broadcaster to Mary Somerville. Later she became controller of talks for the BBC and retired with an Order of the British Empire in 1955.

Chapter 23 / Return to America

The foreign service of the *Public Ledger* and *Evening Post* was discontinued in 1934, and with its end, my life as a foreign correspondent also came to a close. I must confess that I was despondent. I tried to find an acceptable post abroad on some other newspaper, but by then the interest in world affairs in America was swamped by domestic affairs. Once again I tried to join the New York *Times* foreign staff. There were no vacancies. So I prepared to go home and find a new way to make a living. I was forty-seven, had a wife and five children to support and educate—two from my first marriage—and no prospects for employment. I was sure that my days as head of a European bureau were finished. I thought I might end as copy reader on a New York daily. I was more than disheartened.

Ernestine Evans, a friend from her college days at the University of Chicago, and a magazine writer and authority on children's books, lifted some of the pall from my arrival by meeting me at the dock with two suggestions. One was that I apply for the position of minister to Ireland, then vacant, with the understanding that I should have some freedom to travel and to report on European conditions to Raymond Moley, Assistant Secretary of State under Cordell Hull, and member of President Roosevelt's "brain trust." This was in 1934, when the Nazis had been in power for a year in Germany, and the deterioration of European conditions was easy to foresee. Miss Evans predicted that a professional reporter of my experience would be of use to Mr. Moley and she had arranged an appointment with him.

The other suggestion was that I might join the *Nation*, this time as member of the editorial board. Miss Evans had made soundings which were favorably echoed.

The idea of becoming minister to Ireland naturally was alluring, as was the idea of reporting personally to Mr. Moley about conditions in Europe. Nowadays, such an appointment would be preposterous. I do not even now quite understand why it was not so in 1934. Mr. Moley's appointment to the State Department had been no kindness to Mr. Hull, and the two men were not on particularly cordial terms. Mr. Hull could not be expected to approve an appointment Mr. Moley wanted and recommend it to the President, and certainly could not be expected to sponsor someone who was going to move about Europe and report from there directly to Mr. Moley.

But this preposterous thing nearly came to pass. Mr. Moley liked the idea, and when I went to see Mr. Hull, he, surprisingly, said he would support me, too. So the recommendation of my appointment actually reached President Roosevelt's desk. I do not know if he had been informed that I would be Mr. Moley's man in Europe and a new kind of diplomat-journalist. For a little while, it looked as though I might be named. But Congress recessed before Mr. Roosevelt could send in my nomination. Then political influence was brought on the White House to reward some deserving party man with the Irish post, and the President decided not to make any appointment for the time being. That ended the extraordinary dream.

The *Nation*, through its history, had been a periodical of dissent, and as such fed the arteries of American political vigor. It was a magazine of limited circulation, less than 40,000 at this time, but with an effectiveness of much greater dimensions. Oswald Garrison Villard, who had inherited the paper and a considerable fortune from his father, the railroad magnate Henry Villard, had conducted it in the creditable tradition of liberal dissent, and by this time had turned over the management of the paper to his editorial board, with

Freda Kirchwey as managing editor. He became contributing editor and wrote regular articles under his own signature.

The position in mind for me was Washington correspondent with membership on the board of editors, the other members being Miss Kirchwey and Joseph Wood Krutch. I was to write a weekly Washington letter and go each weekend to New York to attend the editorial conference and write either editorial notes or one of the leading editorials. Miss Kirchwey, Mr. Krutch, and, so far as I know, the associate members of the board, favored my appointment, as did Mr. Villard.

My time with the *Nation* was relatively brief. I joined the editorial board on September 12, 1934, and left on January 8, 1936. In the meantime, Mr. Villard had sold the magazine to Maurice Wertheim, a wealthy investment banker, who promised to give the editorial board a free hand. I am sure he meant to, but he was dissatisfied with me for being what he considered too friendly to the New Deal. On the face of it, this sounds as though a wealthy businessman found me too radical. The opposite is the case. I was too conservative. Mr. Wertheim was not against the New Deal because he was a recalcitrant banker, but because he at that time stood farther to the left. And as the months progressed, he wanted to see me replaced by Max Lerner, who in those days was considerably more radical than he has since become. I was finding it hard to make ends meet, and my salary had to be supplemented by outside work. When I asked for an increase, Mr. Wertheim turned it down in a way that made me decide to look for work elsewhere.

My friendliness to the New Deal was a bone of contention at some of the editorial conferences in which I took part. Being an organ of dissent, the *Nation* naturally experienced dissent among its own staff. Certain associate editors were disposed to find the Soviet government and its policies more to their liking than their own. Miss Kirchwey, Mr. Krutch, and I, while not rabidly anti-Communist, profoundly preferred the political principles of the United States to those of the Soviet Union and were able to criticize the Soviet Union editorially, to the disgust of one or two of the associate editors. I speak of this because my service with the *Nation* later proved to be a handicap to me with people who did not know that I myself was under attack there for being not radical enough, and ultimately severed my relations with the magazine because its new proprietor found me too conservative.

Of Miss Kirchwey, on whom the chief responsibility for conducting the magazine rested, I wish to say that she was one of the best and most likable journalists with whom I ever worked. I am tempted to call her the best woman journalist I ever encountered, but hesitate to rank her ahead of Dorothy Thompson, who was a better writer. But she was among the superior women journalists of her time.

I had few close friends in the entourage around President Roosevelt and hardly deserved the appellation of being an out-and-out New Dealer. Some aspects of it disturbed me, for before the passage of the Wagner Act, the position of labor in the "first" New Deal was weaker than that of management. The growing centralization of control in the government through the National Recovery Administration gave the structure a disconcerting similarity to aspects of fascist movements in Europe. I wrote in the *Nation* in January, 1935: "Unless labor is given equal power with management in the dispensation, ours will be a fascism of the European brand. There is no escape from it."

There was some outright fascist thinking and activity in America outside the Roosevelt administration, and I do not mean to attribute to it any influence on New Deal planning. But the thesis of central control in the "first" New Deal, and the creation of the NRA, did not altogether satisfy me. I was happier with the promulgation of the social services, and then with the return to the system of competition in business. Certainly the NRA was not intended to be fascist, but it reeked of authoritarianism, and as such it worried me. When it was found unconstitutional, the "second" New Deal could be initiated with the Wagner Act, and I was gratified.

I had other reasons for fearing fascism, and one I wrote about in the *Nation* produced comment from many quarters. It was an article entitled "The Strike of Capital." Bank deposits were rising, business was holding up commercial loans and even refusing to invest normally in private securities. Banks were investing in government securities, which drove the government to finance many enterprises ordinarily handled by the banks. "Unless the strike is broken," I wrote, "there seems to be one of two possible endings. The State becomes the fountain-head of business and controls it either for social purposes, which is socialism, or to guarantee the profit system, which is fascism. The more the State interferes in business," I predicted, "—even if it is to take the place of striking capital—the more capital will go on strike." I did not describe the strike of capital as conscious. I also did not believe it would end in socialism. "That the country as a whole wants the profit system," I wrote, "goes without saying. The end of this growing tendency makes us much more certain to be fascist, and a titanic effort must be made to save the crumbling economic structure by a state guaranty of business returns." I attributed the strike of capital to fear and urged that President Roosevelt allay the fear by telling business the maximum of his economic program. I was commended in a column-long editorial in the *Wall Street Journal* for arguing with intelligence and restraint, and it found me "curiously sound from the conservative point of view." It agreed with me that fascism was hopelessly wrong. It also agreed with me that President Roosevelt should disclose the maximum of his economic program. It defended capital and its behavior, as one would expect. But such treatment of an article in the *Nation* by the *Wall Street Journal* testified to the sensitivity even businessmen felt toward the potentialities in the economic situation.

I do not believe I was inconsistent in reassuring the Europeans in another article, contributed to the February, 1934, issue of the *British Fortnightly Review*, that the New Deal was neither fascist nor Bolshevik, to which the New York *Times* devoted its lead editorial on February 18 of that year. In this I pointed out that President Roosevelt had done nothing without the authority of Congress. "In other countries where dictatorship has sprung up," I wrote, "there has come with it a new philosophy of the State, and the diminution of the individual. Of this America has heard nothing. President Roosevelt remains democratic in his nature and daily life, and if he achieves his objectives he intends to have saved the essence of American democracy." I pointed out that there is no militant left wing in America, "ready like the Bolsheviks to take over from a Washington Kerensky, no Right Wing listening with growing fury to the rhetoric of an American Hitler or Mussolini. Instead, American democracy, whatever it may be uncertain about, is sure of itself and in no mood for recantation." Stanley Baldwin already was calling the New Deal a dictatorship, and democrats in Europe were alarmed about what they were being told about it. The danger of fascism may have been latent, and it was well to call the attention of Americans to it if it was to be averted. But the basic situation in America, at least ideologically, was sound. By now the pitfalls of the early Roosevelt era are forgotten, and historians attest that he did succeed in preserving the system of free enterprise in the face of the most stubborn obstruction from those who wanted it most.

It was during this time that I first made friends with Harry Hopkins and Felix Frankfurter. The association with Hopkins lasted until his death; and shortly before his fatal illness, he had me in mind, he told me, to be the editor of his papers, a service that was, however, performed by Robert Sherwood, whose exciting book *Roosevelt and Hopkins* was superior to anything I could have produced.

My association with Mr. Frankfurter was frequent and intimate, but this was before his appointment to the Supreme Court, after which I seldom saw him.

# of American Demagogues

Two subjects I wrote about for the *Nation* were of special interest to me, and these articles created a good deal of discussion. One was about Huey Long, the Louisiana "Kingfish," written under the heading "The Menace of Huey Long." The other was about Governor Alfred M. Landon, of Kansas, whom I visited as a possible candidate for the 1936 Republican nomination and liked much better than an editor of the *Nation* might have been expected to.

I went to see Huey Long as the first subject of a series of articles on the potential fascist leaders then making themselves felt on the periphery of American affairs. My request to him to receive me produced a letter from the Reverend Gerald L. K. Smith, at that time Senator Long's unofficial right-hand man, and head of his "Share Our Wealth" covenant. The Rev. Mr. Smith responded warmly and promised to give me every assistance. When I arrived in New Orleans, he welcomed me with an enthusiasm that astonished me. He assured me that Huey Long would be found to be the *Nation's* man. He himself, he said, had been brought up in Wisconsin on *La Follette's Weekly*. He promised me that I would find Louisiana under Long's dominion all that the *Nation* could pray for in generous liberalism.

At that time, Senator Long was generally considered the buffoon of the American political stage. He was vulgar, ill-mannered, and amusingly impertinent. The man who plays the fool and is not counts on being underestimated and profiting from it. At the time I went to see Huey Long, the American public in general did not take him seriously. It knew virtually nothing about his accomplishments, his power, or his potentialities. The clergyman Smith, who gave up a wealthy pastorate to serve him, did. I think that at the time he genuinely believed that Long was a liberal and that as an editor of the *Nation* I would recognize it. What convinces me of this is that he vouched for me without reservation to Senator Long, so that I was admitted to anything and everything I cared to attend, including a two-hour session he held with his county organizers in his bedroom.

This occasion was beyond doubt the most informal meeting of a political boss with his menials that one could hope to watch and listen to. The Kingfish, in green pajamas, stretched out on his bed part of the time, occasionally rubbing his itching toes, stood part of the time, hitching up his sagging nightwear, and on one occasion, in the midst of an outpouring of orders and comment, went to the open bathroom and urinated as he continued talking. The dozen or so local political leaders present spoke up to him freely, argued with him about local sentiment, and found that he knew their districts better than they did, and could tell them how to manage the upcoming election. If I had printed the dialogue I heard, it might well have convicted Huey Long of being a crooked politician. But that fact was not news in Louisiana, and if printed elsewhere about the Senate's leading buffoon, it would not have disturbed the country. The fact that the conversation was being held in my presence did not inhibit the party men; I was Huey's guest. And it did not inhibit Huey; I had been vouched for by Gerald Smith.

I attended two other sessions with his approval, one of a special meeting of the legislature in the skyscraper statehouse at Baton Rouge, the other of the Ways and Means Committee, both called to take care of thirty-five bills introduced by the Long machine. The Senator was at both meetings running things without the slightest right of membership. Nobody objected. This was Huey's legislature, his committee, his statehouse, his state. At the special session of the legislature, he answered questions from the floor. When one of the minority opposition objected to the speed with which the bills were read, he promised to have them printed before the meeting of the Ways and Means Committee the following day. He was the only lively and articulate man in the room, waving his arms, grimacing with eyes protruding, face flushed.

In the committee meeting at nine the next morning, Senator Long read and explained each bill, then the chairman put it to a vote, smashing down his gavel. Here, too, he had no right to take part in the proceedings, but no one objected. The committee consisted of fifteen Long supporters and two oppositionists. Three bills were approved in the first six minutes, thirty-five were acted on in seventy minutes, all but one being approved. The rejected bill was one that Long scowled at when he looked at it, passed back to the chairman, and said: "We don't want that. Let them come to us," a remark which no one explained. The bill was shelved.

This was dictatorship in the guise of the democratic process. And as the session proceeded, the dictatorship added to its power, grabbing patronage it did not yet control, gaining control over the appointment of schoolteachers, obtaining authority to remove the mayor in a town where Long had been showered with eggs, putting its grip on Baton Rouge, which he had failed to carry at the election, by gaining authority to name extra members to the local government board. It plastered an occupational tax on the refining of oil by Standard Oil, which Long had fought throughout his career. Subsequently, the company resisted by laying off a thousand workers. The workers held a protest meeting. Senator Long, threatened with revolt, rushed back from Washington, called out the militia, summoned the legislature in a special session, and struck a bargain with Standard Oil that he would remit some of the tax if Standard Oil would refine more Louisiana oil. He remitted four-fifths of the tax, which the legislature ratified. But the occupational tax was on the books to be used to gouge any business the Long machine cared to exploit or punish.

I confess that Huey Long puzzled me. How could the legislators—who looked like ordinarily decent men—put up with him, his blasphemous language, his unsavory conduct? They did not show fear of him; they seemed to like him. In his way, he was their buddy—but a hundred times smarter than any of them. The dictators of Europe were explained as fulfilling the father-yearning in their peoples. Huey Long was no father image. He was a grown-up bad boy. The Rev. Gerald Smith undertook to explain the Long dictatorship. "It is," he told me, "the dictatorship of the surgical theater. The surgeon is in charge because he knows. Everyone defers to him for that reason only. The nurses and assistants do what he tells them, asking no questions. They jump at his commands. They are not servile, they believe in the surgeon. They realize that he is working for the good of the patient."

This has to be said for Huey Long: he had strong liberal instincts and left to his credit a list of reforms not to be matched in any other Southern state. He shifted the burden of taxation from the poor to those who could afford to bear it. To finance his reforms, he increased the state's indebtedness from $11,000,000 to $150,000,000, but met each increase by new taxation. He passed legislation postponing the payment of private debt. He laid out a system of highways and bridges, and, above all, he dedicated himself to improving the state's education. He remodeled the school system to enable eight-month terms to be maintained in the poorest parishes and provided free textbooks. He strongly supported the Julius Rosenwald campaign against illiteracy, so that 100,000 adults in Louisiana, white and black, learned to read and write in his first term as governor. He backed Louisiana State University, assured it a good faculty, added a medical and dental school, and increased its enrollment from 1,500 to 4,000 in his first term as governor. As governor, he fought the public-utility companies and forced down power and telephone rates. He obtained a reduction of electricity rates in New Orleans. He built a five-million-dollar statehouse, an impressive high-tower building rising on the bank of the Mississippi.

Some of these are solid benefits, which attest that Huey Long knew the good he sought to accomplish. But I concluded that he wanted to do good because he knew it was the way to achieve power.

I had so recently come from Europe, where Mussolini dominated Italy and Hitler, Germany, that in my private talks with Huey Long I sought to have him acknowledge his likeness to them. Mussolini not only made the trains run on time in Italy, but he introduced agricultural co-operatives and other social advances. Hitler restored the wrecked German economy, and in his speeches, which I had heard by the score over the radio in London, talked about power resting with the people, as did the early leaders of America. He was assuring the lower-middle-class Germans that through him, the power was theirs, something it had never been before. In a sense, the appeal of the two dictators was the same appeal as Huey Long's. Huey did not, like the European fascists, believe in war, or, like the Nazis, believe in racialism. He was not anti-Negro. But his movement, in a crude way, was designed to win national power by the same appeal as that of the Italian fascists and the German Nazis.

In my talks with Long, he showed no knowledge whatever of what was happening in Europe. He was interested, even fascinated, to hear me talk about it. But he denied having derived any inspiration or borrowed any techniques from the fascist masters abroad. I am sure he was sincere about it.

When my articles on Long appeared, under the title "The Menace of Huey Long," I received a handwritten note from the Rev. Mr. Smith, expressing his utter dismay. But in another three weeks came a second scrawled letter. In it he said he had changed his mind. My article had done Huey Long a great service: it had elevated him from being a clown into being a menace. I was told that Long thereafter always bought a copy of the *Nation* if something of mine appeared in it.

In my articles I was trying to recognize the demagogues without whom fascism could not come into being, and identify their following and their ideas to discover how much fascism was latent in them. A good deal was to be found in the dogma of Father Coughlin, some in the appeal and techniques of Huey Long. I also wrote a chapter on William Randolph Hearst, which did not appear in the *Nation,* and an analysis of the nature of fascism, and made a book of them all called *The Forerunners of American Fascism.*

I did not call Dr. Francis E. Townsend a potential fascist, though I should have, for he later joined Gerald L. K. Smith. But at the time I wrote, he was simply an engaging crackpot. I chose him for a topic in the *Nation* because I wanted to show what kind of nonsense the economically harassed public was ready for.

I did not consider Hearst a conscious fascist. But he was whipping up public fear of Communism, without which fascism could not come to life. His anti-Communist campaign in 1935—with its drive against academic freedom and campaign for loyalty oaths—died away under the second New Deal and with the outbreak of World War II. It was to come to life in a new guise under Senator Joseph R. McCarthy. If in McCarthy's time America had been as poor as it was in the early 1930's, he, too, might have discovered unmistakably fascist potentialities in the country and himself.

My book, on the whole, was favorably reviewed, but it went through only two printings. The book-reading public at that time was not much interested in fascism or disturbed by its demagogues. Even after Huey Long had won control of a group of Southern states and loomed as a bizarre but undeniable national political power, American intellectuals failed to see any likeness between him and Mussolini and Hitler, just as they had failed to identify Father Coughlin as a preacher of fascism. Moreover, some American business and financial leaders liked European fascism and believed Europe would benefit from it.

James A. Farley said that if Long had lived to found a third party in the 1936 election, he would have polled six million votes. That would not have defeated Roosevelt, as it turned out, but it would have launched an American version (or perversion) of fascism on a scale that no one would have dreamed possible before the Kingfish entered the Senate.

Chapter 25 / Affable Alf Landon

My next—and final—articles in the *Nation* were on possible Republican candidates, and I wrote about Alf Landon, of Kansas, and Colonel Frank Knox, then publisher of the Chicago *Daily News*. The Landon articles, written after extended conversations with the Kansas Governor in Topeka, were frankly commendatory. I found Governor Landon as attractive as anyone I had personally encountered in American public life and said so. His views appeared to me nearly as attractive as his personality. He was being praised by Hearst as a Kansas Coolidge who had balanced his budget, and it was with these words ringing in my ears that I first met the Governor. He was so different that I went far, in my articles, in emphasizing the difference. The Landon I met was a Theodore Roosevelt Progressive, an intimate associate of William Allen White, a believer in civil liberties—he had chaired a Norman Thomas meeting in Topeka—and he was at odds with almost all the conservative Republican dogmas excepting reduction in the cost of government. He wrote privately, as reported in Arthur Schlesinger, Jr.'s *The Politics of Upheaval*: "I do not think there is anything new or revolutionary about the distribution of wealth theory. Every wise statesman in every period of history has been concerned with the equitable distribution of property in his country." At his inaugural address in 1935 he said: "America bids fair to join in the procession of nations of the world in their march toward a new social and economic philosophy" (this from the only Republican governor to have been elected in the previous November). "Some say this will lead to socialism, some communism, others fascism. For myself I am convinced that the ultimate goal will be a modified form of individual rights and ownership of property out of which will come a wider spread of prosperity and opportunity." In a time when the "hate-Roosevelt" campaign inspired most Republicans, such moderate and liberal ideas were outstanding. I found that the Governor believed in social insurance and collective bargaining, which to me were the two essentials of a new era.

I did not realize that my Landon articles were to prove embarrassing to the *Nation*, but they did. Paul Ward, of the Baltimore *Sun*, was sent to Kansas to write an article telling *Nation* readers another side of the Landon story. The fault with me—as an editor of the *Nation*—was that I was not suspicious enough, and in a sense that fault was borne out by subsequent developments. I kept in touch with Governor Landon by letter and maintained close relations with Charles P. Taft and Ralph Robey, who were his speech-writers, after his nomination. The Governor asked me to send him drafts of two speeches, one on social security, the other on labor, the subjects he knew interested me most, and on which we had been in general accord in our conversation. I did so, but the speeches were not delivered. Instead, the Governor made a speech in Minneapolis which seemed to me to amount to a disavowal of his liberalism. I asked him why he had not used the draft of my labor speech. His answer was: "You ought to realize that I can't make a speech of that kind at this time."

I had by then left the *Nation* because, as I have explained, I was too conservative for the publisher. I left Governor Landon for the opposite reason. I am sure that his basic views had not changed, but he felt he had to trim to satisfy old-line Republicans. I am convinced that he did so reluctantly. Certainly the line between expediency and principle is proverbially blurred. A man leading a party, unless he is abnormally self-assured, is bound to feel at times that he must curb his own beliefs for the sake of the party. It takes unusual faith in himself to be confident that what he believes is sure to be good for the party, even if his party leaders tell him otherwise. I was disappointed in Governor Landon's submission to the needs for expediency, and I silently bade him good-by. I did not write him again during the campaign, and when election returns came in, I was convinced he would have carried many more than two states if he had remained throughout the campaign the outspoken man I first met in Topeka.

I did not see Governor Landon again until twenty-six years later, in the spring of 1962, when I was invited to have breakfast with him at the home of Arthur Schlesinger, Jr., with whom he was staying on a brief visit to Washington. The Governor was back in his liberal harness—without a buckle loose—for he was openly supporting President John F. Kennedy's request for power to eliminate tariffs in negotiating with the European Common Market, and looking forward to economic union with Western Europe. While in Washington, he gave a strong address along that line before the National Press Club, which, I think, was somewhat startled to behold a former Republican presidential candidate so far from his party's traditional doctrinal rectitude. But it was not far from Mr. Landon's traditional rectitude. He advocated tariff reduction and freer trade in his campaign for the governorship before being nominated for the presidency.

Governor Landon told me when we breakfasted in 1962 that he had been finding Kansas sympathetic to his trade-expansion arguments and that nearly all the leading Republican newspapers in the state were supporting tariff reductions.

Meeting Governor Landon after a lapse of twenty-six years turned out to be a most agreeable and gratifying experience. He was as easy and rewarding to talk to as when I first conversed with him in his Topeka home. He was energetic and liberal. Had he continued to be so in 1936, he would not have won the election, but he might have contributed for many years to an enlightened leadership of the Republican party.

After leaving the *Nation* I accepted an appointment as New York correspondent of the London *News Chronicle*. My twelve years in London had not made an English-type journalist of me, but they had schooled me to some extent in what it is that a London editor expects from a foreign correspondent. The *News Chronicle* could not use a steady outpouring of political news and news analysis, though being the leading liberal newspaper in London at that time it did want something more than was sent by the correspondents of the *Daily Express* and the *Daily Mail.* All three newspapers had to cater to large circulations, hence they wanted spicy news that reflected the current judgment of the British masses on American life, which was not well-informed or overly friendly. The importance of the Roosevelt administration and the New Deal was not rated highly, and there was no sustained interest in domestic affairs in America or American foreign policy.

I took these handicaps into consideration. They should be tolerable under the chairmanship of Sir Walter Layton, whom I had come to know well as editor of the *Economist.* I knew that I should have to accustom myself to a brevity not demanded by the *Public Ledger* or the Chicago *Daily News.* But I am afraid that my sense of the importance of events got the better of me, and more of my dispatches were simply not used than those of any predecessor. However, I was not scolded for my profligacy, and I served the *News Chronicle* for well over a year, until other occupations claimed my time.

Before the year was out it gave me one premium; Geoffrey Crowther (now Sir Geoffrey), who had succeeded Sir Walter Layton as editor of the *Economist,* asked me if I would take over the Washington correspondence for that periodical, which I did for over a year, including the campaign months of 1936. I regarded the *Economist* then—and still do—as the best periodical of its kind in the world, and I was indeed grateful to be associated with it. I was happy to have the opportunity to discuss the presidential campaign for a foreign public, and to do so objectively.

One report I wrote drew the ire of Felix Frankfurter, because it pointed out the disparateness of Roosevelt's support, which rested on liberals in the West and Middle West, the conservatives in the South, and the big political machines in the cities. Mr. Frankfurter thought he detected a note of disparagement in this analysis and chided me for it. It was his concern at that time that nothing should be published anywhere which detracted from the President's greatness. His rebuke attested how carefully he read what newspapers and periodicals were saying, both at home and abroad.

During this time, I also wrote an article once a fortnight for *Ken,* a serious magazine issued for a while by the publisher of *Esquire,* and I had to fly to Chicago to consult about it with Arnold Gingrich, then editor of *Ken* and later to become the guiding spirit at *Esquire. Ken* was a courageous enterprise which failed because it did not have quite the right formula. Perhaps it was a shade too highbrowed, and I often thought the publishers were trying to demonstrate to themselves and the American public that they could be high-toned as well as amusingly vulgar, as so much in *Esquire* at that time seemed to be.

I was pressed for time and often wrote my fortnightly article on the plane, and was delighted to find that altitude somehow expedited and clarified the writing of it. I would come into the *Esquire* office with the piece in my hands, ready for the hasty, eleventh-hour conference with Mr. Gingrich.

I remember on one occasion telling him that the subject for a perfect *Esquire* cartoon was to be found in the magazine's reception office. This was a room whose walls were crowded with *Esquire* drawings, and certainly a feast for those hungry for suggestiveness. The receptionist sat placidly at her desk in the midst of this supersophistication, reading—of all things —*Science and Health.*

/Part Two

Chapter 26 / I Become a Broadcaster

My professional life falls naturally into two nearly equal parts, newspaper work and broadcasting. At the time of this writing, I have been broadcasting for much or most of the last twenty-seven years. And this is the same number of years I have made my living writing for newspapers and periodicals. To me, one aspect of my broadcasting seems unique: for nine years of it, I lived in that glare of national publicity which is the lot of a successful broadcaster. The other years were spent in almost total obscurity. During some of these years, to be sure, I was learning my job. During some of them, radio news had not yet become an urgent national service. But during twelve of my broadcasting years, due to special circumstances, I was broadcasting as well as I ever did, but was not heard about in my own country. Let me say that I consider these years of obscurity preferable to the preceding years of publicized success.

Not that I am so ascetic as to disparage success; far from it. I enjoyed it immensely. It was intoxicating, challenging, and rewarding in many ways. One of them was that it brought me into contact with the men who were leading the country. It gave me status and won me respect. But I am more normal and spiritually better off being obscure. A successful news commentator is, after all, only a journalist magnified by a mechanical device, the microphone. He is not well known for his statesmanship or his artistry. He is not creating enduring works. He is not going down in history. But because he is well known, he is constantly tempted to accept as valid the exaggeration some others give to his importance, even though the microphone has not added to his stature or made him wiser and more responsible.

There are a few great journalists in every era who do not need a microphone to stand out. The name of Walter Lippmann leaps to mind. With his thinking, he has affected his times. He reached his public through his newspaper columns and books. So does the name of John Gunther, some of whose "Inside" books have instructed his generation and will be read for years to come by students and historians. But the microphone makes the lesser journalist well known. He becomes a factor of value to the radio industry, to advertisers, to newspapers, to the general public, and, inescapably, to himself. If he has a heavy charge of humility, it does not puff him up. But he is kept on the defensive against the effect it might have, and for a man to live defensively against overestimating himself can be a handicap.

The obscurity of the greater part of my better broadcasting years was owing to reasons having little to do with the quality of my work. To jump ahead in my story, six of those years were spent in association with Edward R. Murrow, for whom I wrote for two years some of the commentary sections of his daily broadcasts, and for the other four years, a greater part of them. I also made some contribution to his "See It Now" programs and for two years edited the "This I Believe" program over CBS. Murrow was at the time perhaps the busiest man in radio-television. He did not have the time to write or create all his programs. I shall relate in due course why I went to work for him. But I wish to say now that I was content to write for him because we agreed on most of the issues at home and abroad. On his programs, I was saying what I wanted to have said. Thus it was an unusual opportunity and association.

The other six years of broadcasting in obscurity have been with the Voice of America, for which I served as "first political commentator" from 1951 to 1953, and again from 1959 to 1962, when I reduced my schedule to a single weekly commentary on reaching my seventy-fifth birthday. A year later I stepped up my contribution to two broadcasts a week. VOA broadcasts play no role in domestic American life. Congress has forbidden the American public to be addressed directly by them, fearing that the administration in power might use its radio facilities for its own political benefit. I consider the Voice of America, along with the United States Information Agency of which it is a part, to be the most extensive international communications operation in the world—and an essential service to the American people, even if they know next to nothing about it.

My broadcasting career actually began in an exceedingly small way in England, when I was head of the Philadelphia *Public Ledger* bureau and did a series of broadcasts for the BBC on America and American affairs for the schools.

I have said that these broadcasts also were liked by Sir John Reith, managing director of the BBC, with major consequences in my life. For when Sir John came to Washington in 1934, he was invited to the White House by President Roosevelt, who complained to him about the misrepresentation of the New Deal in all Europe, and particularly in Great Britain. It had been typical of this criticism for Stanley Baldwin to denounce the New Deal as a dictatorship which Britain never would accept. Mr. Roosevelt proposed to remedy this by an exchange of broadcasts between the BBC and an American network. Sir John agreed on the condition that he should choose his own American broadcaster, and the American network his British counterpart. This point being agreed to, he chose me, although I was virtually unknown as a broadcaster at the time in the United States. So in a sense I owe my start to Mary Somerville, Sir John Reith, and President Roosevelt. Some years later I was able to thank the President for his part in it in the only private conversation I ever held with him.

I should record that the exchange idea, though adopted, had a brief life. CBS was the network that undertook to co-operate, and it chose Wickham Steed, then retired from the editorship of the London *Times*, to give the British commentary. His talks were good, but they were discontinued before a year was out. This was not to his disparagement, for in 1934 and 1935 American interest in British affairs was limited, as it was in other affairs in Europe.

My first broadcasting after my return to America was a weekly talk on foreign affairs made for the CBS School of the

Air. This continued for a year, when I encountered one of the most bizarre difficulties of my broadcasting experience. The executive vice president of CBS, Edward Klauber, took a strong dislike to my voice. Mr. Klauber was a man of unusual stature in the radio field and not given to impulsive decisions. I was told he liked what I said, but my voice offended him.

I should say that before I began the CBS assignment, I asked for the use of a studio and an engineer, to listen to my own voice under all varieties of studio conditions, so that I could find the one most satisfactory. And I was just as dismayed the first time I heard my voice as Mr. Klauber could have been. I now know this is a common experience. Many speakers are unpleasantly startled the first time they hear themselves over a loud-speaker. What I wanted to achieve in broadcasting, first of all, was a presentation in which I seemed to address myself to a single listener. I believe I learned early that good broadcasting is a compromise between prose and conversation. It cannot be all conversation because that uses too many words and so takes up too much time. It cannot be all prose because that sounds too much like reading from a book. A happy medium is called for between a certain amount of informal speech and a certain amount of simple but condensed writing.

I also strove to learn to put stress on the important words of a phrase so that what I said, while not conversational throughout, gave a sense of communication. And I worked to avoid any emotional overemphasis, as used in speechmaking. In my studio tests, I tried to find the volume, level, pace, and moderate intensity of delivery that expressed me. The natural pitch of my voice was low. Specifically, what Mr. Klauber disliked was that my tonal volume tended to peter out at the close of a sentence and become a whisper. To some extent, I found this was true.

But it could be corrected. A kindly former clergyman named John Carlisle was at that time on the staff of CBS and rated as a speech specialist. He offered to help me increase my vocal volume and so overcome Mr. Klauber's objections. He prescribed his cure, which was to whisper out loud, first softly, then as strongly as possible, for at least a quarter of an hour a day. This exercise, he promised, would strengthen my vocal cords and would maintain tonal volume to the end of sentences. He said I would notice the improvement within a couple of weeks.

He was right. My sentences soon were ending with unfailing volume. But when Mr. Klauber was told of the improvement, he either did not take the time to listen to a recorded demonstration of it or did not like my voice even without the whisper.

In 1936 the position of director of talks at CBS became vacant and I applied for it. I was accepted. But I did not wish to give up broadcasting; and, as an afterthought, I inquired if I would have to do so in the new position. I was told that I would. Reluctantly, I declined the job. The position thereupon was offered to an attractive young man in charge of the student-exchange program of the Institute of International Education. He accepted it. His name was Edward R. Murrow. He, too, had to refrain from broadcasting, and did not begin his remarkable career on the air until he had been moved to London to head the CBS bureau during the war.

I met Murrow almost at once, and a friendship began that was to become one of the most important in my life. He wished me to continue to broadcast for CBS and planned to use me to do the nightly summing up of the day's developments at the Democratic National convention at Philadelphia in 1936. But he received a sharp order from Mr. Klauber that I was not to be heard over CBS.

By this time, my broadcasts for the BBC had begun; and they were to continue, with some interruptions, for nine years. For two of these years, I also did regular commentaries for the Canadian Broadcasting Company. Sir John Reith had chosen me because of my long acquaintanceship with the British public, as well as my familiarity with American and world affairs. And I can say without reservation that the assignment for the BBC was the most gratifying of my whole broadcasting experience. There was nothing else quite like it. I, an American, was permitted once a week to explain my country and its policies to the British, with whom I had lived for twelve years, and to do so at a time when they approached and then faced the most severe test in their history. As the crisis of the late 1930's came to a head, the attitude of the United States grew to be a matter of vast importance to the British, of which all of them were conscious. They felt that the crisis was one of life or death, as indeed it was. In this time, the Roosevelt administration was skillfully preparing American opinion for the abandonment of isolationism, not, be it said, out of tenderness for the British, but out of the increasing certainty that American self-interest made it mandatory. To be broadcasting to Britain during this time was to be sure of a wide attention. I was not in a position to make predictions or give hints about American intentions. But a record and understanding of the actions of the Roosevelt administration, and the changing sentiment in the United States, was news the British were eager to hear. The audience for the weekly American commentaries at one time was estimated to be well over thirty per cent of the entire population in Great Britain. And since the BBC also short-waved my talks to all parts of the Commonwealth, the number of my listeners may well have been unequaled for an international broadcaster. I was told that members of Parliament formed a "Swing Club" to listen to the commentaries in the parliamentary lounge on Saturday nights. I have in my files several cablegrams from Prime Minister Churchill, commenting on broadcasts he had just heard. An official of the household of King George VI wrote me to say that His Majesty was a regular listener, and desired an autographed photograph. I sent it, but I must admit I did not receive one in return.

The years of the most absorbing British interest in my commentaries were 1939, 1940, and 1941. By the end of 1941 we were in the war, and Great Britain was lifted out of its extraordinary position of tragic loneliness. The nature of the news from America changed, and many other commentators from the United States were asked to speak. The BBC, hoping to draw the Commonwealth together, dropped my own broadcasts for a year, to give the time to Commonwealth broadcasters and thus exploit the possibilities I had demonstrated, and so strengthen Commonwealth relations. But they abandoned this experiment within a year and invited me back. By then I was so burdened by my broadcasting schedule in America that I undertook to speak to Britain only fortnightly, the alternate weeks being used by Elmer Davis. I gave up the commentaries altogether in 1944 because of the press of my work at home.

Chapter 27 / With WOR and Mutual

To go back in time, when I was banned by Mr. Klauber from CBS in 1936, I called on Julius R. Seebach, Jr., at WOR. Probably in part because he knew I had been chosen by the BBC as its American commentator, he engaged me for a weekly broadcast. Mr. Seebach was an intelligent, friendly, hard-boiled Southerner, with whom I had unfailingly good relations. WOR served an area with a population of forty million and was the key station of the Mutual Network. My weekly broadcast was not at first made available to the network, and Mr. Seebach did not hold out any promise that it would be. He paid me forty dollars for it; and said that if conditions in Europe grew worse, he might add a second broadcast a week, which later he did. And then he added a third, fourth, and fifth, and I was made available to the network. But to keep my feet on the ground, Mr. Seebach told me flatly that I never was to expect a sponsor. I had to understand that I was one of the luxuries of radio, not one of its financial assets.

By the time I had a national audience, I was not so sure that I might not find a sponsor, and decided to employ an agent. I was recommended to Thomas L. Stix, a Yale graduate with offices in Rockefeller Center, on whom I called. It was an odd meeting. When I told Mr. Stix what I wanted, he looked bewildered and said frankly that he knew me only from reading my articles in the *Nation*. He asked what I was doing on radio. Then we had a pleasant chat; he agreed to study my problem and see what could be done. We did not draw up a contract, and none was ever written between us. I knew his rates; and as things turned out, he eventually brought me more income than he cost me, which is what one expects from a good agent.

Mr. Seebach was, however, mistaken about my not getting a sponsor. In fact, his own advertising office ferreted out the business. The sponsor was the General Cigar Company, which wanted to push the sale of White Owl cigars. Why listeners to my analysis of world news—surely half of them women—should be considered a lucrative market for cigars, I did not care to question. By that time, war had begun in Europe, and radio was experiencing its pretelevision experience of being the most far-reaching medium of communication man had ever known. Since the sale of White Owl cigars went up during my sponsorship by their makers, they knew what they were doing. They began, however, in a tentative way, buying time on only three stations for two nights a week. Even this modest beginning overjoyed officials at WOR. In their elation, however, they solemnly warned me not to expect ever to earn big money. They said I would probably never gross more than $40,000 a year. This again proved a wrong estimate, for in the last year of my sponsorship by the General Cigar Company, 1941, I was paid something over $87,000.

As a result of addressing a larger national audience, my name, by 1938, appeared for the first time in one of the polls of radio editors voting for what they considered the best programs on radio. I came in third after H. V. Kaltenborn and Lowell Thomas as the best news commentator. Later other names were to appear in these wartime polls and in the radio columns: Elmer Davis was one of the most competent and concise judges of events American radio ever produced; John Gunther, with his terse and knowledgeable discussions, was outstanding; Quincy Howe had both good presentation and solid intellectual value, as did Joseph C. Harsch. Later, Edward R. Murrow came into his own from London, and ultimately from New York; William R. Shirer performed outstanding service from Berlin. There were many others. Each had his different background, different style, different impact. Many of them were highly competent. It was a good epoch for commentators.

It was to the credit of the General Cigar Company that I was to say in my first sponsored broadcast: "My sponsor is permitting me to give my talks, as I have been doing for the past three years over this station and network, without any censorship whatever of my script." Commenting on this, *Radio Daily* reported: "This was said to be the first time such a statement has been made over a network." This was in September, 1939, just after the outbreak of World War II.

The issue of freedom of speech by broadcasters had not yet raised its head. WOR never interfered with anything I cared to say. Actually, the station employed no one who knew my subject as well as I, or who knew national policy better. I was given credit for taking my responsibilities seriously and so was left alone. It probably established an explicit principle for the first time for me to insist that my sponsor should have no control over what I said. But as I recall, there was no reluctance on the sponsor's part to forego such control. The company was willing to have it that way and raised no objections.

I was to give what was called a fifteen-minute broadcast, which meant about twelve and a half minutes, since commercials filled up the remainder of the quarter-hour. There was a brief commercial to begin the program, another to wind it up, and there was the middle commercial. I planned my broadcasts to allow for the middle break. I reported straight news for six and a half minutes, and usually discussed some one subject after the middle commercial for six minutes.

However, I found the middle commercial highly distasteful. It broke into the mood of listeners, jarred their nerves, and spoiled their concentration, damaging any rapport I might have established with them. But the middle commercial was so firmly embedded in broadcasting habits that I made no effort to have it omitted. I am quite sure the General Cigar Company would not have agreed to sponsor me without the middle commercial, for this ranked as the best selling time for the advertiser.

But I grew to abominate it. It always started with the booming words: "More men smoke White Owl cigars than any other cigar in the world!" The announcer had a deep, sonorous voice and launched this declaration with compelling force.

But I finally did get rid of the middle commercial—though it was not until May 10, 1940. That was the day the Nazis invaded Holland, Belgium, and Luxembourg, in opening their western offensive. For me this was the most poignant event that had occurred during my work. I knew I should have to write a tragic broadcast. The wanton, simultaneous attack on three peaceful nations militarily incapable of withstanding the Nazi assault was something that had to be discussed with solemnity and sadness. As I faced the task, I realized that my broadcast was going to be interrupted by the blatant roar of the announcer that "More men smoke White Owl cigars than any other cigar in the world!"

I decided against it. I telephoned the vice-president of WOR, Theodore Streibert, that I was not giving my broadcast that evening. Naturally, he was taken aback. I explained to him what the news was, and that I could not bear having a discussion of it interrupted by the booming statement that more men smoked White Owl cigars than any other cigar in the world. Mr. Streibert had been a teacher at the Harvard School of Business Administration, and later was to serve as director of the United States Information Agency under President Eisenhower. He was a cut above the administrative men I had met in radio, as he demonstrated by saying that he agreed with my decision. He promised to undertake to get rid of the middle commercial for that evening. I told him I hoped he would succeed, but assured him that I would not broadcast if he did not. He knew I meant it.

I wrote my script as though Mr. Streibert were going to succeed. But I did not hear from him until 7:00 P.M., three hours before my broadcast was due to be aired. He then told me that he had been trying all day to reach the man who handled the General Cigars account for J. Walter Thompson, the advertising agency, but he was out of the city. He finally had managed to catch up with him in Albany by long-distance telephone. Mr. Streibert induced the account executive to authorize the program to proceed that evening without the middle commercial, on the stipulation that the concession was not to establish a precedent.

As it turned out, no middle commercial was again used in any of my sponsored programs. General Cigars agreed to drop it; and my next sponsor, Socony Vacuum (Mobil Gas), wrote it into my contract that there should be no middle commercial. This for me was a deep personal gratification, and I hoped that radio as a whole would benefit. I was mistaken. For both radio and television have failed to give listeners the privilege of hearing their news and analyses without interruption. I believe the listeners have not raised an outcry because they have taken it for granted that the men in charge of radio and television really cared for their best interests.

Chapter 28 / A Day in Prague

I want now to turn back to 1938 and the Munich crisis. I was on vacation and in Europe when it came to a head, so that I did not handle its development in my broadcasts. But I knew the gravity of what was happening and turned up in Prague on the very day that Czechoslovakia mobilized as a protest against the surrender of the Sudetenland to Nazi Germany. There I encountered colleagues hard at work, among them some of my good friends, such as H. R. Knickerbocker, M. W. Fodor, John Whitaker, and Vincent Sheean. They were in constant touch with the Czech Foreign Office; they all knew President Eduard Beneš well, and Ambassador Jan Masaryk in London even better. They understood fully the infamy of the Munich agreement and its evil portent for the future of Europe.

On the evening of my arrival, my colleagues and I occupied a large hotel room with a balcony overlooking Wenceslaus Square in the heart of the city. Hundreds of young men already were marching and shouting in the square. Knickerbocker explained to me the position. Beneš had given in to the French and British on the Sudetenland issue, but his ministers had rejected the decision, as he foresaw, until it could be ratified by parliament. Beneš then told the French and British that he was powerless and could not keep his promise. Thereupon, the French and British told him that if he did not,

Czechoslovakia would be branded as the "guilty" party in any trouble to follow, and France's treaty to defend Czechoslovakia against aggression would not go into operation. Beneš thereupon called in his ministers again, and they bowed to the decree from Paris. Knickerbocker said that Czechoslovakia would have to fight, not only for itself, but for all of us and our children. Apparently, Beneš had intended to delay acceptance so as to force Hitler to attack his country. Then both France and the Soviet Union would be required to defend Czechoslovakia by their treaties with that country. But he had not succeeded.

Only by evening did the people in the streets have wind of the news. The first few hundred marchers in the square were shouting in unison "Down with Beneš!" and "Long live Sirovy!" (the head of the army). This number quickly grew, and in two hours the square was packed with thousands. Fodor thought they numbered at least a hundred thousand. It was like the crowd on an election night in Times Square, New York. We watched from our balcony, trying to gauge the mood of the crowd. Fodor remarked regretfully, "This is not a revolutionary crowd. I can tell a revolutionary crowd." Maurice Hindus, who spoke Russian, came up from a sally into the throng. He reported that he had heard the expression of only one sentiment: "We shall never give in!" News of the mobilization was now generally known. We saw an officer hoisted to the shoulders of marchers. We heard the cry: "Down with Hitler!" There was passion in the crowd, but it was difficult to measure.

Suddenly a new sound filled the square. It was a tremendous mechanized voice that emanated from the government's public-address system in the downtown area. It was making the first public announcement of the government's decision to surrender. "It is not cowardice that has moved our leaders to their decision," said the voice, and continued:

This is a decision that has pierced our hearts. Even the bravest man must retreat before the fury of an avalanche. God knows it often requires more courage to live than to commit suicide. God knows that no honest man can say that we were frightened and cowardly when we authorized the foreign minister to tell France and Britain: "We have chosen to sacrifice ourselves for the peace of the world, just as the Saviour sacrificed Himself for the welfare of mankind."

The loud-speakers exhorted the crowd to disperse. They were at first answered by shouts of anger and dissent. Then came another voice. It was that of a cabinet minister, pleading with the crowd to go home. Then still another voice spoke. It was that of none other than Jan Sirovy, Inspector General of the army. If he urged the crowds to go home, he probably would be heeded. He identified himself and made his plea. And thereafter the crowds began to thin out. In an hour, all passion had died away, and the square was empty.

Late that evening, I went to the home of the distinguished leading soprano of the Prague State Opera, Olga Forrai. I had made her acquaintance in London when I was working there and she was a soloist at the Covent Garden opera house. She also had been with the Chicago Opera, though I had never heard her there. She was married to an attractive Czech dentist, Frank Demant, and with them that evening was Peter Herman Adler, conductor at the Prague Opera, who later was to become director of the National Broadcasting Company opera in New York, and, after that, conductor of the Baltimore Symphony Orchestra. We talked in great excitement of the events of the day and their meaning to the future, not only of Czechoslovakia, but of the three with whom I was talking. I pleaded with them to make arrangements to go to America at the earliest possible time. All three were Jewish, and the shadow of Hitler already darkened the horizon of Czechoslovakia. Madame Forrai agreed with me; so did Mr. Adler. Dr. Demant was not so sure. If he went to America, he would have to take another complete course in a college of dentistry to be able to practice there. He already had his DDS, also an MD, and was loath to lose three years before starting out as a practitioner again. We did not settle the question that night, and I had to leave—it was long after midnight—to start the round-about route I had decided to take to make sure of reaching Vienna late that night. But they made their decision the next day, and did so in time to leave the country in safety. All three have practiced their professions with distinction in the United States, and I number them among my closest friends to this day.

I hurried back from Europe to New York, where I gave a special broadcast devoted to the Munich settlement, in which I openly accused elements in the French government of perfidy in their abandonment of their treaty obligations to Czechoslovakia. I rang out the most solemn warning as to the consequences of such a settlement. I was given an award for this broadcast by the Institution for Education in Radio, the first of several I was to receive from that organization.

I also went to Washington to see Secretary of State Cordell Hull. I had read in news dispatches that President Roosevelt was contemplating a public statement taking a share of the credit for the Munich settlement on the ground that he had cabled Hitler, urging him to be peaceable. Prime Minister Chamberlain was enjoying his brief period of exalted popularity for having assured "peace in our time." This may have affected some of the thinking in Washington. I warned Mr. Hull in the strongest language I could muster against President Roosevelt's giving a grain of approval to the Munich settlement. I remember saying: "Munich stinks! It will stink throughout history. And anyone who identifies himself with it will stink." President Roosevelt did not make any statement taking any credit for the Munich settlement; I must assume that others passed on the same counsel.

Chapter 29 / The Coming of the War

As I look back on the events of 1938 and 1939, the steps toward war appear so clear and inevitable that I wonder at there having been any misunderstanding of their meaning. On the whole, I read the events correctly as a commentator, though I made a few misjudgments of important details in my broadcasts. One mystifying factor in the equation was the Soviet Union. I believed it was in the interest of Moscow to line up against Hitler and establish a formidable deterrent against aggression, for the Nazi leader was more likely to strike against the Communists than anyone else. But Moscow had been cold-shouldered in the negotiations of the Munich settlement, and some strong anti-Communist predilections in the West were making themselves vocal. Still, Hitler was the arch anti-Communist, so that the ultimate association of the Soviet Union with the West was logical.

But to expect simplicity from Moscow in its dealings with the West had previously been an error. During the street fighting instigated by the Nazis in their campaign to overthrow the Weimar Republic, the Communists repeatedly took sides with them and actually fought with them in the streets against the adherents of the Republic. The Kremlin at the time was basically against Hitler, but it also was against the Weimar Republic because it was social-democratic. Obviously the Kremlin believed it was safer to deal with one antagonist at a time.

The British were busy all through early 1939 trying to negotiate an agreement with the Soviet Union. Even up to the stunning surprise of the Von Ribbentrop-Molotov pact, a success in the British negotiations was awaited. The Poles were against it; they wanted no truck with Moscow. But I thought the British-Soviet negotiations would succeed in spite of the Poles, and said so.

Now that this is all in the past, one sees that Stalin signed the pact with Hitler for two reasons, one being to partition a hostile Poland and annex a part of it, the other being to buy time to prepare for an attack Hitler might launch against the Soviet Union. This makes the perfidy of the Von Ribbentrop-Molotov pact no less venal, but perhaps a little less stupid than at first appeared. It would have served mankind far better for Stalin to have joined in deterring Hitler, instead of giving him the green light to make war. But when it comes to attributing blame for Hitler's war, France and Britain bear part of it for selling out Czechoslovakia at Munich.

As the crisis of war drew near, I had to work double time, broadcasting not only at my usual hour but also in the middle of the day. This meant writing and voicing 4,000 words a day, with a repeat of the ten o'clock evening broadcast for West Coast stations. I had never been so busy in my life.

On the afternoon of August 21, 1939, the news was flashed that Hitler was to sign a nonaggression pact with Moscow. It came later in the day. My commentary was already partly written. I had to spend half an hour on the telephone, confirming the news, and then write a new 2,000-word commentary in just under two and a half hours. I am not naturally a swift writer and usually go over my scripts repeatedly, interlining with improvements. I also rehearse them; I do not believe I have often gone on the air without rehearsing the commentary at least once. But that day there was no time for corrections or rehearsal. I judged the past aright, for I wrote a broadcast full of foreboding.

The next month, my sponsorship by the General Cigar Company began. After the long siege of working on simultaneous jobs and lecturing, it was a decided financial easement to be grossing $800 a week. I could give up the lecturing altogether, which had begun to swamp me. In a letter to my mother, written October 29, 1938, I said:

This last week I spoke in Delaware University Monday night; in Philadelphia, Wednesday; and Chicago, Friday. Friday I did a broadcast for schools in Britain, and then my regular British broadcast Saturday night. In addition I wrote a piece for Ken. In Chicago I missed my train, the first time I've done anything like that for fifteen years. I had to fly. I wrote all but the last minute of my British broadcast in the plane, with the typewriter on my knee, finishing over Buffalo sometime after midnight.

This week I have a still harder schedule. I broadcast over WOR tonight. Wednesday I speak for the Foreign Policy Association in New York, rush down for an evening lecture in Bryn Mawr, lecture the next noon at the Cosmopolitan Club in Philadelphia, and then get back in the evening to speak at the Harvard Club in New York. The next evening I speak in Columbia University, and the following day do my broadcast to London.

The rush will soon be over, and I shall try to quiet down to a little regular work.

With the General Cigar income, I could forego this kind of scramble. I could afford a secretary to copy my scripts and answer my mounting mail. I no longer had to worry about the expense of sending my children to college.

Also, I found that sponsorship gave me an unexpected kind of status. I no longer counted simply as a tolerated highbrow. I had become a business asset. And while there was an intellectual segment in America which I considered it a distinction to serve, my advertisers were sure there was a still larger public which I was reaching, and I was gratified to be serving it.

When I started with General Cigars, the company, as I said, bought time for me on only three stations on two evenings a week. When my contract came to an end in June, 1942, General Cigars was buying time for me on ninety-seven Mutual stations, though only for two evenings a week. My next contract, with the Blue Network, was to pay me substantially more; but what was more important, it was to buy time for me four nights a week. The fifth I kept free for my work in Great Britain and Canada. I was doing a fortnightly broadcast for each and a weekly cable on American affairs for the London *Sunday Express*.

The nominally large salaries I was paid really amounted to something less than they appeared to. By the time I was broadcasting for Socony Vacuum (Mobil Gas) over the Blue

Network, I received what seemed to me a fantastic sum—$2,500 a week to start, and later $3,000. My agent received twenty per cent of this; my taxes were in the top bracket; and I had to bear all my office expenses. By that time I had four assistants: someone to read current books and magazines for me; someone to read the newspapers; someone to edit the incoming news wire (for which I also paid); and a secretary. To be sure, after the deductions, the salary still was fantastic. This was part of the wine of success.

I worked ten hours each day on my commentary. I spent the forenoons reading the news and making contact with the sources of news—in the White House, State Department, War and Navy Departments, and Congress. I usually lunched with someone with whom I could discuss what was happening in Europe and the Pacific. By 3:30, I shut myself off and began writing.

I think it is time to say that I am not an abnormally diligent person; the work I did was motivated not so much by a sense of duty as by the responsibility of talking about the world crisis and the war to a large number of my countrymen. The nation was in grave danger. I knew it; everyone in Washington knew it. By now, I believe, some may have forgotten how close they were to disaster. But there was a time before Pearl Harbor when only Britain stood between us and a future dominated by authoritarianism. And after Pearl Harbor, there was a time when it appeared as though the Nazis, fascists, and Japanese militarists could not be prevented from winning the war. The victory in the Pacific was the fruit of a colossal effort against great odds. The victory in Europe was long delayed, and it was precarious up to the final year. For one thing, if the Allied air forces had not early bombarded Peenemünde, where the V-2's were being made—doing so at the urging of a still insufficiently sung heroine in the map-studying department of the British air force—the invasion of Normandy would have been impossible. One can only guess how Hitler could have been beaten if that invasion had been prevented. The bombing of German cities, unlike the same exercise in Japan, would not have brought victory. German industrial production actually went up during the worst of the bombing. I worked hard in that time because it was the least I could do. Countless Americans were working harder, millions of them at high personal risk, and relatively few were being rewarded.

I had a great deal of help from men in the administration and close to it. I received a flow of advice and information from Alexander Sachs, chief economist of the Lehman Corporation, whom I consider one of the wisest men of the time. It was he who later was to induce Dr. Albert Einstein to write the letter to President Roosevelt on the German work on atomic fission, which led ultimately to the establishment of the Manhattan Project and the coming of the atomic era.

I had access to several top leaders in the administration, including Secretary Harold Ickes, Secretary Frances Perkins, and Secretary Henry L. Stimson, whom I saw repeatedly, busy though he was. One of the friendliest and most helpful consultants was the Chicago attorney Secretary Knox had brought into the Navy Department as his personal assistant, Adlai E. Stevenson, and I was to watch his rise to eminence with particular satisfaction.

One of my friendliest sources in the government was Harry Hopkins, who never was too busy to answer the telephone or see me in an emergency. I visited him often, and during his illness talked with him more than once while he occupied the celebrated Lincoln bedroom in the White House.

I wish to add a comment about Harry Hopkins. I consider him only temporarily debarred from recognition as one of America's invaluable men, and am confident historians will rediscover him and his stature among the great world leaders during World War II. Possibly one reason he is not yet so regarded is that personally he was brash and indifferent to social niceties. He was playfully a kind of tough guy, talked like one, dressed carelessly, and made no salaams to the great proprieties which most men in public life take for granted they must do.

The public distrusted him for being a professional social worker who suddenly came to execute high government policy under the New Deal. That the policies he helped create turned out to be beneficial and preserved the American way of life, free enterprise included, will in time be recognized.

It was his position as President Roosevelt's chief assistant in World War II that, in particular, needs to be better appreciated and valued. He was not Mr. Roosevelt's closest friend, for the President of the United States does not have friends in the true sense of the word. He cannot have loyalty to individuals, since he has placed his loyalty to the country first. And to be his first assistant calls for humility as well as devotion, and an ability almost on a par with his leader's. In the innumerable conferences Harry Hopkins attended abroad as the President's emissary, he was blunt of speech, adroit of mind, and dedicated to the requirements of victory. It is well to recall that Prime Minister Churchill, in a burst of cordiality, told him that after the war he must come to live in England so that he could be given a peerage and be known as "Lord Heart of the Matter." As chief of the Munitions Assignment Board he had some control of strategy in the war; and because the United States was a member of a coalition, he had some control of world strategy. He was an invaluable liaison between the Pentagon and the White House. It was he who proposed General George C. Marshall to be chief of staff. He also was constantly concerned about the work of cabinet offices. His relationship with the President made such activities inevitable. The amount of work he did would have staggered a healthy man, but he carried the load without complaint until his cancer brought his services to an end.

Chapter 30 / A Visit to London

My most gratifying personal experience during the whole war came from a visit to Great Britain in July, 1941. I was invited by the BBC and the *Sunday Express* for a two-week stay. It was arranged that the broadcasts for my American program were to be relayed by short wave, and that I should make five additional broadcasts for the BBC. It was a heavy schedule. I did twelve broadcasts in the fourteen days, saw innumerable friends, old and new, and had luncheon with Prime Minister Churchill at Chequers on a Sunday.

The trip to England was made in a B-24 lend-lease bomber, unheated and provided only with bucket seats. The other seats on the journey were taken by air officers. I was the only civilian. I was awake all night, and spent much of the time thinking through a speech I would have to make the day of my arrival at a luncheon being given by the *Sunday Express* at the Savoy Hotel. I do not like making important speeches I have not written out. My mind pulls its ideas together more smoothly in written words. I usually can ad-lib without disgracing myself. But I believe I can read a written speech to make it sound fairly spontaneous, through the facility gained by broadcasting. However, there was to be no time to write a speech for the *Sunday Express* luncheon, and I had to work on it in the cold and dark of the B-24.

The trip was uneventful until we passed over some islands at dawn. They rose green and lustrous in the sea beneath us. I thought we were passing over Ireland. Evidently the navigator and the pilot of the plane thought so, too. But after Ireland comes England; and as we flew on, England did not come. That this should be was startling, to say the least. The explanation was that the islands we had seen had been the Orkneys, north of Scotland, and somehow we had missed Ireland altogether. So instead of making for England, we were headed straight for Norway. At the time, Norway was occupied by the Germans; and if we had continued much farther in the same direction, we should have brought a swarm of German fighter planes around us and been shot down. We were defenseless, for the B-24 was unarmed.

Fortunately, the pilot reasoned correctly about what had happened and turned back. Presently, England did appear. So we found our course and came down at an airport near Glasgow.

The Savoy luncheon turned out to be an impressive event. It was the first formal luncheon of any size given in London since the start of the war. The guests numbered 267, among them eighteen ministers of government.

I sat between John Gordon, editor of the *Sunday Express,* and the Labour leader Clement Attlee, then in the cabinet. Forty-five were seated at the long speakers' table.

One guest who had been invited, George Bernard Shaw, did not attend, but he sent a handwritten message on a pink-hued postcard, addressed to the editor of the *Sunday Express.* "I shall not be in London on the 10th," he wrote, "and if I were, I should hardly venture to be presented to Raymond Gram Swing, who must desire to be received by his contemporaries and not by the usual collection of spectral back numbers. If he ever heard of me you may assure him that I always listen with special attention when he broadcasts." The card was signed "GBS." His handwriting was distinguished by a legibility at his then eighty-four years of age that I cannot begin to match at my present seventy-six.

The week before the luncheon, the United States had landed military forces on Iceland to assure the safety of lend-lease deliveries. In my speech I played this up and christened Iceland "Gretna Green," for it seemed to me that American troops so close to Europe and for such a purpose represented a tie with Britain that went further than anything yet experienced in the war. I also praised President Roosevelt for his solicitude for the common people of America.

One thing I did not do was express my appreciation to Lord Reith (formerly Sir John), then Minister of Information, who sat at the speakers' table, for having made my broadcasts to Britain possible. It would have been a gracious and grateful comment on my part. I was later told that Lord Reith repeatedly whispered to the colleague next to him, "Now he is going to say it." But in thinking out my speech in the cold darkness of the B-24, I was absorbed with the political message I had to deliver to my listeners, and the opportunity I would have to say "Thank you" to Lord Reith did not cross my mind. It was a lapse on my part.

My speech was well received and fully reported. I have recently read it again, and must say I was disappointed with it. I have given much better speeches in the United States. I wish I might have done one of the best ones there. But I excuse myself on the ground that the better ones were not "thought up" in the middle of the night in an unheated bomber flying the Atlantic.

The luncheon at Chequers as guest of the Prime Minister on Sunday noon was the accolade of the trip. I sat at the right hand of Mr. Churchill, in a room filled with about two dozen diners, among them Harry Hopkins and Averell Harriman, who were in England on a lend-lease mission.

Ever since World War I and my experiences at the Dardanelles, I had hoped that one day I might have the opportunity to tell Winston Churchill in person how correct he had been about the possibility of forcing the straits, and how the advantages won in the great naval attack on the land fortifications had been thrown away. I knew, for I had been in the fort on the Asiatic side the night of the great attack, and could testify there were not enough shells to hold off the fleet, had it returned. Mr. Churchill had been condemned up and down his country for the catastrophe of the Dardanelles and the subsequent Gallipoli campaign. I had often wished that I might testify to him how right he had been. Now, by luck, I was sitting next to him at his own luncheon table. Naturally, I told him. The Prime Minister's mind was filled with other considerations than World War I, but he pulled himself away from them to listen to my brief story, which I am sure pleased him. By that time, of course, he knew quite well how right he had been, and how his overcautious contemporaries had thrown away the most decisive victory of the war. But he was pleased to listen to my authentic substantiation of it.

After the meal, the Prime Minister invited me to take a walk with him in the garden. This turned out to be the occasion for an unexpected and, I must say, somewhat disconcerting exposition to me of the terms on which Britain at that time could make a separate peace with Nazi Germany. The gist of the terms was that Britain could retain its empire, which Germany would guarantee, with the exception of the former German colonies, which were to be returned. The timing of this conversation seemed to me significant. Rudolf Hess, the number-three Nazi, had landed by parachute in Scotland less than two months before, where he had attempted to make contact with the Duke of Hamilton, whom the Nazis believed to be an enemy of Mr. Churchill and his policies. Hess was, of course, safely stowed away in a British prison. But if he had had anything fresh and authoritative to say on Hitler's behalf about a separate peace, his imprisonment would not have silenced him.

Mr. Churchill said nothing to me about Herr Hess. But he expounded to me the advantage of the German terms; and he seemed to be trying to arouse in me a feeling that unless the United States became more actively involved in the war, Britain might find it to her interest to accept them. I may be ascribing to him intentions he did not have. Later I was to learn that Hitler himself had proposed broadly similar terms to Britain before the war actually began. But I was under the impression that the allurements of peace had been recently underlined by Rudolf Hess, and that Mr. Churchill was impatient with the United States, lend-lease and Iceland notwithstanding. I did not have the impression that he meant me to convey what he was saying to Washington. Both Harry Hopkins and Averell Harriman were at Chequers at that moment. They would be message-bearers, not I. But it troubled me to have him give me his exposition, which must have lasted a full twenty minutes. For my part, I believed that the United States's interests made our entry in the war imperative. But I did not believe it would spur the country to come in to be told that if it did not, Winston Churchill would make a separate peace with Hitler and put his empire under a Hitler guarantee of safety. As a matter of fact, I told nobody but the closest associates about this conversation. I did not pass it on to anyone in the White House or State Department after my return.

Many years later, the opportunity finally came to me to ask Mr. Churchill some questions about this conversation. This was in Strasbourg, where he had come for a session of the European Assembly. I was there to see the Assembly at work and had run across Randolph Churchill, whom I asked if he could arrange for me to talk with his father for a few minutes. As always, he was helpful, and he arranged an appointment.

When I was alone with the Prime Minister, I told him I wished to remind him of what he had told me in his garden at Chequers, back in 1941. He said he had no objection. So I asked him bluntly whether the peace terms which he had outlined to me on that occasion had been offered at that time, directly or indirectly, by the Hitler government. He said they had not. So I asked him whether Rudolf Hess had brought any terms of that nature. He said he had not. What he had told me, he said, was the result altogether of his own presumptions, based on a knowledge of Nazi thinking as he understood it. In other words, he had been still cogitating what Hitler had offered before the war, and he wanted me as an American to cogitate it, to help speed my country into the struggle. What he did not take into account, it now seems to me, was that the United States was much more likely to join up with a steadfast and gallant Britain than one weighing the advantages of a peace with Adolf Hitler. President Roosevelt had gone the whole way from isolation to lend-lease with guaranteed deliveries, which was a long distance for a president to traverse in so short a time. I can understand that Mr. Churchill was impatient. But that was not a subject I cared to tell Americans about.

Chapter 31 / Communists and Fascists in America

A characteristic has developed in America—and undoubtedly has helped develop America—which I do not believe exists to the same measure in any land in the world. This is the civic activity of citizen groups organized in local and national committees or societies. It is an admirable and necessary activity. The constitutional contribution of private citizens to their own self-government is limited to the ballot and the right of petition. The propagation of ideas and the discussion of them is, in a sense, part of the exercise of the right of petition in national affairs, and a vital instigation to action in local affairs.

Under the surface of American political life, there has grown up a bewildering conglomeration of private groups, busily endeavoring to sway either community or national opinion. How these groups form probably has made more than one interesting study. A few neighbors or associates may find they want something done, or not done, in the community or the country, discuss it and say, pertinently enough, they ought to do something about it. So they organize a committee or a society to do it. This committee or society then holds meetings. This gives its members a somewhat larger platform on which to voice their views, and plans can be laid to spread the ideas in newspapers, or on the radio or television, or through further and larger public meetings. Officers are chosen, money is raised, and those identified with the cause to be promoted come to count as civic leaders.

In the eighteen years I had lived abroad, I had not taken part in any of these civic enterprises, or even realized the extent to which they existed. But coming back to my country, I found I had fervent convictions and wanted to see accomplishments which the activity of private groups could promote. I was alarmed by the symptoms of fascism in the United States and concerned over the general indifference to openly practiced race discrimination and the failure to establish collective bargaining in labor-management relations. Later I came to believe also in the necessity for some form of world regulation of atomic and other armaments, which would end the still unchallenged practice of nations resorting to war to settle dispute. So I had two seasons of extracurricular activity outside my broadcasting. One was in connection with the Council for Democracy, the other—after the war—with the World Federalists.

To many, the aims of the Council for Democracy will sound platitudinous today, for the dedication of those in public political life to democratic standards and practices, and the public insistence on them, has widened and deepened since 1940. Only in some sections of the country, where the full equality of the Negro is still obstructed, is there something of a lag. I find on reading over the publications of the Council for Democracy that they were outspoken and true to the American ideal, but I am somewhat surprised to realize now that they were called for at all. But they were. In 1940, in particular, many Americans were still so isolationist as to think tolerantly or even approvingly of National Socialism in Germany and fascism in Italy. And they were ready to see democracy languish in this country and defeated abroad if only American isolation could be preserved.

I do not remember the preliminary personal conversations that led to the formation of the Council for Democracy. The initiative must have come from Henry Luce, for he was ready to lend the services of C. D. Jackson, vice-president of Time, Inc., as its chief executive for a year, and to contribute $25,000 to get the Council started. Leonard Lyons wrote in his column of July 30, 1940: "A group will meet at the Waldorf today for the purpose of coordinating all the separate committees which have been formed in defense of democracy. The group is composed of Henry Luce, Raymond Gram Swing, John Gunther, Freda Kirchwey, and Robert Sherwood." The list must be far from complete. But that Waldorf meeting, in the best American tradition, led to the formation of an organization which, in the prewar and war years, stoutly and effectively propagated the principles of democracy.

As first conceived, the Council for Democracy was simply to be a co-ordinating body to pull together the work being done by a number of small organizations. But as it got under way, it became clear that a central organization supplanting many of the smaller ones would be more effective, and that is what the Council became. Later, after the United States entered the war, it became for a time the Council for Victory. Of both organizations, I was chairman of the board, and, for a time, honorary chairman. I was not in a position to devote as much time as the administration of such an organization needs, even if adequately staffed. The hard work during the first year was done by C. D. Jackson. Then Ernest Angell, the New York attorney, took over. Professor Carl Friedrich, of Harvard, was a faithful and inspired leader in his particular field of publishing studies on the workings of democracies written by specialists. He faded from the picture after American entry into the war, simply due to his own German origin. The roster of the executive committee of the Council included as distinguished a body of civic leaders as I can recall belonging to any private organization. The names covered two pages in fine print, and the members came from educational and religious institutions, journalism, the arts and sciences, motion pictures and radio, organized labor, the law, business and finance, and patriotic and social-welfare agencies. One could hardly conjure up a group of more certain patriotism and reliable judgment.

Europe was at war; the United States was not. The war in Europe was one of the least complicated wars to understand; it was one of both conquest and ideology, waged by fascists. Democracy in Europe was in the most dire peril, which meant that in time it might well be in dire peril in the United States, too. The need for a Council dedicated to the preservation of democracy was incontestable. It had work to do; and within its means, as I now look back on it, it did that work. There was some indifference to democracy in the United States, as I assume there always has been. There was little outright fascism, but an inclination among not a few to be tolerant of it, which was the equivalent of being indifferent to the defense of democracy. Certain dogmas of democracy, like race equality and collective bargaining for labor, had their outspoken opponents. When the Council held a rally in Carnegie Hall on election night in 1940, over which I presided, the Chicago *Tribune* described it as part of a drive to drag America into the war, "by the so-called Council for Democracy." The Council, the *Tribune* said, was backed by prominent pro-British figures; and as observers of the propaganda trend declared, "their sponsors are attempting to force this country into a military adventure on the side of England."

I had asked a number of prominent men to send brief telegrams to be read at the rally, saying we wished "to urge both political sides to get together under the next president to build a strong, free nation." It had been arranged that a Republican would be the chief speaker if the Democrats won the election, and a Democrat if the Republicans won.

The attack by the then-isolationist Chicago *Tribune* can be contrasted with one by George Seldes (a former *Tribune* correspondent in Berlin in my time there who then was considered an extreme left-wing writer), who called the Council a fascist organization financed by Henry Luce.

When, in 1940, the Soviet Union was attacked by Hitler and, so, automatically became an ally of the West, ideologies were scrambled into a hodgepodge of confusion that did not clarify until the opening of the Cold War by the siege of Berlin in 1948 and when the Soviet Union refused to join the Marshall Plan. During this time of confusion, I kept my values simple and did not stray from my faith in democracy. But I did not attribute to democracy virtues it had not yet won. To me it meant unfinished business, and the freedom to finish it. I had known Communists well during and after the war. I found all of them fixed in the belief that Communism meant the promise of finished business, which freedom would prevent from being completed. I knew the record, both good and bad, of capitalist imperialism. I also knew the conviction of Communists that anything that advanced their cause was permissible, no matter what its ethical price. Like many others watching the flow of history, I had had to ask myself if the era of democracy was ending and an era of Communism or fascism was taking its place. With social democracy I had sympathy, but I also wanted the retention of at least the central functions of the free-enterprise system. I imagined that an eventual merger of the two might be coming, though I could not guess how it would be brought about. But I had decided for myself before I returned from Europe that I could become neither Communist nor fascist.

My first work on returning to this country in 1934 was on the *Nation*, where I found that two or three staff members were staunchly pro-Communist, so that policy debates at meetings of the editorial board were often heated. The chief editors, Miss Kirchwey, Joseph Wood Krutch, and I, were not on their side.

I was identified for a time with the effort to help the Spanish Loyalists, but not after I saw the Communists take over the American organization and the movement, and finally the Loyalist cause in Spain itself. In the American committee, the Communists did not outnumber the non-Communists; they simply worked harder. When I realized what was happening, I got out.

I can give a quotation from one of my speeches made at this time which expresses what I thought of Communists. At Brooklyn College, the campus was ridden with them; and President Harry Gideonse, in 1941, asked me to deliver the commencement address, and in it, if possible, deal with the problems the college faced. I shall quote some paragraphs from that speech.

"If I understand correctly," I said,

some of the liveliest hours you have spent in Brooklyn College have been produced by a conflict between the advocates of Utopia and the defenders of an imperfect democracy. It is a conflict in which the Utopians have a certain advantage. You can always outargue the apologist if you can rest your case on a blueprint. For there are no imperfections in a blueprint. And there are imperfections in the United States, Great Britain, and in any country with a long or short experience in self-government. There are many of them. But what is notable about this country of ours is not its completeness, but that the opportunity remains to complete it. The Utopians do not see this, for their blueprint is complete. And as long as it remains a blueprint they seem to be winning all the arguments. When they come to do the building FROM the blueprint, they will make imperfections, too, and their dialectical advantage will begin to melt away. . . .

I do not believe that a Utopia can be made out of bad building material. I do not believe the Utopias are really ever made from blueprints. In social building, what is of value is the soundness of the materials. What each of us has to contribute to society is himself or herself, his honesty within himself, his faith in sincerity, his own sincere dealings. If any of you believe you are going to achieve Utopia by deceit, by raising false flags, by willful misrepresentation, by conscious misstatement, by guile, conspiracy, and fraud, and finally by giving over to someone else the power to think and judge and study the evidence for you, you know little of the ways of progress. For Utopia is no different from democracy. It, too, is never completed. The task of constructing it is infinite. If it were otherwise—as some young people today believe—they might succeed in their sophistry. It might be so that the ends justify the means. One might arrive at a destination of a perfect society, and then, in a great celebration, make a vast bonfire of all the lies and surreptitious trickery which had been resorted to in reaching the destination, and then start life anew on an elevated plane of social decency. . . .

If you think you are building a better society by temporary deceit, you will be astonished to find that deceit is not temporary, it is a permanent part of the society you have built. Social immoralities never buy anything but social immorality. They do not buy Utopia.

A senior had been suspended from Brooklyn College for Communist activity, and the pro-Communists were picketing the commencement services, with the police present to preserve order. This was before Hitler had attacked the Soviet Union, and the Communist movement was ordered to be antidemocratic. When Soviet Russia came into the war, the order was reversed. The problem of sorting out the truth then became complicated. Winston Churchill immediately accepted Soviet Russia as an ally. America sent lend-lease help. One of the actions which later was to be held against me in the McCarthy period was that I put down my name to sponsor a dinner—which I was unable to attend—given in honor of the Red army. This was three weeks after that army had joined the alliance. I thought then, as I continue to think, that the Nazis, fascists, and Japanese militarists could not be defeated without the services of the Red army. But it was confusing to have Communists as allies, and that confusion would have to be clarified after the first objective of the alliance—the defeat of the common enemy—was achieved. It could not be done while the fighting remained to be finished.

Chapter 32 / A Change in Sponsors

The negotiations which ended in my transfer from the Mutual to the Blue Network in 1941 were without reference to a sponsor, and I did not know until after they were terminated that Socony Vacuum, maker of Mobil gasoline, a Standard Oil product, was considering sponsoring my program. When the contract with Socony came under discussion, I asked for freedom from censorship by the sponsor and the elimination of the middle commercial, both of which the sponsor was prepared to accord.

But even with these assurances, I was not at peace with myself. In my boyhood I had been a reader of Ida Tarbell and had been thoroughly immersed in the muckraking of the time. Even though I knew that Standard Oil no longer indulged in the practices of the Rockefeller in the Tarbell saga, still I was not a little astonished, and indeed disquieted, to find myself on the point of becoming a broadcaster for Standard Oil. Early in the war Standard Oil had bought my broadcasts to short-wave to South America for a year, but this did not make me feel like a Standard Oil employee. Now I was going to be one, and I wondered if unconsciously I was slipping into a compromise with my own earlier principles. So, before my contract was signed, I asked for a personal interview with John A. Brown, president of Socony Vacuum.

He was gracious about it and invited me to luncheon in the Standard Oil executive dining room. This was at 26 Broadway

—the fateful address of Standard Oil in its unsavory past—
and as I took my place at the luncheon table, I found myself
sitting under a bronze bust of John D. Rockefeller close to the
table. Mr. Brown had invited some of his associates to eat with
us, and the conversation did not skirt upon the matters uppermost in my mind. But with luncheon finished, Mr. Brown took
me to his private office. He was a robust figure, with a healthy,
rosy complexion, a quiet and pleasant man, and a strong
one. He asked me what it was I had come to discuss with
him. I said that I found the terms of the contract as drafted to
be satisfactory, but that I had one misgiving. Mr. Brown asked
me what that could be. I said it had to do with my freedom to
say what I wished without censorship by the sponsor. "But," he
said, "that is already agreed to. It is in the contract." "I appreciate that," I said, "but I want to be quite sure that you understand what the language means to me." "I don't quite follow
you," Mr. Brown said. "I want it to be understood," I said, "that
I have the freedom to criticize Standard Oil in my broadcasts
if I consider it to be in the public interest."

Mr. Brown did not speak at once. Indeed, he did not move.
I suspected that the blood in his veins had turned suddenly
cold. He remained motionless and silent for a full three minutes. Then he asked quietly: "If you say anything critical about
Standard Oil, is there any reason why we shouldn't answer
you? Do you agree to that?" "Certainly," I said. "Then that
should settle it," Mr. Brown said, and shifted in his chair. He
rose, and shook hands warmly, indicating that the conversation had ended in agreement.

I record this episode because I think it marks a laudable
recognition by the executive of a great corporation of the value
and meaning of free speech in the life of the country in which
he functioned. I do not deny I was surprised by the soundness
of Mr. Brown's ethics. Possibly the story will not surprise others
to the same extent. But I consider it one of the best stories I
know about American big business.

There is a sequel to it which came close to being far from
agreeable. In the first week that I began broadcasting under
Socony Vacuum sponsorship, the newspaper *PM* carried a
front-page article written by I. F. Stone, reporting that Standard Oil was refusing to deliver to the Soviet Union an oil-
refining plant which had been promised. I read this with con-

sternation. If it was true, I felt I should have to say something about it, and so should have to celebrate my first week as a Socony broadcaster with the disagreeable duty of criticizing my sponsor.

I telephoned Harry Hopkins and asked him to find out whether the facts as set forth in Mr. Stone's article were correct. I told him about my plight, that this was my first week with Socony, and that I specifically had the freedom to criticize Standard Oil by the terms of my contract. I said that under ordinary circumstances I would not have handled the story, but I felt under a kind of special compulsion about it under the circumstances.

I still have the confidential memorandum I wrote at the time on Mr. Hopkins's reply. He phoned me late in the afternoon. "He said there was a great deal to the *PM* story," my notes read,

but that it was not correct as written. The Russians could not have new cracking machinery short of two years because it takes that long to make it. We could only give second-hand machinery. It was the Russians who dragged out for months in deciding to take this second-hand machinery in Texas and Louisiana. And it was to be remembered that we have sent huge quantities of aviation gasoline to Russia. But, he said, there was much in the *PM* story as to reluctance to supply secret processes to a future competitor, and there definitely had been obstruction. However, he did not think it would do any good to have the matter discussed on the air.

I felt his answer "took me off the hook," and relieved me of the responsibility to refer to the *PM* story.

I had only one further experience with Mr. Brown, which was likewise to his credit. It grew out of a broadcast I made on the subject of the available supply of nutrition in the United States. I was briefed for it by a nutrition expert in one of the California universities (whose name I regret not to have found in my records). The Soviet Union at that time was receiving a considerable amount of American butter under lend-lease. My broadcast stated that we had an ample supply of fats for our own population because of our production of margarine, which, I said, on my expert's authority, contained about the same nutritional value as winter butter.

This assertion infuriated the dairy interests in the country, and their official association wrote to Socony Vacuum that unless I retracted it, its members would boycott all products of the Socony Vacuum Company, no insignificant threat. Mr. Brown sent me this letter, along with his reply. In the reply, he said simply that under the terms of the contract Socony Vacuum had with me, the company had no control over anything I said in my broadcasts.

Mr. Brown did not add in his letter to me any requests or suggestions. I at once sent him a full report of my authority for my assertion about margarine, and that ended the incident. The dairy association did not resort to a boycott.

I might, at this point, make a generalization about my experience with censorship throughout my journalistic career. The only regular and overt censorship I experienced was in Germany during World War I, and this I considered legitimate. During World War II, none of my broadcasts was censored, though at the Blue Network they were read prior to delivery by someone on the staff. That was, and is, standard procedure in radio and television today; and I find it not only unobjectionable, but proper, since the station is legally responsible for what its broadcasters say. Indeed, the Federal Communications Commission regulations hold the network or station responsible for everything in its programs.

Once, in my early days as a reporter on the Indianapolis *Star*, I reported a sermon; and when the pastor demanded a correction of an assertion as I reported it, I was ordered to write the correction and did so. I had not misquoted the parson, and if I had had enough self-assurance in those days, I should have refused to write the correction.

Throughout all my newspaper service abroad, my copy was consistently used as written by the newspapers for which I wrote. I have recorded that a series of articles I submitted to the New York *Herald* on my observations in the Soviet Union was suppressed, likewise a series I wrote for the Philadelphia *Public Ledger* and the New York *Evening Post* predicting Britain's abandonment of the gold standard. I believe that the publishers were within their rights in not using these articles. They did not misrepresent me in not publishing them. They were scrupulous not to misrepresent me by deletions from my copy.

The question of censorship did arise in respect to my broadcasts to the BBC as soon as Great Britain was at war. Instead of my talks being received from New York "live," as had been the practice, they had to be transmitted in advance and recorded. The recording then was submitted to the proper authorities for censorship. It is difficult to strike sentences found objectionable by a censor from a broadcast and have it keep its unity. So I asked the BBC not to use any broadcast if any part of it was censored. This was agreed to; and for my remaining years with the BBC, only one of my talks had to be omitted. This one made a reference to a coming meeting between President Roosevelt and Prime Minister Churchill which the censor had blue-penciled. There was a lack of coordination in the censorship in London, for the *Daily Mail* had published the same report in London without trouble from the censor—so the episode was somewhat ridiculous. However, I do not question the right of governments at war to censor news and comments.

I am simply reporting that I had remarkably little interference with my freedom to say what I wished throughout my life as a journalist and commercial broadcaster. I suffered interference when I joined the Voice of America, where different conditions prevailed, but I want to testify that I have been remarkably free, and that my right to this freedom has been respected and protected all through my career as a commercial journalist, outside of the government.

I wish I could go on to say that my successors in television and radio are now as free. They are not. The right of free comment has been seriously abridged on the three largest networks, and anything said that affects any considerable and vocal contingent of the public produces a panic and retreat by the network executives. This is a perilous weakness in our communication system, and is not, I think, the fault of the public as a whole. I believe it knows that the freedom of dissent is one of the foundation stones of American life.

Nothing I have said in appreciation of the good fortune I have experienced in my career should be construed to indicate complacency on my part with the present state of radio and television. The treatment of news, perhaps the most important reason for my discontent, has deteriorated to a degree which I regard as hindering the function of American democracy. Radio and TV, to a substantial extent, have replaced the press as the source of news for the great majority of the public. But the newspapers, too, have distorted the object of free discussion, so that the conservative and reactionary point of view is often predominant in them.

Political comment on radio was largely uninhibited during its first years and throughout World War II. Then television came and clamped down on it, and radio, now by far the weaker of the two media, has felt it must follow suit.

The overwhelming popularity of television is, as it happens, a drawback to full and free news discussion, for television has never found a satisfactory formula for presenting news in depth and commenting on it. The news programs, other than documentaries, consist of a brief headline summary of the news, with its newsmen forbidden to express personal opinions about it. In this way the news commentary has virtually disappeared. It does not belong naturally on TV, for the picture of a single person discussing the news for more than a few minutes is likely to become boring. Even Elmer Davis's talents did not make his reading of a commentary before the camera arresting. The commentator must introduce pictures, guests, and discussion with guests, as Howard K. Smith did in his year of guaranteed editorial freedom with ABC. But if his subjects or his guests became genuinely controversial—to the point of being unpopular—as sometimes was the case with his program, the network executives cringed with fear of losing listeners or sponsors, and proceeded to exorcise the freedom.

The documentary on TV is supposed to redeem the medium from the guilt of suppressing free discussion. But since the disappearance of Edward R. Murrow's "See It Now" program, documentaries have not consistently been editorially vigorous. They usually consist of good pictures of a news situation with an array of the persons involved in it and a safe amount of exposition by them. But there seldom is any basic probing by them or the commentator. Eric Sevareid, who is Murrow's successor on CBS documentaries, is no coward when it comes to dissent, but his network does not encourage the expression of opinions by its staff, Sevareid included. And NBC and ABC have adopted the CBS standards, rather than try to live by better ones.

Radio is the more natural medium for thought and discussion. Since it appeals only to the ear, it requires the listener's concentration. If it could get on its feet financially, it could exploit this advantage over television and again assume an important place in the political and cultural life of the nation. News and music are in its true domain and do not naturally belong to television. Radio should be able to sustain a good and useful life developing the two to their utmost serviceability. But I know of only one national commentator of stature left on radio, Edward P. Morgan, sponsored by the AFL-CIO on ABC. And I imagine that the executives of the industry probably consider him a kind of dinosaur surviving in the outlands.

If the United States were internationally secure, if its domestic political life were wholesome, one would not need to lament with such concern the state of the communications industry. But we live in a time of the most profound change that mankind has ever undergone. It needs to communicate within itself and with all the world. The communications media themselves are symptoms of the change, but it is my guess that it is their executives who are in danger of becoming the dinosaurs. They are not aware of the future and its awesome perils and potentialities. They have simply substituted the amassing of wealth for the proper defense of man's right to know, to question, and to change with the times.

Chapter 33 / A Meeting with FDR

Though I worked in and out of Washington for ten years while Franklin D. Roosevelt was president, I held only one private conversation with him. I attended many of the half-jesting and half-serious news conferences he held around his desk in his White House office, and I asked my share of the questions. He knew me by sight and by name. It had been he who decided at the beginning of the war that I should continue broadcasting instead of taking a job with the State Department, for I offered my services to Under Secretary of State Sumner Welles, who told me he would have to ask the President to make the decision, and later informed me that the President had told him I would be more useful as a broadcaster. I was rated a New Dealer, and some of my friends took it for granted that I enjoyed personal relations with Mr. Roosevelt. But I made no attempt to see him and felt more comfortable not to be under obligation to him.

In 1936, I was critical of his decision not to press his proposal to enlarge the Supreme Court. At that time I regarded the Court, as then functioning, as the chief roadblock to social progress in the United States and wanted to see it enlarged by Roosevelt appointees. I thought President Roosevelt compromised too easily in this matter, for political reasons—and while I did not vote for Landon in 1936, I did not vote for Roosevelt either. It was only after the second New Deal was under way that my earlier enthusiasm for Roosevelt returned, and it mounted and continued mounting as war came and his capacities for leadership were unfolded. And as to the Court fight, I was to learn that I was mistaken, for the very threat of enlarging the Court had been sufficient to liberalize the tenor of its rulings after 1936.

I also was to discover that President Roosevelt's readiness to compromise for domestic political advantage did not carry over into the realm of principles in foreign affairs in an important instance, in 1942. This was something of an eye opener to me, for it had to do with recognizing the sovereignty of the Soviet Union over the occupied Baltic states, Latvia, Estonia, and Lithuania. The British had become convinced of the advantage of making this concession for the sake of good Allied relations with Moscow, and Sir Anthony Eden had drafted a treaty to that end. U. S. Ambassador John G. Winant had come to Washington to lay it before President Roosevelt for his approval. The British case was that the Western Allies might as well recognize the accomplished fact of the Soviet assimilation of these states, since to do so would promote better confidence in Western friendship in the Kremlin. The Baltic states had been part of the Russian Empire before World War I and had been carved out of that domain in the peace that followed to serve as buffers against the Communist regime. There were historic reasons, too, but this had been the outstanding one, and it was over this that the Communist leaders were most sensitive.

Mr. Winant discussed the subject first with Harry Hopkins, whom he found to be in agreement on the treaty. A long afternoon appointment for Mr. Winant with the President was arranged. They went on a two-hour drive through the capital. I saw Mr. Winant soon after his return. He told me that President Roosevelt was immovably opposed to the treaty. The President told him this was a matter of principle on which no compromise could be made lest an intolerable precedent should be set. Mr. Winant did his best to dissuade him, for the success of his own mission in London which, while not at stake, was at least affected. But the President would not budge. And by refusing to do so, he upheld the right of the Baltic countries to independence, along with all countries suffering a like fate. The Baltic states still maintain embassies in Washington, tokens of the decision Mr. Roosevelt made that day.

My one private meeting with the President was in the evening of May 24, 1942, and came about through Harry Hopkins. I had just finished a broadcast which was largely devoted to a speech by Hermann Göring on the ardors of the Nazi winter campaign in the heart of Russia. Mr. Hopkins called me at the studio. "How would you like to come over to the White House," he asked, "and meet the President? We have just been listening to your broadcast." Naturally, I said I would be there as quickly as my car could bring me. I arrived shortly before 10:30.

I was at once ushered into the President's office, where he had been working in shirt sleeves, his desk piled high with papers. He greeted me warmly and asked what I should like to drink. "I am going to take a gin and tonic with a slice of lemon rind," he said. I do not remember what Harry Hopkins took, but I joined him in a gin and tonic.

The President opened the conversation by discussing my broadcast and the difficulties the Nazis had experienced with the Russian winter.

Then he told me I had been asked to come over for a particular reason. He wanted my opinion of Elmer Davis as possible head of the Office of Facts and Figures, a position then occupied by Archibald MacLeish. I liked MacLeish and asked why he should be replaced. "Archie is a poet," Mr. Roosevelt said, with what seemed to me a tone of disparagement. I missed my cue at this point, and it did not occur to me until I was on the way home. I should have replied that John Milton, also a poet, had lost his eyesight working overtime as Latin Secretary to the Council of State under Cromwell. But I did speak up to voice my admiration for Elmer Davis. Mr. Roosevelt asked me if I thought newspaper correspondents would consider him a good appointment, and I assured him that I did not believe any colleague would be held in higher esteem. Davis's nomination to head the Office of War Information (replacing the OFF) followed within a week or so.

After talking about Davis, the President let loose what I should call a stream of conversation. I did not keep notes of it, but what interested me most was his account of the efforts he had been making to convert Winston Churchill to the idea of granting independence to India. As a talker Mr. Roosevelt went rapidly from one subject to another, almost by a kind of compulsiveness, not actually conversing with me or with Mr. Hopkins. I had the impression that in his way he was garrulous, which is certainly no fault, but it nevertheless astonished me to find a trace of it in as great a man as Franklin Roosevelt. Both he and I had a refill of gin and tonic. I did not miss the opportunity to tell the President to what extent he had been responsible for my broadcasting career in making his proposal to Sir John Reith for an exchange of broadcasts with the BBC, and I warmly thanked him. By midnight I knew the time for my departure had come, and I left. The visit had been a rare treat, and I knew that Harry Hopkins had engineered it as a special favor to me.

This was the only time I saw President Roosevelt and Mr. Hopkins alone together. I knew they were as nearly intimate friends as that term could be used to describe the association of anyone with the President. But I was struck by the deference Mr. Hopkins showed to his chief. He did not speak familiarly to him at any time and always addressed him formally as "Mr. President."

I met Mrs. Franklin D. Roosevelt on numerous occasions, but did not get to know her personally until after her husband's death. I was included in one luncheon invitation she issued to the news corps at the White House during the war. She was good enough to mention my broadcasts as among her favorite radio programs in an interview in the *Ladies' Home Journal*. It was after this that I made an attempt to arrange an appointment with her. I knew that a few of my colleagues saw her frequently, to their great professional and personal benefit. But her secretary vetoed my request.

Years later I crossed to France on the same boat with the United States mission to the United Nations, of which Mrs. Roosevelt was such a distinguished member. This was when I was commentator for the Voice of America. I had several long and memorable talks with Mrs. Roosevelt on this voyage. Later I met her twice in the home of John Gunther. I am sure she was the most important woman I could know, just ahead of Jane Addams. Somehow, she always said the right thing,

in the right words, at the right time, and did so with gracious-
ness. This is commendation that few deserve. Her service on
the Commission of Human Rights of the United Nations is of
enduring value, even if that code is long in coming into effect.
She led world thinking into channels into which it never had
flowed before. This was pioneering of a most valuable kind.

My esteem for President Roosevelt had not been without
certain reservations. I have mentioned his readiness to be
guided by purely political advantage in domestic questions.
He also said things to callers which apparently were meant to
be misunderstood as agreement with them in a way that
stirred the roots of my puritanical disapproval. But he was a
complex person, and out of this complexity rose a stature in
national and world affairs that both astonished and ultimately
overwhelmed me. I came to regard him as one of the greatest
men of his age. Though he was an aristocrat, he liked common
people. He enjoyed meeting them, and he put their welfare
uppermost in his domestic policy. When I had to write my
commentary on the day of his death, I was too deeply moved
to use more than two-thirds of my time and had to ask the
studio to fill the remainder with music. And having written it,
I threw myself on my bed and wept as I had not done since I
was a boy.

Eleanor Roosevelt's influence on her era also calls for special recognition. She was one of the three persons closest to
Franklin Roosevelt, all of whom had been active in social service. The other two were Harry Hopkins and Frances Perkins.
Many of the reforms that marked the Roosevelt administration
could be called social-service reforms, and the thinking of those
in his circle was predominantly social-service thinking. This
was peculiarly American, and may to a great extent have
saved America from didactic radicalisms of European type,
such as extreme socialism and Communism. I have the impression that Americans of the post-Roosevelt years have not appreciated this enough to bestow credit for it where it is due, on
Eleanor Roosevelt, for one, and on Hopkins, a close second.
Being a social worker of her era, Mrs. Roosevelt was not primarily a feminist. Thus she actually opposed equal pay for
equal work for women because she feared that it would bring
hardship to mothers who had to accept less than standard

wages to provide or supplement the family income. By now the social worker's outlook has pretty largely become the national outlook on social problems, something for which Eleanor Roosevelt and Harry Hopkins were as much responsible as Franklin Roosevelt himself.

Chapter 34 / 1944–1945

My contract with Socony Vacuum came under negotiation for renewal at the end of 1944. By that time the war in Europe was drawing to a close, and I believed that the center of news interest would disperse and not be concentrated in Washington, as it had been. I suggested to Mr. Stix, my agent, that he propose a new arrangement, one which allowed me for at least a year to travel and make my broadcasts from outside the United States. I do not doubt that the idea arose as much from growing weariness caused by the drudgery of the Washington broadcasts as from anything else. But it was not a plan on which Socony Vacuum looked favorably. If I wished to tell listeners about problems in foreign lands, the corporation was not interested in a renewal of the contract. I could understand its point of view. But I said I wanted a change, and the contract was not renewed. Socony thereupon bought "Information Please."

Thus my hope of financing a year of broadcasting from abroad disappeared, and my agent was not sanguine about reviving it.

The decision of Socony Vacuum not to renew my contract did not, as it turned out, greatly affect my earnings or stature as a broadcaster. The Blue Network had been working on a device for financing some of its programs co-operatively, that is, supplying the programs to local stations which then could sell them to local advertisers.

From the commentator's standpoint, the scheme was highly

advantageous, because single local sponsors could not exert editorial pressure. If they did not like what was being said, they could cancel, but the commentator might not even hear of it. The plan was put into operation shortly after my connections with Socony ended. The Blue Network offered me a contract for five broadcasts a week, guaranteeing me $100,000 a year, and then turned me over to its local stations. Small stations charged ten dollars a week and more for each program; in New York City the price was $750. I read in *Variety* in July, 1945, that 120 stations with 129 sponsors were taking my broadcasts, and mine was the biggest co-operative venture up to that time. The total paid by sponsors was stated to be close to a million dollars and I was said to be grossing about $160,000 a year.

As the war drew to an end, the problem of relations with the Soviet Union began looming up toward the large dimensions it was to assume. Some time before the discovery of nuclear energy, it already clouded the future. If there was to be peace, it would have to rest on the foundation of a workable understanding between the United States and the Soviet Union. These were the two great emerging powers; they would be virtually the only great powers; and unless they could collaborate peacefully, a war between them would be World War III. Great difficulties beset them as partners in such a co-operative responsibility. Communism was the religion of the Soviet bloc, and there could be no confidence that the Communists would show restraint in extending their power. We know today, almost nineteen years after the end of the war, that the Communists intend to dominate the world. They believe this is their destiny. We know that they long believed that they would come into their destiny through war, either with the capitalist countries or as the result of war between capitalist countries. We also know that the same kind of legal and ethical disciplines which the democracies have learned to respect do not appeal to them.

But as the war was ending, the situation was not the same as it is today. The Cold War had not begun. Nuclear power had not become the decisive destructive force of the future. The Western powers were allies of the Soviet Union; they had jointly won the war over Germany and Italy; and once Japan was beaten, they faced together the great issue of preserving the peace. As humans educated in the school of so dreadful a battle, they could not easily evade common action aimed at stabilizing the peace.

The agreements reached at Dumbarton Oaks to form a United Nations were certainly inadequate beginnings, and Soviet policy in Eastern Europe was open to suspicion. Prejudices against Communism agitated the Western countries. Those who then argued that peace could not be made and maintained with Communism as the Kremlin was practicing it may have been fully justified, but some historians probably will write about the period at the end of the war and immediately afterward with a modicum of forbearance toward Communist behavior. They can be expected to set forth that if the West did not trust the Kremlin, the Kremlin had some reason not to trust the West. There is one striking example of this. Secretary of State Edward R. Stettinius offered the Soviet Union a rehabilitation credit of a billion dollars, which the Soviet Union accepted. The acceptance, however, never came to light in official American policy-making. Notification of it was "mislaid" in the State Department for a full year, as ultimately was officially admitted. The action was no doubt personal on the part of the official responsible for it. That is, it was not known to the Secretary of State and the President. But the Kremlin would not know this. It wrote off the offer of aid as a hypocritical beguilement. And since the Soviet Foreign Office read American newspapers with zealous fidelity, it could record a spate of statements hostile to the Soviet Union. The anti-Communists in the United States at that time were particularly voluble. When the Cold War came to be openly waged, the anti-Communists of the days prior to it could and did contend that its coming was inevitable, and no possibility for peaceful understanding with the Soviet Union had existed or could exist. They may have been right. But that is hypothesis only. It was not knowledge based on experience, on which American policy could be firmly based. So long as there was some hope of co-operation for peace, the United States was obligated to try to cultivate it.

It was in this period that I was arguing on all possible occasions—though not in my broadcasts—that the peace of the world depended on the United States and the Soviet Union working for it together. Covering the conference in San Francisco, where the United Nations was organized, I had the opportunity to speak on a "Town Meeting of the Air" with Senator Tom Connally, Harold Stassen, Joseph C. Grew, H. V. Kaltenborn, and William Shirer, and used this as my theme. It also was the thesis of the Newton D. Baker lecture I delivered in Cleveland in 1945, in which I analyzed the different world then emerging from the one in 1918. The League of Nations consisted in the first place of eight powers pledged to collective security. In theory, keeping the peace depended on action of seven against one. Now the eight no longer were powers; only two and a half of them were, counting Britain as the half. The possibility of collective security on a seven-to-one ratio was not present in the United Nations. As the war drew to an end, only the United States and the Soviet Union were great nations militarily. And unless they found a way to collaborate, peace would not long endure. I had seen Communism and thoroughly disliked it, but to me that was not the first issue. I disliked war more. I believed that every possible effort had to be made to find ways to co-operate with the Soviet Union, and that failure to do so would be unforgivable.

At San Francisco I was only one of thirty-seven news and camera specialists from my own network, and the number of my journalistic colleagues was greater than the number of delegates. It was the most lavishly covered event in the history of international affairs up to that time. But it was not a congenial conference. There had been a doubt about the Russians even sending their Foreign Minister; and when Mr. Vyacheslav Molotov did put in an appearance in Washington en route to California, he received a tongue-lashing from President Harry S Truman, instead of a welcome. In San Francisco I listened to one high American official telling some newsmen, off the record, that the Russians were not to be trusted, thus actually stirring up distrust for them. It was an inauspicious way to go searching for peace, and, as I felt, peace was what really mattered. We had gotten along with Czarist Russia for a century and a half, despite its being the worst kind of a police state. I felt it was not the existence of Communism in a country that the world had to fear, but aggressive action by Communism to expand. What the world needed was the disarmament of nations, a system of law, and an international power to enforce it, which the United Nations might ultimately provide. But this certainly was not in view when the United Nations was established at San Francisco.

What now needs always to be kept in view is that a disarmed world with international control over disarmament has by now become policy espoused, at least formally, by both the United States and the Soviet Union. The Cold War has not yet ended, but both the great powers agree on what it must be like when it ends. The United States has to this time, 1963, not changed or whittled away from the principles agreed to with the Soviet Union and submitted to the United Nations on September 20, 1961. "The goal of [disarmament] negotiations," the two nations stated,

is to achieve agreement on a program that will ensure that a) disarmament is general and complete and war is no longer an instrument of settling international problems, and b) such disarmament is accompanied by the establishment of reliable procedures for the peaceful settlement of disputes and effective arrangements for the maintenance of peace in accordance with the principles of the United Nations Charter.

The program for general and complete disarmament shall ensure that States will have at their disposal only those non-nuclear armaments, forces, facilities and establishments as are agreed to be necessary to maintain internal order and protect the personal security of citizens; and that States shall support and provide agreed manpower for a United Nations peace force.

To this end, the program for general and complete disarmament shall contain the necessary provisions, with respect to the maintenance of military establishments of every nation, for

a) Disbanding of armed forces, dismantling of military establishments, including bases, cessation of the production of armaments as well as their liquidation or conversion to peaceful uses;

b) Elimination of all stockpiles of nuclear, chemical, bacteriological and other weapons of mass destruction and cessation of the production of such weapons;

c) Elimination of all means of delivery of weapons of mass production;

d) Abolishment of the organizations and institutions designed to organize the military effort of States, cessation of military training, and closing of all military training institutions;

e) Discontinuance of military expenditure.

When the Cold War ends, such a program might be carried out. It is utopian, but the men who drew it up and signed it were not utopians. They knew what would be required to assure peace to the human family. Their joint affirmation should be kept before every American and every Communist of the bloc countries as an objective. It is not a note of nonsense in a world of reality. It is reality in a world of nonsense.

These objectives are strikingly like those set forth in the encyclical of Pope John in April, 1963, addressed—something new in an encyclical—not to Catholics alone, but to all mankind, and appealing to men and women of every religion, and every political system, to create the kind of world order that could assure peace in the atomic age. The Pope advocated a central authority to deal with economic, political, and cultural issues; in other words, he went the whole way to world government, a fact widely ignored in the news reports that summarized what the Pope had advocated.

Having myself for a time been an advocate of world government, I was greatly struck by the failure of the State Department, in its praise of the encyclical, or the press, in its exposition of it, to call attention to this precise proposal of the Pope. I myself had come to believe that the maximum of world government needed was one that had the power to enforce disarmament throughout the world after it had been agreed to and carried out. I came to feel that a central authority ruling on the economic, political, and cultural affairs of all men would inevitably be authoritarian in character, and that a federation with full autonomy for all members in precisely these spheres of economic, political, and cultural activity would be highly preferable. However, I welcomed the encyclical for its promised support of the achievement of complete disarmament, and I am confident that it has been brought nearer by the remarkable and eloquent document from the Vatican. The issue for years to come is not whether the United Nations is to be an out-and-out world government. The issue is whether Communists and non-Communists can agree on disarmament and fulfill their pledges to carry it out. When that happens, a new utopia will have dawned, and the further evolution of that utopia can be left to those who live in its sunshine.

Chapter 35 / The Atomic Era Dawns

It had not been logic or good will that induced the Soviet Union to proclaim a policy of a disarmed world under international control. Soon after San Francisco, an event was to occur that would change the very nature of international relations, that would make obsolete the accepted right of nations to settle by force disputes not amenable to diplomatic agreement. Wars had grown progressively more devastating since the Civil War in America. Now they were to become so destructive as to threaten the survival of civilization itself.

News of the destruction of Hiroshima by an atomic bomb was the first confirmation that the scientists had succeeded in splitting the atom. The similar fate of Nagasaki followed, and the Japanese war came to an end. The nuclear age had begun.

Before going into the details of the effect this event had on me and my life, let me interpolate what effect it had on the mind of President Truman. Ten days after the first atomic explosion in the New Mexico desert—the test explosion about which he was one of the few to know the astonishing secret— he went to receive a doctorate of law from Kansas City University. None of his listeners could realize the special significance of what he said on receiving his degree. "We live," he said, "in an age of law and an age of reason, an age in which we can get along with our neighbors. Now we must do that nationally. It will be just as easy for you to get along in a republic of the world as it is for you to get along in the republic of the

United States." These were the thoughts that rose in his mind, along with the thoughts he must have had about his coming decision to use the bomb to hasten the end of the war with Japan.

I was on holiday at the time Hiroshima was destroyed, and did not go on the air again until three weeks later. I was as greatly affected by the atomic bomb as by any event in my lifetime. I felt that along with every member of the human race I was personally involved, and being involved had a personal responsibility. I was a news commentator with the duty of explaining the great issues of the times. This was, I knew, the greatest that had yet arisen. "Early in the morning of August 24, 1945," I wrote at the time,

I went for a long walk, in the course of which I came to a decision to announce that night in my regular broadcast that thereafter I should devote each Friday's talk to the influence of the release of atomic energy on our time. During the walk I saw certain problems clearly. The atomic bomb had changed warfare, and must change all social life. I recognized that I should have to discuss world government, since only through a world sovereignty could war be abolished and civilization preserved. It would not be easy for me to do this. As a news analyst I had never before espoused any cause or doctrine in my broadcasts, as I believe that I did not have the right to do so. Now I should do so because I did not have the right not to. The atomic bomb blew up any good reason I once might have had against taking such a course; I was driven by a larger logic into a lesser inconsistency. I could rationalize the decision by saying that the atomic bomb was the most important news of the age, and that discussion of it was newsworthy. But I knew quite well I was changing the concept of my work, and that I really had no alternative. I did not, I trust, puff up my own importance. What I value primarily is the freedom to express myself without outside interference, which to the credit of American radio—and my sponsors, I might say—I have been allowed and indeed encouraged to do. So I made my decision out of loyalty to my own vision of the truth. On that long early-morning walk I saw that the human race was having a single chance to survive, and every member of it must do what he could to use that chance. I could answer for only one member, myself.

The first twenty-one of these Friday broadcasts on the atomic era were promptly published by Harper & Brothers under the title *In the Name of Sanity*, and the quotation just made is from the opening of the introduction to that little book.

I did not tell anyone at the Blue Network what I had decided to do in my Friday broadcasts. The first news the officials of the network had of it was my announcement. I assume that the top officials did not listen to it, for I did not hear immediately from them. In fact, I did not for three weeks hear any reference at the office to my announcement, and then only noncommittally. I was neither censured nor praised. Ultimately, however, the network submitted some of the Friday broadcasts to the Institute for Education in Radio for a possible award, and in fact the Institute, on May 4, 1946, gave me two awards: one for news interpretation, one for furthering international understanding.

At about this time I joined the Americans United for World Government, which later was merged with other organizations with the same aims into the United World Federalists, which I served for a time as chairman of the board of directors.

This was my second venture as officer of a nationwide civic group. As I now look back on its program, I think it would have been wiser and indeed more accurate not to have used the far-reaching phrase "world government." "World federation" was an improvement, but even this suggested decisions by a central authority governing the conduct of individual citizens of member states on other matters than disarmament and keeping the peace. This went beyond what most of us thought practicable. We wanted peace. And we knew the way to peace was through total disarmament under international control. Since both the Soviet Union and the United States, in their joint statement of September 20, 1961, had agreed that this was their ultimate objective, it seemed to me that the work we set out to do was accomplished insofar as private efforts counted. The world situation had changed in that the United States no longer had a monopoly of nuclear power, and the Cold War was on. The Soviet Union may not have as great a nuclear power as we, but it has enough to destroy our civilization, as we have to destroy that of its people, and we live in a time of what I hesitantly call grace. Mutual deterrence of nuclear destruction is not automatic or complete, but it is in effect. A nuclear world war is unlikely—one hopes that it is highly unlikely—under present conditions. This mutual deterrence has bought for the human race time to solve the highly complex and sensitive problems of disarmament and international controls. How much time? Not much, for it is only until there is a proliferation of nuclear weapons, when the decision of peace or war will not rest principally with the President of the United States and the Chairman of the Soviet Council of Ministers. It is time enough to proceed with what most World Federalists meant when they launched their campaign.

It is to the credit of the United States that it took seriously its responsibility in possessing the secret of atomic fission, even though it did not at once understand all the implications. The Acheson-Lilienthal report, drafted on behalf of the government, recognized the desirability of an international monopoly of the production and use of atomic energy and advocated it. Bernard Baruch, representing the United States at the United Nations, made his celebrated proposal to the General Assembly to this effect. It may be forgotten by now that after this proposal was made, the Soviet Union agreed to inspection and control of all weapons of wholesale destruction without veto once the Security Council had adopted a program for the international control of atomic energy. The United States at the time insisted on a veto, while Mr. Molotov, then Soviet delegate, swept aside the veto as irrelevant. This curious reversal of the 1963 national positions no doubt was due to the consideration that at that time United States power rested on heavy armaments and the ability to make them, the atomic bomb in particular. Soviet power rested on its vast army. The United States was the country that would be subject to the most important inspection, something which the Soviet Union wished to take advantage of.

I was to experience many attacks because of my advocacy of peaceable relations with the Soviet Union. The Brooklyn *Tablet,* writers in the Hearst press, and the *New Leader* called me Communist or pro-Communist. I admit I was resentful, and I begged Morris Ernst, my attorney and good friend, to bring suit for libel. I was familiar with the British courts, where such libels could be severely punished. But Mr. Ernst always refused. He said that it was exceedingly difficult to win a libel action in an American court, and that my opponents would make the trial the occasion to publicize every conceivably disagreeable innuendo about my private life. He was sure I would lose much more than I could expect to win.

But if I felt unfairly mishandled by the passionate anti-Communists, I had far more than adequate consolation from the recognition my work was given from many sides. I had received the highest honors open to news commentators, including the DuPont and Peabody awards. Six universities and colleges bestowed honorary degrees on me—the one pleasing me most being a doctorate from Oberlin College, which had suspended me at the end of my freshman year. I was even given three votes by a panel of seventy-five advisers of *Newsweek* as one of the ten Americans who had made the most valuable contribution in the first two years of the war. In fact, I was the only person in radio mentioned.

Chapter 36 / Recollections of Einstein

When I was a guest on Howard K. Smith's television program in 1962, he asked me whom I considered to be the greatest man I had met in my professional life, and I replied that I had to choose among three, Churchill, Roosevelt, and Einstein. The choice between Churchill and Roosevelt was difficult to make because both had been great political and war leaders. I said I thought Roosevelt had been the greater humanist. But for Churchill's leadership of England at the start of World War II, without which it could not have been won, and because of his historical writings, I was inclined to place him first. I did say that I thought Dr. Einstein had more nobility, hence more spiritual greatness. And if I had had time to go into the matter, I should have said that I saw more of him in the course of my work than of the other two, and found him to be touchingly kind and thoughtful and of remarkable humility, a man imbued with generosity and devoid of vanity.

I wrote two interviews with Dr. Einstein for the *Atlantic Monthly* on the atomic bomb and the meaning of the nuclear age, one in 1945, the other in 1947, which permitted me to spend the better part of several days at his home on Mercer Street in Princeton. But I had visited him before, and he frequently wrote brief notes of appreciation for certain broadcasts. His residence itself was plain and homey, cluttered with books and periodicals like that of any elderly professor in a small college. I had seen other homes like it in Oberlin when

I was a boy. It badly needed a coat of paint, and the furniture was old-fashioned, but it was conducive to comfort and relaxation. Most of our conversations were held on the back porch overlooking a stretch of lawn.

But Dr. Einstein was not the professor type. He was unique. With his long, white, uncut hair, his drooping white mustache, his huge, expressive eyes, his deeply lined forehead, and his oversized nose, his countenance was not like that of common mortals, even professors. I often thought that he looked like a great Jewish prophet, and of course that was precisely what he was. His religion was not orthodox, since it would be perverting the language to call mathematics or physics a religion. But in this language he had opened the doors of the mind to the cosmos.

The very concept of relativity is difficult for the layman to grasp. It is a little easier for the layman to see the significance of the great Einstein formula that energy is equal to mass multiplied by the square of the speed of light. This formula is the key to the nuclear era in which everyone lives, whether or not he realizes how nearly incredible it is.

A visit with Dr. Einstein did not plunge the caller into mathematical whirlpools. He did not try to overpower me with his special knowledge. He loved to chat about current national and international affairs. And when the time for my visit ended, he often would escort me to the railway station, wearing sandals and no tie.

I believe the most characteristic experience I had with him was the result of a passage in a manuscript I brought him to read of one of the *Atlantic* articles. It was made up of our conversation the day before. I had inserted an idea that grew out of something Dr. Einstein had said, but which in fact I had expanded. I knew he would agree with it, and he did; but he had not expressed it, and he said that on that account it did not belong in the article. It was not originally his, he said.

This led me into a brief argument with him about originality. I must explain that Dr. Einstein made one feel so much at home that such an argument was conceivable. I had been reading something recently about creative thinking and how, as a rule, it always was derived from the thinking that had preceded it, and I argued with Dr. Einstein that originality was not an essential criterion. If he agreed with what I had written, that was enough. He beamed on me with his benign friendliness and said I was right; originality was not an essential criterion, and the sentence in my manuscript could stand. It was not until I had left him that I realized the impertinence with which I had addressed the man with the most original mind of his times, and his complete failure to resent it.

In the first *Atlantic* interview, Dr. Einstein, despite his formula that energy is equal to mass multiplied by the square of the speed of light, told me he was not the father of the release of atomic energy. "My part in it," he said, "was quite indirect. I did not, in fact, foresee that it would be released in my time. I believed only that release was theoretically possible. It became practical through the accidental discovery of chain reactions, and this was not something I should have predicted. It was discovered by Hahn in Berlin, and he himself misinterpreted what he discovered. It was Lise Meitner who provided the correct interpretation, and escaped from Germany to place the information in the hands of Niels Bohr."

I learned later that Bohr, in three weeks, went to New York, where he passed the information on to Enrico Fermi and Leo Szilard, who were working along the same line and were able to confirm the possibility of chain reaction with uranium. But I could tell in one of my atomic-era broadcasts how Dr. Einstein had written the historic letter to President Roosevelt, delivered by hand by Alexander Sachs, starting with the words: "Some recent work by E. Fermi and L. Szilard, which has been communicated to me in manuscript, leads me to expect that the element uranium may be turned into a new and important source of energy in the near future." He went on: "This new phenomenon would also lead to the construction of bombs, extremely powerful bombs. A single bomb of this type, carried by boat and exploded in a port, might very well destroy the whole port together with some of the surrounding territory." This letter was the first of a series of steps that led to the Manhattan Project and the development of the atomic bomb.

Dr. Einstein later told me that he had written this letter only because the Germans might develop the atomic bomb first and win the war with it if the United States did not already possess it. After Hiroshima, and in the years of the United States monopoly in possessing the atomic bomb, he was more disturbed by the ultimate consequences of its existence than its immediate significance. Some well-known individuals were in favor of giving the secret of the bomb to the Soviet Union, Henry L. Stimson among them. This Dr. Einstein opposed. He proposed instead giving it to a world government consisting, to start with, of the United States, the Soviet Union, and Great Britain. But he also wished the authority of this world government to be limited to issues of world security. That is, his proposal was similar in substance to the one the Soviet Union and United States ultimately subscribed to in the joint statement of 1961. That is to say that the international control of total disarmament, and the abolition of all nuclear weapons under such control, was what Dr. Einstein meant by world government. In his talks with me, he considered it the only way to be sure of preserving civilization. He did not advocate a world government dealing with local national issues or economic subjects.

But what he said was enough to get him criticized, even by many persons who considered themselves forward-looking, on the ground that he was unrealistic and too easily inclined to trust the Soviet Union.

Chapter 37 / A Change in Activities

It was in 1946 that my health began to fail, not precipitately, but sufficiently to force me to cut down my work. I had trouble with circulation in my legs and was subject to severe cramps, which sometimes set in after I had walked as far as fifty feet. I received first-class medical care and went under prolonged treatments, but the condition did not improve. So in that year I reduced my broadcasts to three a week; and Elmer Davis, being free from directing the Office of War Information, took over the other two, which was fortunate for my listeners.

It was after a long siege of ineffective treatments that my attention was attracted to a German refugee physician, Dr. Max Gerson, who undertook the treatment of a number of major illnesses by a stern protein-vegetarian dietary regime. Dr. Gerson had had the dietary supervision of the postwar Prussian army and was also a friend of Dr. Albert Schweitzer. His primary, and indeed obsessive, interest was to prove that cancer could be controlled and cured through his special dietary treatment. A good many of his cancer patients undoubtedly benefited from it for a time. John Gunther's son, who died of a brain tumor, and about whom he wrote his deeply moving *Death Be Not Proud*, was a Gerson patient for some time and actually improved to the point that he could go back to his preparatory school and graduate, though his other physicians refused to attribute the improvement to the Gerson treatment.

However, I responded to the treatment. My cramps ceased within six weeks after I went on the Gerson diet. I continued faithfully to follow the regime for nine months, and became well enough to count on doing three months of lecturing. I hoped to earn enough income by lecturing for two or three months a year to forgo broadcasting altogether and so spare myself its exacting requirements.

As to Dr. Gerson, I regret that he later came into disagreement with his medical associates in New York by claiming actual cancer cures in cases in which orthodox medical controls had been neglected, perhaps largely through his impatience. I shall always thankfully acknowledge my debt to him as a physician, but I had to disassociate myself from any assurance by him that he could cure cancer.

With my improvement in health, I set out to fulfill a season of lecture engagements, while Elmer Davis took over the remaining three nights of my broadcasting contract. The Blue Network made an undertaking to allow me to do a year of Sunday news commentaries in 1948, which I did. Thereafter, I did no more broadcasting until I returned to WOR during the Korean crisis.

I found lecturing to be a refreshing and instructive experience. It took me into virtually every state in the union, which by itself is an education. I was brought face to face with a large number of audiences, which every speaker knows provides two-way communication. These audiences, as a rule, were predisposed to agree with me and did not represent a sampling of the general public. But I had the experience, never to be enjoyed at the microphone, of knowing what response my words were receiving and what passages were being found arresting. No doubt, the genes of my academic and ministerial forebears were finally having their way with me. I also learned what was in the minds of some of the listeners from the question period following the address. The question period not only gave me an opportunity to explain details of policy and events for which there had not been time in the main presentation, but also to criticize or justify what listeners found difficult to accept in American policy.

The lectures also resulted in my meeting a great many people. There were receptions, dinners, and private hospitality. These can be tiring on top of the constant travel, but they proved to be one of the rewards of the lecture tour. I made not a few acquaintanceships which developed into friendships, some of which are precious to this day.

My first lecture tour lasted about ten weeks. I then had a chance to rest and travel. A visit to Panama, Colombia, and fabulous Peru, with its relics of ancient civilizations, gave me my first close-up of Latin America and its endowments and problems.

I also saw a good deal of the Caribbean, and for a time made a temporary home in Jamaica, an exceptionally lovely island physically, but beset by severe economic difficulties. I briefly visited the luxurious north-shore tourist centers, but settled down for longer stays in the less-known heart of the island, in a village called Mandeville, forty miles from Kingston. Here I found good company among both British and Jamaican residents. A vacation in Europe also became possible, with touring by car in France and Italy.

In 1948 came a less relaxing undertaking, a flight into Berlin with a cargo of coal during the airlift of that year. It was then that I was forced to recognize that the siege of Berlin was the formal opening of the Cold War, which postponed any expectations I harbored of co-operation between the United States and the Soviet Union for the maintenance of peace.

My flight into Berlin provided not only a setback to my early hopes for a world of law and order, but also a shock to my memories of this capital where I had worked most of seven years as a newspaper correspondent. I had known abstractly about the damage done to German cities by Allied air raids, but I was not prepared for the reality of the destruction. Large parts of Berlin still lay in ruins. My former office was a shambles; so was most of the center of the city.

My experience in Berlin was one that was to be repeated in other ruined and impoverished places. I was shocked that such dreadful havoc had been caused. Then I was shocked that after a week or two my eyes ceased seeing the ruination and my mind ceased being offended by it. By the time I left Berlin, I could have settled there without suffering any of the horror I felt in the first days. I had similar experiences in other demolished cities. I had it in places inundated by poverty, like

India. The first week or two was unbearable. Then I developed a kind of protective blindness—I ceased seeing what so sharply hurt me. I say that this also shocked me. It signified that I was easily capable of growing insensitive to the effect of disaster on my fellow-men. I wish this were not so. I have mentioned it to a number of colleagues, all of whom have testified to having had the same experience. I think all of them also wished it were not so.

I did a second lecture tour under commercial auspices, and in part of a third year spoke almost exclusively under the auspices of the United World Federalists. These were not as rewarding financially as the first, and I learned that there is an aphorism about lecturing. To speak on current events on a new tour, a lecturer must bring a new set of observations. I did have some fresh material, and my thesis about peace had to be modified. But I came to appreciate that lecturing as a livelihood would require far more preparatory travel than I cared to undertake. What I wanted to talk about most was not current events, but the need for complete disarmament under international control. I began to appreciate that the Cold War could not be ignored, and that the spread of Communism by subversion and conquest had to be curbed, the free world had to be sustained and defended.

But I also knew that the Cold War could not be a permanent condition, or the arms race an unending competition. And I continued to hold up as essential to human survival the early establishment of a world of law, in which war no longer was possible as a means of settling differences between nations, a world in which national sovereignties in the possession and manufacture of armaments were merged into a higher world sovereignty to enforce disarmament and uphold the law.

Chapter 38 / The McCarthy Period Opens

When Senator Joseph R. McCarthy, on February 9, 1950, delivered his speech at Wheeling, West Virginia, announcing that the Secretary of State knew of 205 in the department who were members of the Communist party, an episode was begun in American history which ended with his condemnation by a Senate committee in 1954. In those four years he throve as a demagogue, and frightened many, if not all, diplomats into failing to give their frank opinions to the government for fear of being falsely accused of Communist tendencies. The government thus suffered from a debility among diplomats. Employees in the Information Agency had to smother their political judgments lest they be pilloried by Senator McCarthy's congressional committee. It was a season of terror for which Senator McCarthy somewhat incorrectly bears all the blame. He became the name-symbol of the epoch, not by accident, for that was precisely what he wanted. He found the Communist issue when he needed something to make himself known and powerful. Through his exploitation of it and by his attacks on innocent persons, he did the United States more harm at home, and in democratic countries abroad, than any individual in modern times. Perhaps more harm was done by Alger Hiss, without whose activities there might never have been a Richard Nixon, made glorious for having brought him to book; and without the Hiss episode, McCarthy would have remained obscure and ineffective. So it is not easy to say which man hurt his times more, Hiss or McCarthy.

Even so, I do not think all the blame for McCarthyism was McCarthy's, for it existed before McCarthy gave it its name. There is today a different kind of McCarthyism under different nomenclature, and presumably there will continue to be a threat of this distinctive form of slanderous bigotry so long as the United States permits freedom of thought and speech, or until bigotry itself is reduced by the rise of understanding.

I am more than a little disquieted that McCarthy's condemnation by the Senate and his subsequent death have satisfied so many people that McCarthyism is over. For one thing, I consider that the condemnation by the Senate has given unwarranted satisfaction. It was based on an altogether peculiar sense of the importance of secondary matters. I am profoundly grateful that the committee went as far as it did. But I feel that it left out of account in its condemnation most of what Senator McCarthy had injuriously done. It ignored his roughshod disregard of civil rights and his irrepressible mendacity, and the fact that they existed while he was acting with the authority of the Senate. These transgressions were not specifically and helpfully rebuked at the time or ever. American principles and ethics were not strengthened by the Senate resolution of condemnation. The nation did not become healthier through it. It simply was rid of a menace because some Senate conservatives realized that their dignity was being sullied.

About six months after the epochal McCarthy speech about Communists in the State Department, a book called *Red Channels* appeared, published by the company that issued *Counterattack,* a weekly newsletter purporting to disclose Communists and those favorable to Communism working in radio, and attempting to have them blacklisted by the industry. By this time the country could be said to have been in a fever about the McCarthy charges. So *Red Channels* attracted wide attention. The book did not mention me, nor had I been mentioned in the newsletter at the time the book was published. *Red Channels* did not present proof that any of the persons listed in it were Communists or fellow-travelers. It simply called them that. The appearance of the book was an attempt by self-appointed judges to impose their unsubstantiated judgments of individuals upon the radio industry, and to do so for financial profit. The book both frightened those who cared for civil propriety and comforted those who suspected that Communists were infiltrating some of the key institutions of American life and wanted something done about them.

The Radio Executives Club of New York, to which most of the high-level administrators of radio belonged, scheduled a meeting to hear the two sides of the question, and invited T. C. Kirkpatrick, secretary-treasurer of American Business Consultants, publishers of *Counterattack* and of *Red Channels,* to discuss the book with someone from the performing side of radio. I was invited by Robert Saudek, then president of the club, to appear with Mr. Kirkpatrick and speak on the topic "Red Channels—Pro and Con."

My first reaction was that I was not the appropriate person to speak for radio performers. I did not at the time hold an important position in radio. I told Mr. Saudek so, and said that H. V. Kaltenborn, a veteran broadcaster, was a member of the executive committee of the Civil Liberties Union and so was the natural individual to ask. Mr. Saudek concurred. He invited Mr. Kaltenborn. But Kaltenborn passed the ball back to me, saying that he did not care to enter into a discussion with Mr. Kirkpatrick, but that I was the person best suited to do it.

I must here interpolate that Kaltenborn later was to become one of the most outspoken opponents of McCarthyism in the country, certainly the most fearless among the conservatives associated with radio, and he confirmed my respect for his courage and integrity.

I then told Mr. Saudek that if Kaltenborn would not do it, the logical person to ask would be Edward R. Murrow, then executive vice president in charge of news at CBS. So Mr. Murrow was asked, and he likewise passed the ball back to me. He did not care to meet Mr. Kirkpatrick, he said, but the right person to do so was myself. I told Mr. Saudek that I was not trying to get out of it, and if he could not find someone more suitable, I would accept the invitation. I laid down one condition, that Mr. Kirkpatrick was not to attack me personally in the discussion, and that I would not attack him. We both kept our promises, and the meeting went off decorously.

I am sure that some of the radio executives present ended

up on Mr. Kirkpatrick's side, on the assumption that he was doing the radio industry a service in identifying the Communists and pro-Communists among its employees so that they could be cleaned out. It was dirty work, and probably they were glad to pay somebody to do it for them. Mr. Kirkpatrick certainly presented himself as doing a necessary service.

My own view was quite different, and I have decided to reproduce my remarks:

Let me begin by saying that we are dealing with an unsolved problem. One of the questions we have to answer is whether Mr. Kirkpatrick and his associates and *Red Channels* are the right way to solve it. Let me state the problem as I see it. It is not only how the American public is to be protected from insidious, concealed Communist infiltration in the radio industry. Obviously that by itself is an undeniable necessity of the greatest urgency and importance. But there also is the need of protecting American standards and American freedom, both in radio as an employer and through radio as an instrument of democratic survival. There must not be Communist influence in American radio. But there also must not be the slightest weakening of genuine Americanism in keeping out the Communist influence.

I shall be brief in giving the reasons why I believe the approach of *Red Channels* is utterly un-American. It is a book compiled by private persons to be sold for profit, which lists the names of persons for no other reason than to suggest them as having Communist connections of sufficient bearing to render them unacceptable to American radio. The list has been drawn up from reports, newspaper statements and letterheads, without checking, and without testing the evidence, and without giving a hearing to anyone whose name is listed. There is no attempt to evaluate the nature of the Communist connections. A number of organizations are cited as those with whom the person is affiliated, but with no statement as to the nature of the association.

Furthermore, in addition to *Red Channels* and the news letter *Counter-Attack* which published it, the Kirkpatrick associates offer a so-called screening service to employers, whereby they will tell them whether the names of their employes are on any of their lists. So a profitable enterprise is put together, which makes quite a thing out of pretending to help keep radio safely American by these slipshod and strangely un-American ways.

I could use much of my time in demonstrating that *Red Channels* is one-sided in important particulars. There are cases of inaccuracies which I shall not try to enumerate. I don't want you to think that if

Mr. Kirkpatrick and his associates were more workmanlike I would approve of them. I wouldn't.

The point I want to make is that *Red Channels* does not show that there is any clear and present danger to the people of the United States if the persons it lists work in American radio. And to prove that is, I believe, the only legal or ethical reason that can be advanced in America for not employing these persons. The technique used is that of the blanket smear, against which, as you experts in public relations will appreciate, there is no adequate disinfectant or deodorant. A person once named, however innocent he may be, can never be quite rid of the taint, the taint not of his guilt, but of his having been named. It is the power of people using these methods that an ounce of insinuation outweighs a ton of fact. It is conviction by a private committee without even a trial. Certain persons are declared guilty without weighing the evidence and then punished for life without possibility of sufficient redress even if the most flagrant wrong has been done.

I am not going to use the cliché of saying that if the Founding Fathers had dreamed that this could be done in the name of Americanism they would turn over in their graves. For I don't believe the Founding Fathers would be in the least astonished, not about *Red Channels* or its author. There were some pretty feverish libellers and defamers in their time, and they threw their filth and disseminated their odors most widely and injuriously. A free society is free also to the unworthy, something the Founding Fathers understood quite well. It has always been the history of this country that small groups have tried to gain power by traducing innocent people; they smear their enemies, and play on all the current bigotries and hatred to give themselves an importance they could not otherwise achieve. Democracy is a free market, where anyone is able to seek power in any way he chooses, and can go on doing it so long as he can stay clear of the law. Not all the traders are scrupulous. But democracy is, among other things, a belief that in this free market the unworthy will ruin themselves and truth in time—yes, only in time —will triumph.

The problem before us, and before this country, is not the problem of trying to teach the publisher of *Red Channels* the democratic profundities, or to inspire him with a due regard for the rights of American individuals in radio. That is not the issue, or the way to go about it. The *country* has not chosen Mr. Kirkpatrick and his associates to guard over its ideological safety, nor vested in them the slightest authority to interfere with the conduct of radio entertainment or the nourishment of public opinion. He and his organization and committee chose themselves for that duty, and are doing so to make money out of it and exert power through it. The real problem is how much influence they are able to exert on those who *have* been given responsibility by the American public.

Frankly I think the method of *Red Channels* is indefensible. But I see only one danger in it (other than the danger to Mr. Kirkpatrick's soul), and that is that the men who control American radio should allow it to deflect *them* from a rigorous, rugged maintenance of true Americanism in the radio industry. So I think our real problem, after realizing that *Red Channels* is not the right way to safeguard the American public, is to do it in the American way.

Let me state some of the difficulties of dealing with our problem. Communism is a peculiarly evasive enemy. It operates behind a mask. And it is not a simple task to find out who is a Communist. The Communist will lie about being a Communist, and that tends to make everyone who *denies* being a Communist, a suspect, or at least incapable of being cleared of the charge of being one simply by the process of denial.

But this difficulty should not lead us to lose our perspective. For the danger to the American public and to radio can be pretty easily detected without knowing all the private secrets of every person employed by radio. Remember, it is only by reference to the "clear and present" danger formula of the Supreme Court that the law is entitled to risk infringing the personal rights of those who may happen to believe in the theory of Communism. Under the American system they are free to believe the theory, but they are not free to practice it.

What must be guarded against is whether anyone having to do with radio constitutes a clear and present danger to his country. Let me say at once that anyone selecting and interpreting news or in a position of influencing opinion, as by writing the scripts of plays, should be vigilantly watched, to determine if he is a clear and present danger to his country, by serving a foreign power. There are two categories of danger. There is this category of those who have actual influence over the public by their promulgation of ideas. Then there is a much lesser danger; those who are employees of radio as performing artists. I can mention a third category, which Mr. Kirkpatrick says nothing about, those who actually administer and control radio, the radio executives, or booking agencies, or advertisers in charge of accounts. Don't think I am pulling your legs. It would be quite sinister if Communists were finding their way into the administrative and operating end of radio. I do not *know* that they are, though I have heard that they are—I simply am trying to show the areas of danger.

There is still a fourth category of danger, another one, which Mr. Kirkpatrick's operations do not in any way cover. It is in the technical side of radio. The wrong man at the master controls in a radio station in a time of civil conflict might do irreparable damage. I suggest there might well have to be a security status for such posts, and security clearance for those holding them.

Here, then, is a grave problem. But let us not exaggerate it. There isn't much trouble about deciding whether anyone dealing with news or comment about news or writing tales and plays is commenting freely as an American, or represents a clear and present danger to his country.

If you know what the Communist line is in world and national affairs, it doesn't take much checking to find out whether it is being followed by this or that writer or commentator. It may be mighty easy to practice communism in secret but it is pretty hard to keep the secret by practicing it over the air. Anyone really versed in political theory, and who keeps abreast of the vagaries of Communist theory, can tell you whether this or that speaker is consistently following the Communist line. I should add, however, that judgment about it mustn't be left to political ignoramuses, or to self-appointed power-seekers, or to bigots, or to those who denounce as Communist any idea that they happen to disagree with. It can be done by the exercise of adequate judgment, and it can be done without working an injury on those who may hold views deviating from the extremes of orthodox conservatism. It can be done by the radio industry without fear or favor, and without reference to any book like *Red Channels*.

Now to the second category, the performing artists. There are two kinds of performing artists, as compiled by *Red Channels*, those who appear to *be* Communists, and those having connections with pro-Communist organizations. Here I recommend leaving it to the law of the land, and the law enforcement agencies, to decide whether a member of the party, or someone obviously an outright Communist, should be allowed to earn his living in radio in a capacity where he has no editorial influence on public opinion. Let the government determine what it regards as a security risk for performing artists. Let it decide whether radio is on a par with the State Department, or the Defense Ministry, where an employee has access to State and military secrets, or on par with a labor union, whose officer may not be a Communist.

Perhaps it may be so decided, but so far it has not been. And if the radio industry should anticipate that decision in regard to performing artists, it will injure persons in violation of their American rights.

The other kind of performing artist, the alleged fellow traveler, should be handled with even greater care. For if the outright Communist has not yet been forbidden a right to earn his living in radio

—the person merely associated with Communist organizations surely must not be forbidden to do so either.

Let me point out that *Red Channels* is largely a compilation of the performing artists. There are few commentators in it (and may I say that the two of these I know most about should not be listed at all, and it is an outrage that they are).

In reality *Red Channels* is little more than a blacklist of these artists which borrows a dignity it is not entitled to because it plays on the very true and present danger to America of Communist influence on American political life. Because Communism *is* a danger, *Red Channels* appears to be rendering a public service. The fact is that *Red Channels* really does not take up *much* more than the feeblest category of danger, the category of the performing artists, and does not even refer to the third and fourth categories I have named.

I should mention that Mr. Kirkpatrick and his associates have the backing of a committee which can recruit letter-writers and telephone callers to denounce the appearance of blacklisted persons on the air, they can flood a radio switchboard with protesting telephone calls, they can pretend that they represent a large part of the public. And if a radio executive or advertising agency is pressed for time, and frightened about offending a substantial section of the listening public, he may be tempted to shirk his own responsibility to inquire into the truth himself.

Nothing is easier than to gather together a small group of an identical bigotry and the same political hatreds, and produce telephone calls and letters by the dozens. Everyone in radio knows this. Every Congressman knows it. It is one of the facts of life of a democracy. And it is, as I said, nothing new in America.

But let me repeat that the pressure group is not the danger to American life, nor is the blacklist. The danger from these is not that they exist, but that those who have been vested with the power of safeguarding America yield some of their power to pressure groups and blacklisters. The weakness in American democracy would come from those who, having been given responsibility for one of America's most vital institutions, unwittingly, or carelessly, or timidly, yield some of their authority to people who are not entitled to it. Let the danger of communism be met, not by resort to stealthy weapons, not by blacklists, not by unventilated and often inaccurate charges, but openly and with courageous faith in the due process of law, faith in a civilization which fully protects the free rights of the individual. If, by some bleak and dreadful tragedy, American radio should come under the control of persons intent on producing a single conformity of thinking in America, it will not be the pressure groups or the blacklisters who will be to blame, but those now in charge of radio. They *have* it in their keeping, and what *happens* to it will be *their* doing and *only* their doing.

Afterward Mr. Saudek wrote me:

I am sure you will be greatly interested in the widespread favorable reaction to your appearance before the October 19th [1950] luncheon of the Radio Executives Club of New York. Many members and their guests have gone out of their way to tell me that they feel you made an extremely able presentation of your views on the topic "Red Channels—Pro and Con." To this I wish to add my full concurrence. This luncheon meeting certainly added to the deep interest in the subject, and the discussion went a long way to clear the air.

But I had little enough persuasiveness, for the blacklist grew in power inside the radio networks.

The tide of the new McCarthyism had begun to rise, and *Counterattack* continued its weekly appearance with its carefully phrased assaults on the men and women in radio it chose for professional extinction. Six months after the debate with Mr. Kirkpatrick, it got around to me, as I might have anticipated. Here is what it charged:

Raymond Gram Swing, radio commentator, has supported functions of the Communist magazine *Soviet Russia Today* and *Committee of One Thousand*. The National Council of American Soviet Friendship was cited as subversive in 1947; in late 1948 he was still listed as one of its sponsors.

In 1939 Swing wrote a letter to Secretary of State Cordell Hull urging him to extend the visas of Hanns Eisler and his wife to the United States, and said: "I would not presume to call Eisler's case to your attention if I did not believe Mr. Eisler worthy of asylum in a free country. I believe there is some prejudice against him in your department because he wrote music for workers' choruses." Hanns Eisler composed the official Comintern song. He is a brother of Gerhart Eisler, who was deported in 1948 as an alien communist.

In his broadcasts Swing often followed an appeasement line and defended Russian policy. He wrote in the *Atlantic Monthly* that the people of the United States "can choose whether to work with the Soviet Union as a partner or whether to surrender to memories and fears." In other words, Stalin's Russia has done nothing to impede US-USSR cooperation and friendship—the only deterrent was the attitude of the American people.

In its concluding feature, called "What Can You Do," it advised its readers: "Write to Edward Weeks, editor of the *Atlantic Monthly*, and chairman of the Peabody Award Committee and ask why such a large number of individuals they have honored have front records or are obviously biased or have a confused attitude about communism."

I shall take up these counts in their order. After the Soviet Union became an ally in the war against Hitler, I did sponsor (but did not attend) certain meetings held under Soviet auspices. I thought this was in the interest of winning the war. I still think it was. When the National Council of American-Soviet Friendship asked me to allow my name to be used as one of its sponsors, the Soviet Union had just become an ally, and I consented. I believed it to be in the public interest. When the war ended in Europe in 1945, I requested that the organization remove my name from its list of sponsors, and I assumed that it would comply. I did not discover until early in 1948 that letterheads with my name listed as a sponsor were still being used. This was before the accusation appeared in *Counterattack*; and before its publication I had my lawyer write the society that prompt legal action would be taken unless my name was removed from its sponsor list as I had asked. He received a reply saying that my original request must have miscarried, and my name would no longer be used.

The Eisler letter I confess was a bloomer. I wrote it before the war, and did so at the request of a musician whom I trusted and who assured me that Eisler was completely nonpolitical and was being obstructed in obtaining an extension of his visa by prejudice in the State Department. My musician friend turned out to have been completely wrong. So, I was.

Because I believed that understanding and co-operation between the United States and the Soviet Union were imperative if world peace were to be preserved, I was occasionally accused of being an appeaser. As a commentator I frequently had to explain what I believed Soviet foreign policy to be. I never "defended" it. Nine times out of ten, I disagreed with it.

The final quotation, from the *Atlantic Monthly*, was the republication of a sentence taken out of context from my Newton D. Baker lecture, delivered in Cleveland. In that lecture, there is not a breath of implication that American attitudes were the only deterrent to an understanding with the Soviet Union. I simply was advocating the understanding.

Actually, the accusations in *Counterattack* were mild, and even the worst one, my Hanns Eisler bloomer, dated back to 1939, long before Communist infiltration had become a national issue. But it was not the pertinence of the charges that mattered. To have been pilloried in *Counterattack* would mean to employers in radio that there was a probability of guilt, which would reduce the chances of employment.

However, long before the article in *Counterattack* appeared, I had been invited to join the Voice of America as "first political commentator." My clearance came through within a few weeks after the appearance of the issue dealing with me. But if I thought that my clearance would satisfy all skeptics about my loyalty, I was mistaken. The appointment was denounced in the Hearst press, the *New Leader*, and the Brooklyn *Tablet*, and I was to encounter quiet resistance by the coterie within the Voice which was to become Senator McCarthy's fifth column for his ultimate attack on the United States Information Agency, of which the Voice is a part.

The invitation to join the Voice had originally been extended to me by Alfred J. Puhan, who told me it had been decided that the Voice needed "a name commentator." Mr. Puhan was program manager, and politically he was known as a conservative. He did not seek me out because I was a liberal, but for a practical reason. All my commentaries for the BBC for nine years had been carried to all the Commonwealth by the foreign service of that corporation. I had been broadcast in Latin America for a year, in Canada for two years. And during the war, all my commentaries were rebroadcast abroad by the OWI in English and in sixteen foreign languages. While it was not true, as a gay but maliciously inaccurate profile of me in the *New Yorker* stated, that mine was the best-known voice in the world, I may well have been the best-known professional commentator. Mr. Puhan, as program manager of the Voice of America, was taking advantage of this.

Another of his motives was to have the principal "house" commentary written with a degree more of personal latitude than the rigid policy control by the State Department had been allowing. He told me that he had succeeded in getting for me a higher Civil Service grade, a GS 15, than ever before had been permitted for a writer. I was to have access to everyone I wished to talk to in the State Department, from the Secretary of State down. He also explained that there was a natural limit to my freedom, for whatever I wrote had to remain within the confines of United States policy, something that I took for granted. I was to deliver my broadcasts over the world-wide English service of the Voice, which beamed the commentary in English to Europe, the Middle East, the Far East, Latin America, and Africa. All the language desks were supposed to translate them and have them voiced and attributed to me. My schedule called for five ten-minute commentaries a week. The subjects for them would be agreed to by Mr. Edwin M. J. Kretzmann, the State Department's chief policy officer at the Voice, and the texts would be "passed" by him. That is, I became semiofficial.

Chapter 39 / Working at the Voice

Being first political commentator of the Voice of America was like no experience I had ever had as a broadcaster. To begin with, the Voice is a bureaucracy; and the difference between being part of a bureaucracy and of a professional journalistic enterprise, while difficult to describe, is not difficult to feel. In commercial journalism, I worked individually. I knew my superiors in the front office, my announcer, and producer. Everyone else let me alone. No one knew what I was going to talk about, and no one around the office said anything about it after it was over. I had a speaking acquaintance with many on the staff, but they lived as apart from me as I did from them. At the Voice I found I was working in a goldfish bowl. Since my broadcasts were circulated to the "house," they were subject to comment and criticism from anyone. Editors on the language desks telephoned quibbles about words and phraseology, and occasionally caught me in errors, which made the call worth receiving.

Regular staff policy meetings were held at which the participants discussed the news of the day and how it should be treated. These frequently turned into heated debates between the advocates of the "hard" and those of the "softer" line. These were legitimate discussions in good temper, and they frequently were illuminating, for the Voice employed among its top men persons of political, scholarly, and human insight. But there was nothing like them in commercial broadcasting.

One of the most debated issues was whether to "pour it on" in broadcasts to the Soviet Union and the bloc countries, or to present American policy more quietly and persuasively. Plenty of times there was provocation enough to "pour it on," and on many occasions I did not prefer the gentler approach. But generally speaking, I was not often in full agreement, for example, with Bertram Wolfe, a former Communist and now a strong anti-Communist, and one of the historical and ideological authorities at the Voice in combating Communism, nor with Alexander Barmine, chief of the Soviet desk and a former general in the Soviet military intelligence. I respected and liked them both. They were men of incontestable ability. But I was sure it was not wise to broadcast as pugnaciously as they usually wished at that time. In the debates they could fortify their arguments by reference to the Baltic states and the bloc countries, some of whose people undoubtedly wanted to be liberated from Soviet domination and would feel discouraged by any evidence of American patience with Soviet behavior. But the liberation of the bloc countries was far away, unless war should come. And the Voice also spoke to the rest of the world, and it could be argued that it was not politic always to be engrossed by anti-Communism.

However, the final decision was not Mr. Wolfe's, Mr. Barmine's, or mine. It was Mr. Kretzmann's, as policy officer of the State Department, and of the State Department itself, from which he derived his guidance. These differences were a new experience for me, and I thought then, and still think, they were valuable. Whether or not I contributed anything, I know they were useful to me.

But that is one of the few benefits I can identify from a journalistic enterprise like the Voice of America being managed as a bureaucracy. Since it was under the Civil Service Commission, it did not have the right to dismiss employees for incompetence; there always had to be a much bigger reason. The result was that employees felt secure and were not always driven, as in theory they are in private enterprise, by the motive of good performance. The scale of salaries was much lower than in professional radio, which meant that good English-language writers and broadcasters were hard to come by. The foreign-language desks, being staffed to some extent by expatriates of the countries being serviced, were not so much handicapped in this way, because the Voice probably offered as good a living to these men as they could find in this country. I am sure the great majority of these expatriates were devotedly American in performing their duties, and worked from a sense of serving their adopted country by their particular knowledge of the onetime homelands.

At that time Foy Kohler, later to become ambassador to the Soviet Union, was managing director of the Voice. It was an inauspicious time to be holding that position, for the undercurrent that later was to identify itself as McCarthyism was already in evidence, but, being underground, created problems which no director could effectively cope with. I respected Mr. Kohler and believe I enjoyed his confidence. He had supported Mr. Puhan's desire to have me appointed. And in addition to the duties set forth in my job description, Mr. Kohler wrote me a personal memorandum saying that he intended to call on me for editorial advice and that I was to feel free to offer it to him whenever I wished.

Next in command was Mr. Kretzmann, and my work called for close daily relations with him. We became better than cordial associates; we grew to be friends. Mr. Kretzmann was a graduate of a Lutheran theological seminary, which, while no factor in our relations, must have made me, as the son of a theological father, predisposed to understand him. But what I liked particularly about him was his cool, even temper, his clear mind, his patience and intelligence. And he knew his postwar Europe well, having served as political adviser to General Mark Clark in Vienna. By the time I returned to the Voice in 1957, he had become Deputy Assistant Secretary of State for Public Affairs.

I was to stay with the Voice less than three years on my first association with it, and in that time the two events that stand out most clearly in my recollection are the McCarthy crisis, in the course of which I resigned, and a month's visit to India made in 1953.

The Indian visit was considered advisable because the Voice was being snubbed by the All-India Radio, and good relations with that country, as the most populous democracy in the world, would obviously be an advantage to us, no matter how "disengaged" the Nehru government chose to be.

Chester Bowles was at that time ambassador to India and

had first proposed my trip. I stopped off for a day at Karachi, capital of Pakistan, on my way to India, and was guest at an official dinner given by the Minister of Information. I was to discover that first evening what would be the burning question of my trip: Kashmir. I was subjected to the most intense presentation of the Pakistani claims to Kashmir before, during, and after the dinner. I also was given access to the Pakistan radio for a guest commentary.

When I arrived at New Delhi, I had a talk first of all with Mr. Bowles. I had known him well when he was Price Administrator during the war, and found him in good spirits in his diplomatic post, as stimulating as I had ever before heard him, with alluring new ideas and proposals, one on top of the other. I learned from him that there was to be a meeting in a few days in New Delhi of American diplomatic and information officials of the Near East. I had not come all the way to India to spend my time with scores of American officials, and I begged to be excused from the meeting. What did I propose to do? I told Mr. Bowles I wished to see as much of India as was possible in a month's time. I had an invitation to visit for a few days at the residence of Sir Girja Badjpai, whom I had known well as Indian High Commissioner in Washington during the war. Though he had been a British official, he had been appointed by Prime Minister Jawaharlal Nehru first to the Foreign Office and then to be governor of Bombay. To see him was my only fixed appointment. I wanted to visit some of the villages where farm reforms were in progress; I wanted to go to Kashmir; to see the great Bakra Dam—second largest in the world, then halfway built; some of the extensive public works northwest of Calcutta, and, at opposite ends of the map, Amritsar and Madras. The ambassador undertook to facilitate all these visits. But he advised me to spend at least a few days in New Delhi, making contacts at the All-India Radio and meeting some men in public life and journalism.

One of my privileges was to attend a session of the Indian Parliament during question time—which was a period taken over from the British House of Commons. An official of the All-India Radio escorted me and kept me abreast of the questions as they were asked. At first only members of Mr. Nehru's cabinet replied. I confess that I did not understand a word of what was being spoken. It was English, but the English used even by educated Indians is not easily intelligible to an American. When Prime Minister Nehru came to answer questions, I understood him perfectly, for he speaks the pure Oxford version of the language flawlessly. I whispered to my escort that I was at last able to understand, and later he invented a story which went the rounds in New Delhi in which he said I had whispered to him in astonishment, "But he's speaking English!"

I found to my surprise that my name was well known to many educated Indians. I felt I was even better known in India than in the United States. This was owing largely to the American commentaries that had been broadcast to India by the BBC and my war commentaries sent out by the OWI. Being well known served me well with the All-India Radio, which rebroadcast all the commentaries I wrote for the Voice during my Indian visit. These were the first Voice programs that up to that time had ever been carried on the Indian radio, and this of itself made the trip worthwhile. It paid off for another reason, too, for I made most of my commentaries on the work India was doing under the first Five-Year Plan, much of it with American aid, and thus helped inform the outside world of what Indian-American relations amounted to.

My visit at the palace of the Governor of Bombay was fortunately timed to coincide with a state dinner being given Prime Minister Nehru, to which I was invited. I was housed in a commodious guest cottage in the palace grounds, only a few hundred feet from the cottage occupied by the Prime Minister. Sir Girja arranged an interview for me with Mr. Nehru, which was held in his cottage. Mr. Nehru was courteous enough to give me to understand that he remembered me from a reception held in John Gunther's house in New York two years before. What I recall most vividly from my talk with him in Bombay was the opportunity it afforded me to study his face. He had—if I may use the hackneyed and sentimental phrase—the most beautiful brown eyes I have ever seen in a man. They made it fascinating to watch him as he talked. He already appeared very tired, and the burdens of office were growing heavier by the year. But he spoke with a distinction of thought and language that confirmed his high rating among the outstanding leaders of men.

The state dinner had already begun by the time I reached my place, because my house servant had not called me punctually. I slipped into my designated seat without finding a table plan showing who the guests were or where they were seated. The lady on my left at once engaged me in a lively conversation, in the course of which she mentioned having served time in prison under the English. She was a congenial person, and I wished to know who she was. At last I threw conventions to the winds and asked her. She replied that she was Krishna Hutheesingh, Nehru's sister, and the wife of a Hindu journalist who had recently visited Communist China and written a not-flattering account of what he had seen. Her family lived in the Bombay area, and I was invited to their home, where I spent one of the most interesting evenings I enjoyed in India. Mrs. Hutheesingh was not in government service, like her sister Madame Pandit, whom I had met at the United Nations, but her husband and she were absorbed in political affairs.

Sir Girja Badjpai had a married daughter who lived with him, a vivacious and dark, tiny wisp of a woman. I had met her in Washington, and I felt sufficiently at home with her to propose that we go together to see "Quo Vadis," which was playing at one of the city's cinemas. I said I would ask her father, to make sure he approved, which he did, and he provided us a palace limousine to take us to the cinema. The incident is in no way notable, save for two details. One was that I discovered something that would not have occurred to me otherwise, that "Quo Vadis" is a propaganda film for Christianity, and the young woman I was escorting, not being a Christian, was to some extent put off by it, though I know she liked the adventure of seeing it. The other was that when we emerged from the theater, a thick crowd surrounded the palace car which was waiting for us. The people wanted to see who from the governor's palace had been to a downtown movie. It took us no little trouble to work our way to the limousine and get into it.

Bombay reminded me of Naples. The buildings that curve around the end of the bay are modern, and the city presents a more prosperous appearance than any other that I saw in India. New Delhi has broad boulevards and an array of red-stone and brick government buildings erected by the British in the last years of their rule. Calcutta, the largest city in India and one of the largest in the world, was something of a shock to me. It has many large business houses and office buildings, but these were dilapidated and sadly in need of paint and plaster. The poverty of the people encountered everywhere was depressing. I was there shortly after the sanguinary, sectarian fighting between Hindus and Moslems that followed the partition of the old India between the new India and Pakistan. Vast numbers from each country were migrating to the other, and creating social problems the authorities could not cope with. The day I arrived in the Calcutta railway station, 30,000 migrants were sleeping on its floors, and I had to pick my footing among the ragged bodies with care. The number of people sleeping every night on the streets of Calcutta was stated to be well over 200,000, which sounds just a little worse than it actually was, for the climate of Calcutta makes outdoor sleeping quite tolerable. When I asked the Mayor of Calcutta why the city did not work up some municipal pride and rid itself of its helpless intruders, he explained that the city administration was virtually powerless, since both the housing administration and the police were under the central government.

Everywhere I went in India, particularly when I visited officials and journalists, I was "given the works" as to Kashmir. There already had been fighting between India and Pakistan, and Pakistani forces were intrenched in one part of Jammu, and Indian troops in another part. The Vale of Kashmir itself was still under the Indian government, and its final disposition was to be decided by a plebiscite. Since most of its inhabitants were Moslems, the Indian government kept putting off, and finally canceled, the plebiscite, which it seemed fairly certain to lose. The Indian case presented to me was that whatever was done with the territories now occupied by military forces, the heart of Kashmir had to belong to India. I had heard the Pakistani side, and then the Indian side, and the best solution seemed to me to be to allow those territories now occupied by troops to continue to belong to the country occupying them, while the Vale of Kashmir itself should be made into an autonomous buffer state, guaranteed as to its independence by both India and Pakistan. This was in 1953, and the Kashmir issue has kept India and Pakistan at sword's point much of the time since. Only in 1963, thanks to Averell Harriman's and Ambassador John Kenneth Galbraith's persuasion, did India agree to hold negotiations on Kashmir with Pakistan, which, however, quickly collapsed.

The prime minister of Kashmir and Jammu was Sheik Mohammed Abdulla, who had replaced the Maharaja and proceeded with such reforms as redistribution of the land and the introduction of education. Sheik Abdulla was a veteran Indian independence leader and served in prison as many years as Nehru. In 1953, when I visited him, he had constant and cordial relations with the Indian Prime Minister and was rated among the outstanding younger men in the regime.

It was arranged that I should meet Sheik Abdulla when I went to Srinagar, the Kashmir capital; and I had good journalist's luck, for he was going into the interior of the province that day to visit schools and took me along as his only companion.

The Vale of Kashmir is justly celebrated for its beauty. It is interlaced with a network of waterways which makes it a favorite summer resort for Indians, who rent fully furnished houseboats for their outings. I was captivated by these resort facilities in the heart of the grape-growing country, and still think that spending a month in such a houseboat in such an environment would be an experience not to be surpassed in Europe or the United States. What makes Kashmir so remarkable, however, is not only its streams and horticulture, but its closeness to the Himalayas. The traveler's plane sets down at the airport at Srinagar, and his first vision when he leaves the plane is the lofty heights of the mountains to the east. I am familiar with the Rockies, the Alps, and the Andes, but these mountainous masses beyond Kashmir possess a magnitude and grandeur I had not believed possible.

I found Sheik Abdulla to be a six-footer with the figure of a varsity end on an American football team. Actually, he had attended college in America, and consequently made me feel at home with him. By the time I arrived at his office, he was ready to set out in his official limousine on the day's excursion. He explained to me that he periodically went to inspect schools, since he considered them to be one of the most essential interests of his government. We were to be gone for the entire day, which meant that I should see a great deal more of Kashmir than the normal traveler, and in the ride from one community to another we could talk politics.

At this writing Sheik Abdulla is in prison, having been deposed by the Nehru government on the charge of conspiring with Pakistan to turn over the Vale of Kashmir to that country. His arrest came soon after an interview he had with Adlai Stevenson, in which he told the American that he believed the best solution of the Kashmir issue would be the division of the militarily occupied territory between India and Kashmir and the creation of an autonomous state from the Vale of Kashmir, guaranteed by India and Pakistan alike. I do not know precisely what he said to Mr. Stevenson, but in the day we spent together he asked me how I would settle the Kashmir question, and I put forward the view he is reputed to have expressed to Mr. Stevenson. He listened, was silent for a moment, and then said: "I agree with you. Naturally," he went on, "I cannot say so publicly." He could not advocate this solution publicly because it was contrary to the policy then adopted by the Indian government, which was to keep Kashmir permanently Indian. But I thought at the time that what Sheik Abdulla was willing to accept would be better for India than a plebiscite, and that the permanent deferment of a plebiscite was hurting India through the world, and embittering its relations with Pakistan.

I now have an uneasy feeling that the removal and detention of Sheik Abdulla may be a scandal the like of which one should not expect from the Nehru government. The imprisonment for years of one of his closest political cronies because of his views on Kashmir appears difficult to justify. Whether or not Sheik Abdulla "conspired" with Pakistan I naturally am not in a position to know. But I do not believe that any conspiring he did justified the treatment he received. I cannot escape the impression that he was punished because he advocated some such reasonable settlement of the Kashmir issue as he did to Adlai Stevenson and to me.

Sheik Abdulla's interest in the schools was genuine. Wherever he appeared, he received a happy welcome from both teachers and students. They greeted one another like old friends. I do not recall that we visited any but primary schools, and I concluded that the school system was still in its early development. But he was keenly aware of the importance of education to Kashmir and thoroughly enjoyed watching and helping it grow.

During our conversation in his car, Sheik Abdulla told me how much land reform had meant to his country. Most of the land, he said, had come into the possession of a small coterie of court favorites of the Maharaja and his predecessors. If they did the ruler a service, they were rewarded by a gift of land, so at the time that India gained its independence, most of the useful land belonged to these owners, and was tilled by agricultural workers on a share basis, the worker getting half and doing everything, the owners getting the other half and doing nothing. When he became prime minister, Sheik Abdulla pushed through the local assembly laws confiscating this land and dividing it among the workers. It was done without a pretense of liberalism. The owners were simply dispossessed without compensation. "We could not afford to pay them," Sheik Abdulla told me, without a tone of regret in his voice. He did not conceal his enormous pleasure that the redistribution of the land had taken place. "The owners," he said, "really had no claim to the land. They were not left impoverished. They had piled up fortunes from owning it."

I was told in Srinagar by residents who knew Sheik Abdulla intimately that he lived a frugal life. His income as prime minister was meager and his residence was unpretentious. His office naturally offered opportunities to increase his income by selfish dealings, which I was assured he had not done. His neighbors said he was a dedicated servant of his province in the best sense of the word. He had political enemies who no doubt were gratified when he was removed from office and imprisoned. I repeat that I do not know whether he conspired with the Pakistani government. The charges have never been laid before the country in any detail, and he has not up to this time been brought to trial. That he was more loyal to his beloved Kashmir than to the Indian government may not be inconceivable, but he ranked high among the Indian patriots. And one of the riddles in the complex personality of Nehru is how he could treat one of his old friends so heartlessly while holding onto another, Krishna Menon, so obstinately and at such cost to his country.

Chapter 40 / McCarthy Attacks the Information Service

For Senator McCarthy the USIA and the Voice of America were steppingstones. They elevated him in the public's attention. He made news out of his hearings, for they were the first to be televised. His case against the Voice was not built up convincingly, but he was. When he had finished with the Voice in March, 1953, no conclusions had been objectively established. The hearings simply came to an end and Senator McCarthy moved on to other, more sensational, charges. But he was already a national figure, endowed with dangerous power, capable of ruining anyone in public office whose anti-Communism was vulnerable to public attack or misrepresentation. He had been strong enough to impose Scott McLeod on the State Department as Personnel and Security Officer, which meant that John Foster Dulles and the Eisenhower administration were compliantly on the defensive. He was loyally served by an underground in the State Department, at least ten or fifteen of them employees of the Voice, who swarmed to his office and whispered whatever tittle-tattle they believed might be used in the hearings.

One of the first charges against the Voice was the selection of sites for East and West Coast transmitting stations. The charge Senator McCarthy attempted to establish was that these sites were too close to the magnetic pole and would not be heard without the use of a costly amount of power, or, even then, not at all. If the cost was too high, this showed public money was being thrown away by left-wingers. If the stations could not be heard, then pro-Communists were conspiring to keep them from being heard. The two sites, Baker East and Baker West, actually had been chosen after consultation with engineers from Massachusetts Institute of Technology, which can be assumed to rule out either engineering or ideological incompetence. A strong point was made by the McCarthy committee of the fact that the chief engineer for the Voice did not have an engineering degree, and little heed was paid to witnesses who testified to his unusually valuable inventive ability.

Senator McCarthy early showed his talent for distorting the evidence to make it fit into the picture of evil he was trying to create. With one breath he would affirm his fairness, with the next he would disprove it.

Thus it was characteristic of his methods to misrepresent Reed Harris, Deputy Administrator of the Information Agency, because in his senior year at Columbia Mr. Harris had written a book denouncing the influence of football in colleges, in which, though he was not Communist, he said some radical things. Mr. Harris forthrightly repudiated the ideas he had written as a young man. He did it repeatedly, though Senator McCarthy sought to leave the impression that he still held them and hence was a pro-Communist in a high executive post in the Information Agency. The Senator pressed his case on the ground that Mr. Harris had not at some later time written and published a repudiation of the ideas in the book, as though this were a practice of young men who came to modify their youthful enthusiasms.

One of the charges brought against Mr. Harris was the discontinuance of the Hebrew-language service to Israel. As Mr. McCarthy asked questions about this, it was made to appear to be an act intentionally promoting Communism. The evidence, however, showed that the listening audience to a service in the Hebrew language was too small to be rewarding, while VOA broadcasts to Israel in English were widely listened to. Day after day Mr. Harris was subjected to Senator McCarthy's defamatory inferences, but he kept his temper and defended himself capably whenever given a chance. Shortly after the hearings he resigned, not because he considered himself implicated in disloyal conduct, but because he knew that the Senate Appropriations Committee would slash the budget of the Voice if he remained deputy director of the Information Agency. His resignation was a useful exercise of loyalty to the Voice; and when Edward R. Murrow was named director of the Agency by President Kennedy, he appointed Mr. Harris as his personal assistant.

Actions within any large organization are subject to criticism on account of judgment. Thus an editor of the news desk at the Voice was accused of pro-Communism because he changed the language of a dispatch about demonstrations in Guatemala to read that they were made by pro-democratic elements and not, as the dispatch had originally stated, anti-Communist elements. Senator McCarthy's questions tried to prove that "democratic" in Latin America was the same as "Communist." But since anti-Communists in Guatemala were not as numerous as the genuinely democratic elements, the news editor had been trying to build up the importance of the demonstrations. It may not have been the most enlightened editing, but the editor did not deserve to be branded before the public as a Communist.

Every large organization has a few questionable employees, and the McCarthy committee, through its spies, was able to disclose the views of an employee in the French service who favored a society based on free love. This philosophy was promptly publicized and somewhat ludicrously branded as Communistic.

Another target of the committee was the religious editor of the Voice, a man who had done his work effectively, but who was attacked because, as one witness said, he was an atheist. He was not. He was not orthodox, and his belief in God was of a nature that undoubtedly made his treatment of religious subjects more acceptable in non-Christian countries.

I am not going to review or even mention all of the charges brought in the McCarthy hearings against the Voice. Nothing was revealed in the evidence that pointed to the existence of Communist influence in the direction of the Voice, or to the existence of Communists on the staff. On the whole, the charges were contrived from trivial events. But the consequences of the hearings were far-reaching. The Voice itself was demoralized, no more so by Senator McCarthy's persistent misrepresentations and innuendoes than by the failure of the State Department to stand behind its employees who were being falsely accused.

The most inexcusable instance of this, in my opinion, was the dismissal of Theodore Kaghan, acting Deputy Director of the United States Information Agency in Germany. Mr. Kaghan's work in Germany had been consistently anti-Communist and of outstanding ability. But he had had Communist associations before the war, which he said "phased out" when he joined the staff of the New York *Herald Tribune* in 1939. He then joined the OWI, and at the end of the war was capably representing American policy in Germany against Communism as editor of the American-published *Deutsche Zeitung*. Senator McCarthy allowed him no credit for his work in Germany. The result of the campaign against him was his dismissal by the State Department.

I can testify that the demoralization at the Voice was "so thick one could feel it." In dread of McCarthyism few felt encouraged to represent Americanism in the place of McCarthyism. That was just as true of the State Department, with even more serious consequences, for an intimidated diplomatic service on whose judgment and reports the administration has to rely must not be frightened to tell the truth. Senator McCarthy denied that the morale at the Voice had been damaged. "From the information I get," he said, "the morale of the good Americans in the State Department is at an all-time high; that the morale of those who feel soft toward communism and have been acting soft toward it may be rather low and should be."

I assumed that Senator McCarthy's committee hearings would get around to me, for I had learned after they began that the heads of at least two language desks had issued orders that my commentaries should not be used. It was a sign of the fright that permeated the Voice that such insubordination should have gone unrebuked, as it did. But as it turned out, my treatment by the McCarthy committee was relatively gentle and harmless. I was not heard in public, but was called before the committee just before the luncheon hour. Most of the questioning was left to the committee's general counsel, Roy Cohn. He first asked me about my appointment, and whether I had not been named by the left-wingers in the management as part of a conspiracy to make the Voice a left-wing organ. My reply to this was that my appointment had been proposed by Alfred Puhan, program manager, a person of decidedly conservative political views. Then why had I been made the first political commentator? I explained that because of the world dissemination of my broadcasts by the BBC and the OWI during the war, in Canada by the CBC, and in Latin America by Standard Oil, I probably was one of the best-known broadcasters in the international field. A question was asked about the republication of one of my broadcasts by the Communists in Greece, which I had to answer by saying that since all my scripts were available, if the Communists chose to use one of them, I was not responsible. Senator McCarthy put in an unfriendly question or two; Senator Henry M. Jackson asked a few friendly ones.

The hearing ended in eight minutes. Senator McCarthy told newsmen that I would not be questioned again, so I had not been found useful in his campaign to defame the Voice.

With this appearance before the McCarthy committee over, one obstacle was removed to my resignation. I had come to the conclusion that failure to protest publicly against the treatment the Voice was receiving, from McCarthy and from the State Department, would be in a sense condoning what was taking place. I would not resign under fire. I also would not resign until the money for my salary had been appropriated by Congress and I had been reconfirmed for my position. By May 10, 1953, all these conditions were met. I wrote my resignation to the Voice and sent a copy to the New York *Times*.

The following day the *Times* published the statement that I had resigned on the ground that the agency had been crippled perhaps beyond recovery by slanderous attacks on its integrity, and that the State Department was guilty of spineless failure to stand by its own staff. I also had said that economy cuts by the administration had reduced the Voice to relative impotence. The *Times* added: "It was understood that the last straw determining the 'when' if not the 'why' of Mr. Swing's resignation was the forced resignation of Theodore Kaghan, deputy director of the United States Information Agency in Berlin." I did not mention Senator McCarthy by name in my letter, but no one would be ignorant of the author of the "slanderous attacks on the integrity of The Voice." But it was the failure of the State Department to stand by its loyal workers that seemed to me to make my continued association with it inexcusable.

Chapter 41 / Six Years with Murrow

The person who had most shared my concern about the events at the Voice was Edward R. Murrow, at Columbia Broadcasting System. This was before his celebrated "See It Now" program on Senator McCarthy, which, while it probably did not of itself turn the tide against the Senator, coincided with the rise of the public's disapproval of him. I kept Mr. Murrow informed about events at the Voice, as I saw them, and he several times offered me a spot on his 7:45 P.M. news program to say anything about Senator McCarthy I wished to. However, I did not think this would be a suitable way to combat the Senator. I was a State Department employee, hence a government official, and the only suitable weapon I had was to resign. So when I did resign, the first person I went to tell about it was Murrow.

He congratulated me and then asked me what I would be doing. It was indeed a pertinent question, for I had to tell him I did not have the slightest idea. To this he surprised me by saying that he believed he might have something that would interest me in his office. He had taken on some additional work and would need someone to write two of the commentaries on the 7:45 P.M. radio program each week before the close of the summer. He also spoke of the possibility of my taking over some additional work in his office. Edward P. Morgan, who was editing the "This I Believe" program, which Mr. Murrow broadcast each night, might be moving to another job, and I then could take his post, too. All of this was altogether unexpected. I regarded Ed Murrow as one of my very best friends, but it had never occurred to me that I might ever work for him. But before autumn, Ed Morgan had been made news editor at CBS, and I fell heir to the "This I Believe" program, in addition to the two commentaries I was writing for Mr. Murrow.

I had done a little ghostwriting before this for men in politics. I have told that I wrote two speeches I hoped Alf Landon would use in 1936. At the request of Harry Hopkins, I contributed about 1,200 words on foreign policy for President Roosevelt's main address in his fourth-term campaign—much of the rest being written by Dorothy Thompson. I should have been happy to be a ghost writer for Adlai Stevenson in his 1952 campaign, and there was some discussion of it, but it did not reach any conclusion. Ghostwriting has become a respectable and indeed necessary function in American public life. I recognize there is a technical difference between ghostwriting for a politician and for a fellow-commentator. But Ed Murrow and I saw public affairs eye to eye; and at the time I wrote commentaries for him, I was saying what I would have said on my own program and saying it to a larger audience than would otherwise have been available to me at the time. He did not give me orders what to write. We arrived at the topic of the commentary in a most informal way. Usually I would consult with him in the morning and tell him what I thought the possible themes were, in the light of the news, and what I would suggest saying about them. He then would express his preference. He would sometimes suggest a theme of his own, but if I did not like it I was under no compulsion to use it. Later, when I wrote most of the commentaries, excepting an occasional one of his own and those supplied by correspondents in Europe, and had my headquarters in Washington, our consultation was held by long-distance telephone. I doubt if many ghost writers are in such close fellowship with the speakers for whom they write. Collaboration with Ed Murrow always was based on the understanding we shared on public issues and our trust in each other's judgment. And it was made particularly palatable by the close friendship between us.

By this time Mr. Murrow had become the most influential

as well as the busiest performer in radio and television. His most important program was "See It Now," produced by Fred W. Friendly. Between them, they created a weekly documentary on public affairs that set a standard that in my opinion has only been equaled, on occasion, by Howard K. Smith and Eric Sevareid. His weekly "Person to Person" program did not aspire to the intellectual and political importance of "This I Believe," and on that account was more popular. He himself considered his daily 7:45 P.M. radio program the most important segment of his work. And, in addition, he introduced the statements on the daily "This I Believe" program.

When "This I Believe" was discontinued after the tragic death of Ward Wheelock, its personal sponsor, I became free to write all the commentaries, as well as to collaborate on a few of the "See It Now" programs.

The most interesting of the television programs in which I had a part was the one on automation, for it gave me my first acute sense of the changes ahead in industrial production and of the problems created in employment. It also led me to inform myself on the progress of automation in the Soviet Union and to examine the rapid rise of education in that country. I suggested that the automation program end with a quick review of the Soviet Union's remarkable progress in education and the challenge that this implied to the United States. Mr. Murrow and Mr. Friendly wished to enlist the services of Dr. Vannevar Bush as the chief spokesman on the program, and sent me to Boston to outline to him my ideas and ask him if he cared to co-operate. He listened to my analysis of the Soviet challenge with obvious disagreement. "Are you out of your mind?" he asked me, when I had ended my exposition. He assured me that automation and education would not make the Soviet Union a challenge to us. Naturally, I reported his opinion—along with the "are you out of your mind" question —to Mr. Murrow and Mr. Friendly, and they decided to leave the Soviet Union out of the American presentation. But they did promise that they would do a later program on the progress of education and automation in the Soviet Union, and would schedule it for the early autumn. As things turned out, this documentary was not made that summer, as it had to be if it were to be used in the autumn. But if it had been used at the time proposed, it would have appeared just before the sensational launching of Sputnik. And that would have made it as timely and useful a documentary as one could possibly aspire to.

Ward Wheelock, who conceived the "This I Believe" program, was a Philadelphia advertising agent who was known on Madison Avenue because he had the lucrative Campbell Soup account. His interest in obtaining and publicizing the personal beliefs of common and unusual persons was altogether unselfish, and I was told that he had come upon the idea after a tragedy in his family. He first consulted Mr. Murrow about it and obtained his consent to introduce the speakers. Then he offered the program to CBS, himself assuming the annual cost, which probably ran to about $75,000.

The year that I edited it was marked by an innovation in using the beliefs of twenty immortals, written by authorities on their lives and works. For example, we presented Confucius, written by Will Durant; Socrates, by Gilbert Murray; Thomas Jefferson, by Claude Bowers; Simón Bolívar, by Salvador de Madariaga; Lincoln, by Paul M. Angle; Marie Curie, by Eve Curie; and Gandhi, by Louis Fischer. The contemporary contributors included such notables as Bernard Baruch, Bernard Berenson, Aneurin Bevan, Chester Bowles, Ralph Bunche, Paul H. Douglas, John Gunther, Dag Hammarskjöld, Joseph C. Harsch, Alfred M. Landon, Alfred Noyes, Carl Sandburg, Adlai Stevenson, Harry S Truman, and a host of others. The statements of their beliefs were of such interest that the book of them produced in 1954 was the eighth-best-selling nonfiction work published that year.

The program came to an end because of Mr. Wheelock's untimely death. He owned an eighty-foot yacht and was on the way to the Caribbean with a party of friends, including a Philadelphia banker and his own wife and one of his sons. The yacht had gone into Bermuda to escape a storm. Mr. Wheelock evidently believed that he could avoid the storm by heading south, and so set out from Bermuda. It was the last that was heard of his yacht and its passengers and crew. The Navy searched the Atlantic down to the Bahama Islands, but never found a trace of the vessel.

That was the end of the program, for CBS decided not to continue it at its own expense, which I regarded as a highly commercial application of economy. I was particularly distressed at the interruption of the work of my staff, since we were compiling a "This I Believe" of world figures of all nations, and had about two-thirds of the manuscripts and recordings in hand. But these were the property of Mr. Wheelock's heirs, and they, too, decided not to continue with the work in his name, so that these statements of some of the greatest figures of the time have never come to light on radio or in book form. They would have supplied a remarkable testimonial to the basic unity of world religions.

My most interesting experience in working for Mr. Murrow was covering the Bandung conference for him in 1955. CBS decided not to send a correspondent of its own and agreed that I should make a short broadcast each day of the conference for the network, for which I was paid $25 a broadcast. Murrow bore all my heavy traveling and living expenses. This disproportionate arrangement pretty well testified to the difference in news judgment and sense of public service between Murrow and the network.

The Bandung conference was of novel and major importance. It was the first occasion on which states from Asia and Africa sat down together to deliberate on the problem of their freedom. This was in the era when Communist China was preaching peaceful coexistence with still greater eloquence than Khrushchev was using a few years later, after the rift appeared between the two largest Communist nations.

The feature of the conference was the rivalry for leadership of Asia and Africa between Chou En-lai and Nehru, and Nehru came out second best, owing to the then alluring moderation of the Chinese leader.

It was at this conference that Krishna Menon, Nehru's right-hand man, was particularly enamored of the Chinese, and I vividly recall an instance of it. Bandung, the most fashionable resort city in Indonesia, has a Chinese population of several thousand who were under orders from the local Communist leadership to demonstrate on all possible occasions for the visitors from China. On one morning they duly packed the street at the entrance to the assembly hall and were caught in a torrential tropical downpour which was flooding the street when Chou En-lai's car drove up. Drenched as they were, the crowd pressed around the car, shouting greetings. I watched this odd enthusiasm standing beside Krishna Menon. He was so overcome that he turned to me with face aflame with delight. "Cable that to America!" he cried. "Tell them what the Chinese in Indonesia think of the Chinese Communist government!" Apparently he did not appreciate the misfortune to India of Nehru's failure to dominate the conference, just as he did not anticipate the later danger of Chinese Communist attacks on India's frontier.

I did not have more than a journalist's relations with Krishna Menon, but he did invite me to dinner and gave me a good example of the Menon treatment. For the whole of the first part of the evening, he did not so much converse with me as insult me with a steady flow of jibes. He was bitterly anti-American and wanted me and all at the table to know it. Then, toward the end of the evening, he suddenly changed, became agreeable and friendly, and discussed politics on a high level of intelligence. Krishna Menon seemed to me like a kind of scorpion. He demonstrated this with his ability to awaken the antagonism of all America during his services at the United Nations, where he seemed oblivious of India's dependence on the aid India needed from the United States.

I have gone to dozens of international conferences, but I found Bandung to be the most interesting and picturesque of them all. The assembly of Asian and African dignitaries, most of them in the costumes of their lands, was unique, and gave a glimpse of a new world coming into being. It heralded the explosion of independence that was to open up Africa within a few years. It expressed and certified the approaching end of imperial rule.

I wish I could say that the State Department understood or welcomed the conference. It seems to have decided that it was going to be anti-American and had better be snubbed. The fact was that a lusty conflict was waged on behalf of the United States throughout the conference by its friends, like the Philippines and Thailand, and a more cordial interest shown by Washington would have greatly increased American influence. Nothing can be less genuine than that the peoples of Africa and Asia should seek their true political freedom under the leadership of Communist China. The real significance of the Bandung conference was dimly and tardily recognized in Washington, and an attempt was made to recover lost ground before it ended, but it came too late to be effective.

The correspondents at Bandung were generously treated by the Indonesian government. This was before the sensational shift of President Sukarno to the left. I shall always remember Bandung as a tidy resort city, built by the Dutch to be far more attractive than Djakarta. Most of the correspondents ate sumptuously and lived cleanly in a little white frame hotel. I shall remember the friendly colleague in the room adjoining mine, tirelessly working at his typewriter and tape recorder. I had met him at the United Nations conference in 1946 and knew he was prized in California as a top-notch commentator. It was not long before he was to come to New York and become a national figure. He was Chet Huntley.

When the conference closed, it produced something of a traffic jam which the regional airlines found beyond their powers to cope with. I tried to "hook" a ride to Djakarta in Prime Minister Nehru's plane, but he told me he had just invited the Burmese delegation to accompany him and did not have a free seat left. However, he turned to his aide and instructed him to see if he could get the Cambodian delegation to give me a seat. It did, and afforded me the pleasure of a conversation with Prince Sihanouk, whom I found to be courteous and personable, though we did not travel together long enough for me to gain more than a superficial impression of him.

In Djakarta I managed to get a seat in a plane to Singapore, where I was entertained overnight at the palace of the governor by my old London acquaintance Malcolm MacDonald, then Commissioner-General for the United Kingdom in South-East Asia, and enjoyed some excellent talk. He had come to be one of the most knowledgeable British experts on Far Eastern affairs. I could not linger in Singapore, because I was to keep my absence from New York down to a total of three weeks, of which the Bandung conference had consumed two. I flew home via Karachi, Istanbul, Cairo, Athens, Rome, and London, and thus made my first round-the-world trip. I must confess I found that such hasty travel was more exacting than exalting.

The most important event that took place while I was working for Murrow had nothing to do with him or my duties. It was my marriage to Meisung Euyang Loh, whom I had come to know just before she joined the Voice of America. There she became a writer in the Chinese service, and later Service

Chief of the Asian feed, which sent programs for use by radio stations in several Far Eastern countries. I met her when she first returned to America in 1950 as an employee of the U.S. aid program. She was one of the three Euyang sisters of Shanghai, celebrated for their beauty. Her name, "Meisung," in Chinese means "born in America," and she was a native of Chicago, having been born there while her parents were studying at the University of Illinois. She returned to China as an infant, but retained her American citizenship. She crossed from Shanghai to Chungking as a refugee after the Japanese occupation and took what amounted to a master's degree in the school of journalism set up in Chungking by the Columbia School of Journalism. Previously she had attended, but not completed her studies at, St. John's University in Shanghai. She was the first Chinese to win the scholarship named after Madame Chiang Kai-shek at Wesleyan College, Georgia, which Madame Chiang had attended. When we met, she was a widow, with a young son, her Chinese husband having been killed in an automobile accident. There was no doubt about our wanting to marry, but we had understandable qualms over the difference between us in age and the wisdom of her waiting to marry a Chinese. These hesitations, however, were overcome.

The Voice by this time had moved to Washington, and I was working in New York, which necessitated weekend commuting to Washington during the first year or two of our marriage. Then I prevailed upon Mr. Murrow to let me move to Washington, which I am sure did not reduce the quality of my work for him and certainly added to my happiness.

The work with Murrow continued until his difficulties with CBS reached the point of inducing him to decide to take a sabbatical. He told me about this in confidence a few days before it was announced. He had probably anticipated the coming change and had earlier tried to make provision for me by interesting me in the project of writing a book on Admiral Hyman Rickover and the development of the nuclear submarine. To study this project, I took a week's leave, which I spent as a special guest in Admiral Rickover's division of the Navy Department. This gave me the privilege of long talks with the specialists and several peppery conversations with him. It was a fascinating week, but at the time I was not overly tempted by the prospect of writing the book, which I figured would take at least three years to complete. And while I appreciated that such a book might become a classic of current history, I declined the opportunity.

I was not in doubt about obtaining interesting employment when Murrow left, for two proposals were made to me. One was by former Senator William Benton, publisher of the Encyclopædia Britannica, who asked me to join his staff and edit a special report on the development of Communist China which was being compiled for him by American scholars. I also was to help him on the preparation of his speeches. I am sure Senator Benton made the offer at Murrow's instigation. But the other proposal came out of the blue. I had invited Barry Zorthian, program manager at the Voice of America, to luncheon at the Cosmos Club. Zorthian had been news editor during my first term of service at the Voice, and we had been good friends. During the meal he unexpectedly asked me: "Why don't you come back to the Voice as commentator?"

Nothing had been further from my thoughts. But happening two days after learning that Murrow was going to take a sabbatical, the question seemed to me providential. I knew I would have said yes then and there had Murrow not asked me to keep his plans confidential until he announced them. So all I could do was to express interest, say I would think it over, and show my pleasure at the question. The following week Murrow let it be known he was leaving CBS for a year, and I could tell Mr. Zorthian I was available. Only three months were needed this time for me to obtain my security clearance, and then I became for the second time first political commentator of the Voice of America.

Chapter 42 / Back at the Voice

By this time, 1959, the United States Information Agency, of which the Voice of America was a part, had been detached from the State Department and become independent. Senator McCarthy had been dead for two years; the morale and self-confidence of the agency had been largely restored; and in August, when I resumed my broadcasts, it was functioning with as much smoothness as one is entitled to expect from a vast bureaucracy. I made the mistake of undertaking to give five weekly broadcasts; and though they were only of four minutes' duration, I soon learned it was as easy, if not easier, to write a broadcast of eight or nine minutes about some topic than one of four. The short one had to be both listenable and complete, as well as safely within the policy of the United States government. The amount of time needed to check with the State Department to get the policy clearly in mind, to read diplomatic dispatches and congressional reports, as well as the voluminous periodical material that one needed to go through to keep abreast of world affairs, made for a crowded day's work. A commercial commentator is spared much of this effort. He can read his newspapers, make his telephone or personal calls, choose a subject he wishes to talk about, and give ride to his own opinion about it.

After suffering a serious heart attack in December, 1960, and recovering from it, I reduced my schedule to three broadcasts a week, which it should have been all along, and maintained this until my seventy-fifth birthday, when I reduced my schedule for a little more than a year to one weekly broadcast. In 1962 I increased this to two weekly broadcasts until my retirement on December 31, 1963.

At this point my professional memoirs could understandably come to a close. But I have a little more I wish to tell about and to say. One subject is an episode at the Cosmos Club in Washington; another is the nature and importance of the Voice of America, about which the American public is in strange and virtually complete ignorance.

The Cosmos Club affair has to do with the rejection for membership of Carl Rowan, Deputy Assistant Secretary of State for Public Affairs. Mr. Rowan is a Negro. He succeeded Ed Kretzmann at the State Department, and Mr. Kretzmann thought so well of him that he decided to propose him for membership in the Cosmos Club, thus breaking down the color bar, and asked me to meet him, and, if I liked him, to second his nomination. This I did. Mr. Rowan was an Oberlin graduate who had served many years on the Minneapolis *Tribune* as a journalist, had won two national citations from the journalistic fraternity, Sigma Delta Chi, had been chosen by the Junior Chamber of Commerce in Minnesota as one of the ten most distinguished young men of the state, and later by the national Junior Chamber as one of the ten most distinguished young men in the United States. He had written a number of books, of which one on India has been particularly praised.

He was the first Negro to be nominated for membership in the Cosmos Club with one exception, some decades ago, when a Negro candidate died before action on his application could be taken. Mr. Rowan's nomination came at a time when the subject of segregation in the capital was under the liveliest discussion and when the other leading social club, the Metropolitan, had been in the news because a Negro diplomat had been invited there for lunch and the member inviting him had been censured in writing by the president of the club. President Kennedy, who had been nominated for membership at the Metropolitan, thereupon promptly withdrew his application. He was at once nominated to the Cosmos Club by his ambassador to India, John Galbraith.

Naturally, there was a stir in the Cosmos Club when

Mr. Rowan was nominated. The Cosmos is less of a diplomats' club than one of scientists. But Washington is a Southern city, and a good many in the Cosmos Club were Southerners and opposed to the admission of Negroes.

I was to learn this in a curious way, for I was invited to deliver the address at the annual dinner of the club in 1961. A member of the management committee who was chosen to extend the invitation told me casually that another committee member had opposed it because I had seconded Mr. Rowan's nomination. In voicing his opposition, this other member had said he hoped I would not touch upon the subject of segregation in clubs in my address. I said that this was the last subject I would wish to talk about at the annual dinner, but that it was an indignity for the club to ask me to speak and tell me what I must not discuss. If the invitation were reworded to make it explicit that I could talk about anything I wished, club segregation included, I would accept. The officers of the club, however, declined to agree to this condition, for the invitation was not renewed and I did not deliver the annual address.

It takes nearly a year for the membership committee to get around to consider the nomination of any applicant, and by the time Mr. Rowan's name came up, Mr. Kretzmann was stationed in Bern, Switzerland. However, an unusually large number of letters approving Mr. Rowan, many of them specifically advocating his election because he was a Negro of high qualifications, had flooded the membership committee. So it was clear that the club was keenly alive to the importance of the decision it had to take.

I have been told that the membership committee devoted an entire session to the Rowan case, and the hearsay in the club was that three members voted against him: two, on account of his color; one, on the ground that he was not desirable. Two adverse voters are sufficient to exclude an applicant. I received the news of the result late that night, cabled Mr. Kretzmann in Bern that I was resigning, and also cabled Ambassador Galbraith in New Delhi. The following day I learned that Mr. Galbraith was in the Naval Hospital in Bethesda, where I telephoned him. He immediately got in touch with the White House, which gave out the news that day that Mr. Galbraith had resigned from the club, which meant, of course, that President Kennedy's application for membership was withdrawn. Assistant Secretary of State for International Organization Affairs Harlan Cleveland resigned. Ed Murrow, by that time Director of the United States Information Agency, who had been nominated for membership, announced that he was withdrawing his application. Resignations came in from Howard K. Smith, James Warburg, Bruce Catton, and others. The story was prominently on page one of both the New York *Times* and the *Herald Tribune* for two successive days, and was published all over the country. Some of my good friends in the club, among them Ferdinand Kuhn, Frederick Kuh, and Ernest Lindley, decided not to resign, but to dedicate themselves inside the club to breaking down the practice of segregation. It was essential that they should do so if the club was to redeem itself from the stigma of racialism. It is my opinion that the resignations, with the nationwide publicity they had received, helped stir the club to change its policy. The annual meeting certainly was obsessed with the issue. A slate of new members of the membership committee was elected pledged to removal of the color bar, and the club adopted a ringing resolution pledging itself not to discriminate against any applicant on the ground of creed, race, or color. It was the largest club meeting ever held, and, I am sure, quite the most exciting.

Shortly afterward I was informed that, under the rule of the club, members who had resigned could ask to have their resignations withdrawn within a year if the management committee approved, and that this approval was a mere formality, never having been withheld in the past. I decided at first that I would not apply for reinstatement unless the membership committee reversed its rejection of Carl Rowan. I have been told that a vote of reconsideration was taken and was defeated by the decisive two votes.

By the spring of 1963, three Negroes had been elected to the club, thus amply fulfilling the antidiscrimination decision of the annual meeting. The first was John Hope Franklin, professor of history at Brooklyn College; the second was another professor of history, Rayford W. Logan, of Howard University; and the third was Stephen J. Wright, president of Fisk University.

In the meantime, Carl Rowan had been appointed by President Kennedy to be ambassador to Finland, but he was not elected to the Cosmos Club. My friends in the club urged me to join the others who had resigned over the racial issue in applying for reinstatement, saying that if I were back in the club, I stood an excellent chance of getting Mr. Rowan elected within a year or two. This argument persuaded me to apply to the Board of Management for reinstatement. Eight others also asked for it. Then, to the astonishment of the nine, and our friends, the Board of Management refused all the applications and issued a highly questionable statement that Mr. Rowan had not been rejected on racial grounds and that those who had resigned should have remained in the club if they wished to see the color bar removed. At another annual meeting a strong effort was made to elect another board of management, but this time the issue was not so dramatic or clear, and it was not basic. The old board won the election. We who resigned were not taken back into the fold. In another four years I would have been eligible for honorary membership, which would have exempted me from payment of dues.

I do have the satisfaction, which I believe is justified, of knowing that those of us who resigned over the Rowan issue were probably decisively responsible for the change in the club's racial practices. It is questionable whether the huge meeting which voted against discrimination would have turned out had there not been the national publicity which the resignations produced. So, in this belief, I comfort myself with the thought that, even though no longer a member, I helped do the Cosmos Club a service. An interesting irony of the situation was the appointment of Carl Rowan to succeed Edward R. Murrow as head of USIA after Murrow's resignation due to illness in 1964.

The other point I wish to elaborate is the extent of the work done by USIA and the Voice of America. I have called them the most far-reaching communications setup in the world, and I think it is one of the oddities of American life that the public has not the vaguest knowledge that this is so. In number of short-wave broadcasting hours, the Voice of America ranks third, behind the Soviet Union and Communist China, and for a year or so also ranked behind the United Arab Republic. This, I think, while not common knowledge, has been published a number of times. But what is not at all known is that the placement service of the Voice, that is to say, its supply of tapes and programs for use by local broadcasting stations—either attributed or not attributed, either in English or the local language—multiplies the broadcasting originating with the Voice and the USIA posts nearly twenty times. And this is what makes their combined output the vastest communication operation the world has ever had. It is far greater than that of the Soviet or Chinese radio, even greater than that of the combined network services of the United States or the combined American news services.

Americans, who depend so much on television, are unaware that radio, as a world medium, has prime importance. There are at present about 220 million radio sets in existence, the number having been enormously increased by the development of the Japanese transistor radio. Radio, rather than the press, is the main source of news for the vast majority of the people of Asia, Africa, the Middle East, and Latin America. If the American policy in world affairs is to be presented to the world at large, it must be done, first of all, by radio. And the primary task of the Voice is to acquaint foreign listeners not only with the major news of the day, but also with American policy, and to present the policy in such a way that the listeners come to understand that it is in their interest as well as America's. Radio also is a weapon in the Cold War, but that is not its primary function, regardless of what the warriors of the Cold War may believe. Certainly it exists to combat Communism and promote the belief of people everywhere in the advantages of political and individual freedom. But it has a far more complex purpose. It must portray not only American foreign policy but American life, showing how a democracy goes about dealing with its uncompleted tasks, a process which, of course, is unending. It will be effective in its work insofar as listeners believe it. It will be believed insofar as it tells the truth. So it must not hide or misrepresent the problems the American people have to deal with. Nor can it afford to overstate what America expects to accomplish with its policy of defending the freedom of others, or understate its interest in the needs of developing countries.

The policy of the United States, of course, is made in the White House and the State Department. But it has to be told and expounded by the USIA and the VOA. There is no rule of thumb by which this can be done with utmost effectiveness. To find the best method is, of course, the professional problem of the Voice. Often it succeeds; sometimes it is less than successful. Though I have been one of the chief spokesmen of the Voice, I must not attempt to judge whether such problems have been, on the whole, dealt with wisely. That is for the administration, the Congress, and the public to determine. But I am moved to say that the American public cannot arrive at a judgment unless it knows more about USIA and the Voice, and about the problems of broadcasting to foreign listeners.

The general assumption in America is that the number of listeners to American short-wave broadcasting is necessarily small. It probably runs from five to twenty-seven million a day. In many foreign countries, this number includes the government professionals whose business it is to keep abreast of foreign policy. They listen to Moscow, Peiping, and Washington as a means of knowing how their own immediate policy might be affected. Other listeners include American diplomatic missions abroad, for in this way they hear not only the latest news, but also know promptly what the administration is doing. It is one of the functions of the Voice to inform these attentive experts, and doing so alone would make the short-wave service worth what it costs.

But in the new free countries in Africa, in the Middle East, in India, in Southeast Asia, in Latin America, millions of people own short-wave sets and listen to VOA, not professionally, so as to know how to shape and reshape the foreign policy of the country, but for the same reason Americans turn on their car radios and their TV sets—to keep abreast of the news. If these people receive a competently compiled survey of the news and interpretive commentaries, these affect their judgment and mold their thinking. And since the number of short-wave sets in existence has grown, the value of an American news and feature service has increased.

It puts these generalities into clearer focus to specify some of the figures about international broadcasting. The world total of broadcasting hours was 17,000 a week in 1962, of which 4,000 originated in Communist countries and 7,400 in free-world countries, the remainder in the nonaligned. The United States total of short-wave broadcasts was 760 hours a week. But the placement service of the United States came to 14,046 hours a week. Tapes and scripts provided by the Voice of America accounted for 8,854 hours a week, relays and feeds for 2,030. The balance was supplied by USIA material locally produced and broadcast from local stations. All these 14,000 hours were on local radios.

It will give an idea of the volume of the placement material to say that it was twenty-one times greater than would be the total output of all four American networks if they were on the air all twenty-four hours a day.

About two-thirds of the materials thus placed could be called substantive, the rest being music. That is, the majority of programs consisted of news, discussion, and features, and they were heard at or near prime listening time. Many of these programs were not attributed to the United States, being devised to fulfill local radio needs. The opportunity thus was presented in news and discussion to broadcast an authentic statement of United States policy and the reasoning behind it. To do this over so many local stations is an achievement for which the USIA deserves the highest credit.

The distribution of this placement material in 1962 was uneven. Much the greater part went to Latin America, 10,872 weekly hours, of which Colombia, with 5,402 weekly hours, and Venezuela, with 2,366, used the largest amount. But the figures for Brazil, 637, Ecuador, 655, Mexico, 426, and Bolivia, 253, are gratifyingly large if they are compared with the total short-wave broadcasting hours of the Voice, 760 hours a week, or the BBC, 615 weekly hours.

The area using the second-largest amount of placement service was Europe, with 1,862 weekly hours, of which 1,597 hours went to Italy alone. The Far East received 1,046 hours, the largest amount going to Japan, 378 hours; Thailand ranking next, with 183; and Korea, third, with 103. The placement service to the Near East and South Asia was 177 weekly hours. The African service was in its infancy in 1961, showing a total of only twenty-four placement hours a week. This increased to eighty-eight hours in 1962. By now the figure will be considerably higher, and will continue to grow with the expansion of the service and the installation of high-powered transmitters in Liberia.

I have spoken of my years with the Voice as having been lived in obscurity, but the word applied only to my own country. The number of my listeners abroad was nothing stupendous, but it was in the millions for my broadcasts as voiced by myself, which were repeated to Europe, the Middle East, the Far East, and Latin America. There were other millions of short-wave listeners in other languages; I was often translated into all thirty-six languages used at the Voice. And my broadcasts, too, benefited from placement, not only being frequently used on local radio stations abroad, but also appearing regularly under my signature in translation in newspapers in Japan and Korea, and occasionally in other countries. While I was first political commentator of the Voice, my broadcasts were the programs having the greatest usage of any on the regular menu, the normal figure being an average of over twenty-one for each broadcast. Occasionally I received responses from listeners, but few of them knew how to reach me, and I have always felt, when broadcasting at the Voice, that I was engaging in a wholly impersonal activity. It was a mistake to feel this way, but the contrast with broadcasting commercially in the United States was striking. From commercial broadcasting in America, I received a daily stream of mail, sometimes huge, sometimes small, but continuous. About nine-tenths of these letters were responsive to something I had said, and many of them asked questions that called for answers. The other tenth was abusive. I kept a finger on the pulse of the listener; I knew when the reaction was friendly, which it was most of the time; and I knew when I gave offense. This, for me, was a rewarding feature of my work. I was in touch with people, from one end of the country to the other. But at the Voice, my work, which put me in touch with people from one end of the earth to the other, was devoid of this reward, not through any defect of mine, but owing to the nature of the operation. I do not complain. I received the Award for Meritorious Service in June, 1961, with bronze medal. I am pleased to add that in the following year, my wife received the same award for her pioneer work in the Asian field. The Voice has shown us its appreciation. But the fact remains that most Americans who knew that I broadcast for the Voice of America had no way of knowing what that meant.

Chapter 43 / A Final Word

The subjective experiences which make a person fervently American, or French, or British, or one of any other nationality, are not, as a rule, complex or inscrutable. They derive chiefly from environment, express the influences of local or national opinion, and are as much unconscious as rational. The normal American prefers his country and its manners and habits to those of other countries. But at the same time he has strong dislikes for certain aspects of American life. It is these dislikes which help motivate his political attitudes and often determine his political allegiances. What he does not easily do is see his own country as a whole, to weigh the permanent values in it against his dislikes, and measure the changes that are taking place in it.

A person who goes abroad as a newspaper correspondent for a considerable number of years comes to a slightly different view of his country. If he is an observant journalist, he sees the country to which he is assigned as a whole, and the whole as consisting of segments with differing views, values, and judgments. He does not identify himself with any single segment, but attempts to understand the country as a product of the interplay of the differing forces within it.

In this analysis, he also comes to see his own country as a whole. Not being under the influence of local environment and prejudices, he is able to understand his own country as being the product of the differing forces within it and to evaluate it objectively.

During the eighteen years I served as a correspondent in Europe, I was always aware that the residents of the countries where I worked had biases that I did not share, and in a way I looked beyond them to the nation as an entirety of which they were only fractions. I was not put off by their biases, but learned from them what constituted the whole nation. I consider this to have been a privilege, for I learned also to see my own country for this period without limiting my allegiance to any one set of views. I also came to see my own country as a product of the differing biases of which it was composed, and to judge it in relation to other countries as a whole compared with other wholes.

For the eighteen years I worked abroad, I was detached from the particulars of the differences which swayed my countrymen. And in seeing the United States as a whole and destined to play an astonishing and decisive role in the lives of other nations, I understood that the character of the United States as a whole was in fact the fusion of its own conflicting parts. This produced a character which I not only accepted, but which I admired deeply. And as the crisis which ended in World War II came to a head, I found myself growing patriotic to a degree I had never been capable of before. I think this patriotism was different from mere loyalty. It was a faith which rested on my evaluation of all the political systems I had been studying. I repeat, I came to this faith in some degree objectively. And I was to that extent fitted to broadcast to American listeners with conviction during this period. That is, my life had been lived, though not planned in advance, to equip me in some measure for the work I had to do.

It is true that I did identify myself with factional political action after returning from Europe. I was busy in the operations of the Council for Democracy. I spoke out against fascism when I detected any incipient tendency toward its development. I played some part in the rising advocacy of a new kind of supranational world organization, after the start of the atomic era. At home again, I rediscovered my latent political biases, and I think it was good Americanism to do so if I did not lose my awareness of the value and destiny of the United States as such.

My work with the Voice of America has been like my broadcasting during the war in being based on my faith in the United States and my belief in the democratic process which has molded American life. If I had gone on in commercial radio, I am sure I should have been often critical of this or that policy of the government. But at the Voice, I do not consider it delinquent on my part to present the good in American policy while remaining silent about such shortcomings as I perceive. The Voice carries what the home critics say. That is part of its obligation if it is to be believed. But the Voice's own spokesmen are under no compunction to originate critique themselves. It is their function to present American policy in a way to make its listeners understand it and see how it is serving them in maintaining the possibility of free peoples remaining free, and preventing the successes of those dedicated to achieving their domination.

I should say in conclusion, however, that the Voice cannot be an oracle. It is not able to foresee where the inevitable power of change which rules all mankind is going to lead us. We are now in the years of hiatus which have been vouchsafed us in this nuclear age. In this hiatus there will be no all-out nuclear war, and time has been bought in which to begin with disarmament and proceed with it until its completion, which is the policy of the United States. If this time is wisely used, a different international life will emerge, and the economically lagging nations will be assisted to enjoy the benefits of the unlimited technical bounties that will be available. It will be a resplendent epoch, one of peace but also of further change, the nature of which only a great prophet could foretell.

But if the time that has been bought is not wisely used, our present civilization will be destroyed, and the work of rebuilding it will have to start at the beginning.

I wish I could testify that the hiatus in which there is to be no nuclear war is being wisely enough used. To build a world without national wars, founded on enforceable law, is a task exceeding any that any single generation has been challenged to complete. It requires the solution of problems more formidable than any the human race has yet faced. Unless they are solved, the day of the proliferation of nuclear weapons may be relatively near, not more than one or two decades away. If it comes, destruction may be unavoidable. The will and the wisdom to prevent the dawning of this day are not now in evidence. The joint United States–Russian resolution of September 21, 1961 on disarmament reads like a dedication of the world's two strongest powers to preserve civilization from nuclear destruction and build under it a foundation of peace based upon law. To resolve this in such words is to utter wonderful rhetoric, but so far it is no more. When the Soviet Union violated the nuclear-test moratorium to launch a new series of tests, and later when it installed nuclear weapons in Cuba, it was making a mockery of the resolution, and Americans cannot be chided if they have well-nigh forgotten it. But Soviet greed for power and American scorn for Soviet rhetoric are not going to prolong the period of freedom from nuclear war; indeed, probably they threaten to curtail it. And if the nuclear war comes it will set back civilization by many hundreds of years if it does not end it altogether.

In the past, when nations could not agree about something vital, they fought it out. That possibility is no more. One can almost say it is a pity it has gone, for in the great crises of war men often rose to the challenges of change and accepted it. They staked everything they had, and then through chance and mischance, as well as through purpose, a new status emerged that made peace more rewarding. But a great war over the differences now dividing the human race would not bring out the best in men and would open no new vistas. We do not know just how annihilating a nuclear war would be, but it could kill hundreds of millions now living and might doom to deformity many millions yet unborn.

When I reflect on these possibilities, I have to take refuge in faith. I have been an interpreter of two world wars, and of the interim between them, as well as the period following World War II. I know that both wars led to the explosion of freedom all over the world. The wars stimulated science and were stimulated by it. They hastened the revolution of industrialization. Now, science and industry both promise that life may abound in well-being for all. They have made the planet small and locked all its parts together by interrelated interests. They have made it possible for all the parts to speak to one another and see one another.

I must say, however, that without faith I would be in despair. For science, industry, rising material well-being, and the fabulous means of communication so far are not rebuilding the basic structure of human relations, and at this writing only peripheral actions seem possible to reduce the tensions that underlie international affairs.

I realize that peace in a nuclear world cannot come all at once. It must begin with small steps that build up confidence so that longer steps can be ventured. Both President Johnson, like his predecessor President Kennedy, and Chairman Khrushchev know the pace must be slow and that patience is the essence of progress. Both are under pressures applied by the very existence of the power of their nations. They also are held back by public opinion that is unschooled in the changes now taking place and that adheres to truisms that do not apply to the future, if the future is to be.

As a person who has spent his entire life in the field of communications, I am acutely aware of the quite frightening inadequacy of the communications media to prepare the public for the changes that must be accepted. Perhaps I am not reasonably patient; the technical dimensions of communications have to be stretched before the minds using them need to be. No doubt the technical perfection of communications is still far away, and it will become something undreamed of in competence and service. But the time available, so far as I am able to judge, is no more than a historical moment, and the communications media are only just beginning to appreciate that they have a new function and duty.

Taken at their best today, they are only vaguely alive to the possibilities of international television and broadcasting, while the level of national journalism, though much higher than it was fifty years ago, is far below the demand of our present complex and threatened era. If communications are going to help the human race solve the problems of life in the nuclear age, now is the time to be about it. Social as well as electronic scientists have to be trained and given the guidance of both national and international communications. It has to happen here; it also has to happen in the Soviet Union and Communist China, and to say this is not to express utter pessimism. Good communication begets good communication, and understanding begets understanding, not all of a sudden, not dramatically, but slowly and surely, a stage at a time, as safety can only come in the nuclear world.

If anyone with the vision to have foreseen today's world fifty-eight years ago had told me about it when I took my first job on a newspaper, I could not have grasped it with all the imagination I then had. The changes in my lifetime have indeed been revolutionary, and the revolution is still going on, for we cannot grasp what the world will be like in another fifty-eight years. But this we know today: that never have the stakes been so high, never has the potential of destruction been so all-consuming, and never have the allurements of a world without war, kept peaceful through the operation of law, been so nearly within reach. In my boyhood no such alternatives presented themselves. Now they do. And now I cannot predict how—or even whether—the right choice will be made.

Index of Persons

B SWING, R.
Swing, Raymond, 1887-
"Good evening!"

		DATE DUE